Paddling Virginia and West Virginia

Paddling Virginia and West Virginia

A Guide to the Area's Greatest Paddling Adventures

Johnny Molloy

FALCON GUIDES

GUILFORD, CONNECTICUT

To Keri Anne and all the paddlers of the Old Dominion and the Mountain State

FALCONGUIDES®

An imprint of The Rowman & Littlefield Publishing Group, Inc.
4501 Forbes Blvd., Ste. 200
Lanham, MD 20706
www.rowman.com
Falcon and FalconGuides are registered trademarks and Make Adventure Your Story is a trademark of The Rowman & Littlefield Publishing Group, Inc.

Distributed by NATIONAL BOOK NETWORK

Copyright © 2019 The Rowman & Littlefield Publishing Group, Inc.

Photos by Johnny Molloy unless otherwise noted
Maps by The Rowman & Littlefield Publishing Group, Inc.

British Library Cataloguing in Publication Information available

Library of Congress Cataloging-in-Publication Data

Names: Molloy, Johnny, 1961- author.
Title: Paddling Virginia and West Virginia : a guide to the area's greatest paddling adventures / Johnny Molloy.
Description: Guilford, Connecticut : FalconGuides, [2019] | Includes index. |
  Identifiers: LCCN 2018057130 (print) | LCCN 2019004554 (ebook) | ISBN
  9781493029921 (ebook) | ISBN 9781493029914 (pbk.)
Subjects: LCSH: Canoes and canoeing—Virginia—Guidebooks. | Canoes and canoeing—
  West Virginia—Guidebooks.
Classification: LCC GV776.V8 (ebook) | LCC GV776.V8 M66 2019 (print) | DDC
  797.12209755—dc23
LC record available at https://lccn.loc.gov/2018057130

∞™ The paper used in this publication meets the minimum requirements of American National Standard for Information Sciences—Permanence of Paper for Printed Library Materials, ANSI/ NISO Z39.48-1992.

Printed in the United States of America

Contents

Overview Map

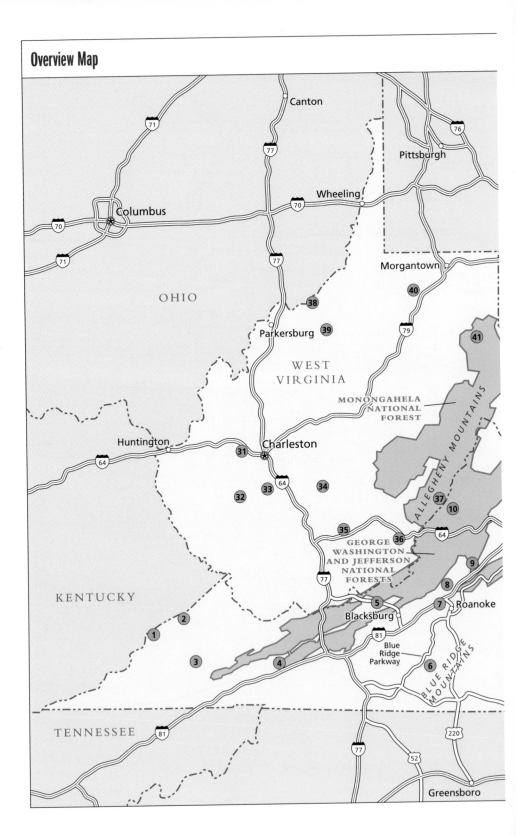

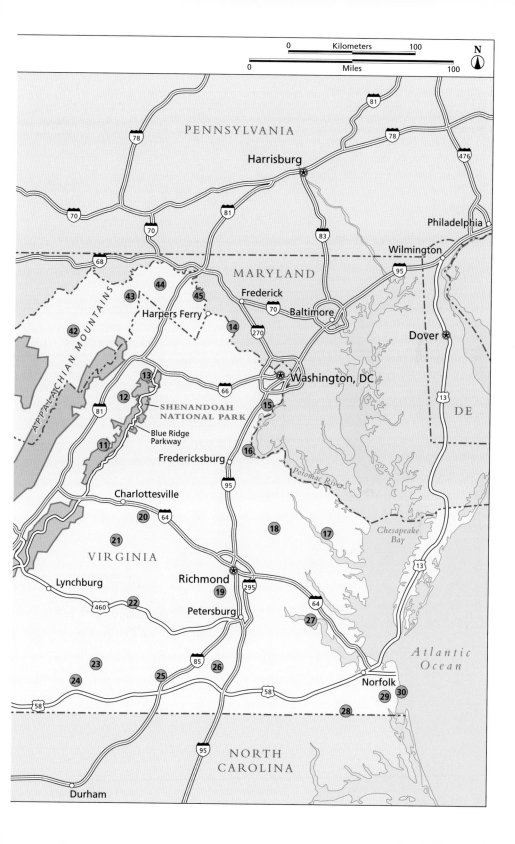

WEST VIRGINIA PADDLES

Acknowledgments

Thanks to my wife Keri Anne. And thanks to all the paddling enthusiasts who have built up the sport in Virginia and West Virginia, establishing paddling trails, paddling clubs, and organizations that help keep our waterways clean and paddler friendly.

Thanks to Sierra Designs for their tents used for camping between and during paddling trips. Thanks to Wenonah for providing me a great canoe to paddle on many rivers—the Spirit II. The 17-footer handled wonderfully, and its light weight made for easy loading and unloading. Thanks to Old Town, too, for my 16-foot Penobscot that can handle the wear and tear of an outdoor writer on the move along the waterways of America.

Introduction

Welcome to *Paddling Virginia and West Virginia*. These two states, paired as one for four score before being divided by the Civil War, present a wealth of paddling possibilities from the Atlantic Ocean to the Ohio River. As an outdoor writer I have had the privilege of authoring several hiking and camping guides to these two states and was very excited about exploring the rivers and lakes of Virginia and West Virginia and then sharing them with you. And there is plenty about which to be excited, including a treasure of expanding paddling trails and blueways. Take Virginia for example, from the Great Dismal Swamp in the east to Virginia's contribution to great rivers of the world, the James, to the Shenandoah River along the Blue Ridge to the mountain-rimmed North Fork Pound Lake in far southwest Virginia, the paddling opportunities are as varied as the colors on a kaleidoscope. Here in the Old Dominion, you can explore tidal creeks, powerful Piedmont rivers, mountain waterways, and regal impoundments in natural settings that allow you to reconnect with nature on nature's terms.

In West Virginia the alluring paddling opportunities start with the New River, brawling its way through the Appalachian Plateau, and other mountain streams such as the legendary Greenbrier River. Paddling trails have been established in the Mountain State, too, along the Coal River, the Cheat River, and still others. Lake paddling,

This is where you begin your paddle at Belle Isle State Park (paddle 17).

too, is a popular pastime here in Almost Heaven. Think of the lakes at Hawks Nest State Park and North Bend State Park, presenting eye-pleasing scenery in a still-water setting. Other waterways such as the Cacapon and South Branch Potomac River present additional rivers to run.

The opportunity arose to write this guidebook and I excitedly jumped on it. I began systematically exploring the waterways of the two Virginias for great paddling destinations. I sought to include paddling destinations that would not only be rewarding but would also be exemplary paddles of the varied landscapes offered in all the geographic regions of the two states. In far West Virginia the Ohio River represents a big-river paddling possibility. The South Branch Potomac winds beautifully through a canyon known as the Trough, while the West Fork River provides a less-visited paddling destination in the northern part of the state.

In Virginia I found Accokeek Creek, a newer paddling destination that explores a companion state nature preserve. It winds through a tidal marsh before opening onto bigger water leading to a panoramic vista of lands and waters extending to the horizon. The unusual Farmville Blueway leads you first to a lake, then a creek, then a river, all in one paddling trip. Want to explore history while paddling? Head out on the Jamestown Island Circumnavigation, floating around the site of the first successful English colony in Virginia. Stroke the Banister River and see Indian fish weirs and wing dams that aided early tradesmen who used Virginia's rivers for transportation. The Roanoke River Blueway allows for a fun paddle down bouncy shoals right through the heart of Salem. Paddle to Emberson Falls, which spill into Philpott Lake.

What can you say about the Rivanna River, where history, waterside scenery, and good floating combine into one paddling adventure? This destination is something you must experience for yourself—with the help of this guidebook of course. Then, when you cobble the paddling destinations together, it presents a mosaic of Virginia and West Virginia beauty and biodiversity that is hard to beat!

This book serves up the information you need to execute paddling adventures in the Old Dominion and the Mountain State. As you may guess, the hardest part of writing this guide may have been picking out the paddling destinations. With each of these waterways, I sought out a combination of scenery, paddling experiences, ease of access—including shuttling when necessary—and a reasonable length for day-tripping. Now it is your turn: Get out there and paddle the two Virginias!

Weather

Virginia and West Virginia experience all four seasons in their entirety, and given the states' elevations—from over 5,700 feet to sea level—they could be experiencing them all at the same time. Summer—the most popular paddling season—can be warm, with occasional downright-hot spells in the eastern lowlands of Virginia and along the Ohio River Valley of West Virginia. The mountains of both states will be cooler. Morning paddlers can avoid heat and the common afternoon thunderstorms of summer. A smartphone equipped with internet access allows paddlers to monitor storms as they arise. Given the mountainous terrain of the two states, do not count on cell service everywhere you go. Paddlers are drawn outdoors when the first northerly fronts of fall sweep cool, clear air across the two states. Crisp, still mornings, ideal for paddling rivers and lakes, give way to warm afternoons. Fall is drier than summer. Winter will bring frigid subfreezing days, chilling rain, and snow, especially in the mountains. There are also fewer hours of daylight. However, a wise choice of paddling days and smart time management will keep you warm and paddling while the sun is still above the horizon. Each cold month has a few days of mild weather, especially in Southside and southeastern Virginia. Make the most of them. Spring will be more variable. A warm day can be followed by a cold one. Extensive spring rains bring regrowth but also keep paddlers off excessively high rivers. However, any avid paddler will find more good paddling days than they will have time to paddle in spring and every other season. A good way to plan your paddling is to check monthly averages of high and low temperatures and average rainfall for each month in which you intend to go.

Flora and Fauna

The natural landscapes of Virginia and West Virginia are inextricably intertwined with their human history (especially since they began as one state). They offer everything from the huge Ohio River Valley in the west, leading to a maze of hills and hollows, to the high mountains of the Alleghenies and Blue Ridge to the rolling midlands of the Piedmont, where big rivers carve bigger valleys, to the gentle Tidewater and onward to the Atlantic Ocean. A wide variety of wildlife calls these dissimilar landscapes home.

Deer are the land animal you most likely will see along West Virginia's and Virginia's waterways. Deer along some lakes and rivers are remarkably tame and may linger on or close to the water as you approach. A quiet paddler may also witness turkeys, raccoons, or even a coyote. Aquatic animals such as beavers, muskrats, and otters may also be seen. Bears can be found throughout most of the two states. They occur in greatest numbers in the mountains and eastern swamps. If you feel uncomfortable when encountering any critter, keep your distance and they will generally keep theirs.

Overhead, many raptors ply the skies for food, including hawks, falcons, and owls. The waterways of the two states are alive with osprey and bald eagles, lording over the terrain below them. Herons, waterfowl, and songbirds are abundant, too. Depending upon where you are, other birds you may spot range from kingfishers to woodpeckers.

The flora offers just as much variety, especially with such a range of elevation and transitioning aquatic environments, from big freshwater rivers of the west to clear, cold mountain streams to saltwater seas. Along the waterways you will find evergreen forests, bottomland hardwoods coloring autumn's landscapes, cypress-filled swamp woods, even spartan beach environments. Wildflowers will be found in spring, summer, and fall along watercourses and in drier site-specific situations.

Virginia is divided by nine major river systems: From the north the Potomac River drains the Virginia portion of the Shenandoah River, while the Rappahannock and York absorb waterways east of the Blue Ridge. The James River takes in waters from the West Virginia state line easterly through the heart of the Old Dominion all the way to Chesapeake Bay, draining 25 percent of the state. The Roanoke flows from the Appalachians southeasterly into Southside Virginia, also going by its historical name of Staunton part of the way. Although the Chowan begins in North Carolina, many of its tributaries start in Virginia, including the Nottoway and Meherrin Rivers. All the above waterways flow into the Atlantic via Chesapeake Bay or Albemarle Sound, while the Eastern Continental Divide separates the aforementioned streams from the New River, the Tennessee River, and the Big Sandy River drainages. These waterways ultimately feed the Ohio then Mississippi River, emptying their waters into the Gulf of Mexico. The New River forms in North Carolina's mountains, then cuts across Southwest Virginia to enter West Virginia and end as it enters the Kanawha. The Tennessee River tributaries such as the Clinch flow from the far southwest Virginia highlands into the Volunteer State, while the Big Sandy River drains a small portion of Southwest Virginia to ultimately meet the Ohio River and onward.

West Virginia's waters flow into two major drainages—the Ohio River and the Potomac, which leads to Chesapeake Bay. The vast majority of Mountain State

Paddlers fixing to enter Lake Drummond (paddle 28)

waterways, including the New, the Monongahela, Cheat, and Gauley, flow into the Ohio and on to the Mississippi, exiting into the Gulf of Mexico. The Monongahela is of special interest. This waterway and its tributaries flow north into Pennsylvania to Pittsburgh, where they join the Allegheny River to form the Ohio River, then turn south. The New River has a large watershed, which starts in North Carolina then flows into Virginia and onward into the Mountain State, where it, along with the Gauley River, drain a substantial number of eastern West Virginia mountain counties. The New and Gauley flow into the Kanawha, passing through West Virginia's capital city of Charleston. The Potomac River system covers northeastern West Virginia, along with portions of Virginia, Pennsylvania, Maryland, and even the District of Columbia before emptying into Chesapeake Bay. Major streams in the Potomac/ Chesapeake drainage are South Branch and North Branch Potomac River, Cacapon, and the Shenandoah River.

Your Rights on the Rivers and Lakes of the Two Virginias

Navigability laws differ in West Virginia and Virginia. In 2015 and 2016 landowners along Johns Creek and Craig Creek in western Virginia fought the notion of paddlers being able to float down their streams through privately owned land, bringing suit. Consequently, the Virginia Marine Resources Commission confirmed that they consider Johns Creek, Craig Creek, and several other whitewater streams navigable and public. The commission determined this based on their policy of assuming streams of sufficient size are navigable unless proven otherwise.

When actually on the water, what does this mean for the Virginia paddler? Paddlers must put in or take out on public property or their own private property (all the paddles in this guide have public accesses). The vast majority of landowners do not mind passage through waters along their property. While paddling, be considerate— do not litter, bother livestock, climb on a dock, or traipse through someone's backyard. If encountered or confronted, be friendly and approachable. However, if you are stopped or you are asked to get off riverside property, then I suggest you paddle on. Adhere to the landowner's request and live to paddle another day. Be apprised that you could be considered trespassing when you portage, camp, fish, or even stop for a lunch break on streamside lands if not on public property. At that point it is not a great time for debate on Virginia waterway law.

The laws in West Virginia are more paddler friendly. Under the Equal Footing Doctrine, the beds and banks of the Mountain State's rivers and streams are a strip of public land, to be conserved for public benefit. Boaters in all kinds of boats are free to use this water and the immediate adjacent land. Again, use common sense and common courtesy when floating down rivers and along lakes. Respect private property rights and use only public accesses. Be a good representative of the paddling community.

How to Use This Guide

This guidebook offers trips covering every corner of West Virginia and Virginia. The paddles of the two states are divided into four regions. Each paddle included in the book is chosen as a day trip, though overnight camping can be done where noted. The following is a sample of what you will find in the information box at the beginning of each paddling destination:

18 Mattaponi River

Follow this blackwater stream as it changes from slender stream to tidal waterway in a short span. A short, easy shuttle can be done on foot or bike.

Counties: King William; King and Queen
Start: Zoar State Forest Access, N37 48.542' / W77 7.280'
End: Aylett Ramp, N37 47.145' / W77 6.180'
Length: 5.0 miles
Float time: 2.6 hours
Difficulty rating: Easy
Rapids: None
River/lake type: Small tidewater river
Current: Slow
River gradient: 1.7 feet per mile
Water gauge: Mattaponi River near Beulahville, VA, no minimum runnable level

Season: Year-round, spring for blooming wild azaleas
Land status: State forest; private
Fees and permits: None
Nearest city/town: Aylett
Map: USGS: Aylett
Boats used: Kayaks, canoes, motorboats on lower stretches of paddle
Organization: Zoar State Forest, 4445 Upshaw Rd., Aylett, VA 23009; (804) 769-2962; www.dof.virginia.gov
Contact/outfitter: Mattaponi Canoe & Kayak, (800) 769-3545, www.mattaponi.com

From the information box we can see that the paddle is in King William as well as King and Queen Counties. It begins at Zoar State Forest. The GPS coordinates for the put-in are given using NAD 27 datum (the base mapping collected by the US Geological Service), which you can plug into your phone or auto GPS for direction finding. The paddle ends at the Virginia Department of Game and Inland Fisheries ramp in Aylett. The trip is 5 miles in length, which I acquired from using a GPS during my research. The paddle should last around 2.6 hours, but this is just an average. The time you will spend on the water depends upon whether you fish, picnic, swim, paddle, or simply relax. Use the float time as a gauge to help you determine how much time you need/want to spend on your particular trip. The paddle is rated as easy since it is slow and no rapids exist along the run. This river difficulty rating system goes from Class I to Class VI. Class I has easy waves requiring little maneuvering and few obstructions. Class II rapids may have more obstructions and require more maneuvering, and the rapids may be flowing faster. Most paddles in this guidebook are Class I–II. Class III rapids can be difficult with numerous waves and no clear defined passage and require precise maneuvering. Classes IV to VI increase in difficulty, with Class VI being unrunnable except by the best of experts.

The water type classification reflects its geographical placement within the two states and what type of river it is where the paddle takes place, in this case a small tidewater river. The current is slow here, and for all paddles can range from tidal to slow to moderate to swift. The river gradient reflects the rate at which the river descends during the paddle.

The water gauge listed will be near the destination and will help you determine the paddleability of the river. Some rivers have minimum flow rates listed so you will get on the river only when it has enough water—or stay off when the water is too high. Others that do not have a minimum runnable level—like this one—can be paddled year-round. Concerning water gauges, the key variable is the height of the river at a fixed point. Gauge houses, situated on most rivers, consist of a well at the river's edge with a float attached to a recording clock. The gauge reads in hundredths of feet. Rating tables are constructed for each gauge to get a cubic feet per second (cfs) reading for each level. Other gauges are measured in height, given in feet. This gauge information can be obtained quickly, often along with a gauge reading of recent rainfall at the same location. USGS Real-time Water Levels for the United States can be found on the web at http://waterdata.usgs.gov/nwis/rt. This in-depth website has hundreds of gauges for the entire country updated continually, and graphs showing recent flow trends, along with historic trends for any given day of the year, available at a click. Consult these gauges before you start your trip.

The best paddling seasons are given, followed by land status. The lands bordering the Mattaponi River are private and public, in this case a state forest as well as county park. Many paddling destinations included in this guidebook border public lands. See above for information about your rights on the river. For this sample paddle, no fees or permits are required. Aylett is the nearest municipality. This listing will help you get oriented to the paddle destination area while looking at a map or looking up map information on the internet. Though quality maps and driving directions are included with each paddle, the Maps section lists pertinent maps you can use for more detailed information, including United States Geographical Survey (USGS) 7.5' quadrangle maps. These "quad maps," as they are known, cover every parcel of land in this country. They are divided into very detailed rectangular maps. Each quad has a name, usually based on a physical feature located within the quad. In this case the paddle traverses a quad map named "Aylett." Quad maps can be obtained online at www.usgs.gov.

Boats used simply informs you of what other river users will be floating. The Organizations section lists groups that charge themselves with taking care of the particular waterway or manage lands included on the paddle. If you are interested in learning more about the river's health and other water-quality issues, as well as simply getting involved in preserving Virginia's and West Virginia's waterways, consult these groups when listed. The Contacts/Outfitters listing will sometimes also give you information if an outfitter operates on the segment of river given. This can help with shuttles and boat rentals.

In addition to the information in the sample above, each paddle has several additional sections. Put-in/takeout information gives you directions from the nearest interstate or largest community first to the takeout, where you can leave a shuttle vehicle, then from the takeout to the put-in. By the way, look before you leap! Some of the put-ins and takeouts use dirt or sand roads just before reaching the waterways. After periods of extreme weather, such as heavy rains or long dry periods, the roads can become troublesome. If you are at all unsure about the road ahead of you, stop, get out, and examine it on foot before you drive into a deep mudhole or get stuck in the sand.

A paddle summary (not shown on sample float) follows the put-in/takeout directions. This does what it sounds like it should do—it gives an overview of the paddle trip, giving you an idea of what to expect that will help you determine whether or not you want to experience this waterway. A river/lake summary follows. This gives an overview of the entire river or lake, not just the section paddled. This way you can determine whether you want to paddle other sections of the river/lake being detailed. It also gives you a better understanding of the entire watershed, rather than just a section of river in space and time. Next comes The Paddling, which is the meat-and-potatoes narrative, giving you detailed information about your river trip, including flora, fauna, and interesting not-to-be-missed natural features. It also details important information needed to execute the paddle, including forthcoming rapids, portages, bridges, and stops along the way, and the mileages at which you will come across them.

Finally, some paddles have a sidebar. This is interesting information about the waterway that does not necessarily pertain to the specific paddle but gives you some human or natural tidbit that may pique your interest to explore beyond the simple mechanics of the paddle.

Fixing to Paddle

Which Boat Do I Use?

This book covers waterways in West Virginia and Virginia, from crashing mountain rivers to massive waterways a mile across to still and silent swamp streams to tidal creeks barely wide enough for a boat. So with such variety, what boat do you use? There are multiple possibilities.

Choosing a Kayak

The first consideration in choosing a kayak is deciding between a sit-on-top model and a sit-in model, such as a touring kayak or whitewater kayak. Sit-on-tops are what their name implies—paddlers sit on top of the boat—whereas a touring kayak requires you to put your body into the boat, leaving your upper half above an enclosed cockpit. Ask yourself, what type of waters are you going to paddle? Are you going to paddle near shore, on calm flat waters, or are you going to paddle bigger waters, such as the lower Rappahannock River in Virginia's Northern Neck? If paddling bigger water, you will need a cockpit. Sit-on-top kayaks are generally more comfortable and allow for more freedom of movement. They also take on water more readily and are used almost exclusively in warmer-water destinations, and are often used by outfitters as rental boats on mild rivers during summertime. Sit-in touring kayaks are inherently more stable, since the user sits on the bottom of the boat rather than on top of the boat. Sit-on-top kayaks make up for this stability shortcoming by being wider, which makes them slower. Base your decision primarily on what types of waters you will be paddling and whether you will be going overnight in your kayak. Sit-on-top kayaks are a poor choice when it comes to overnight camping. However, sit-on-tops do have their place. Smaller waters, such as ponds and gentle, smaller streams, are good for sit-on-top kayaks.

Sit-in kayaks are the traditional kayaks, based on models used by Arctic aboriginals. Some factors to consider when choosing a touring sit-in kayak are length, volume, and steering. These longer touring kayaks are built to cover water and track better. Look for a boat anywhere from 14 to 18 feet in length if overnighting. Sit-on-top kayaks will range generally from 8 to 15 feet. Narrow touring kayaks have less "initial stability"—they feel tippier when you get into them—although their narrowness prevents waves from flipping the boat over. Waves will tip wider sit-on-top kayaks, which have better initial stability. Whitewater kayaks are another matter altogether. Often short and operated with a spray skirt covering the entrance hole, these boats are built specifically for maneuvering through crashing whitewater and not for traveling downriver or on a lake. Consider them the sports cars of kayaks. Whitewater kayakers are diligent about picking the boat that works for them, factoring whether they are paddling down big, brawling rivers like the New or narrow, steep, rocky creeks that you and I as recreational paddlers wouldn't consider going down. These are used for many of West Virginia's and Virginia's wild whitewater streams, almost none of which are included in this guidebook. This volume is designed for the large audience of recreational paddlers.

Kayak materials vary from the traditional skin-and-wood of the Inuits to plastic and fiberglass composites like Kevlar and the waterproof cover of folding kayaks. For touring kayaks I recommend a tough composite model, simply because they can withstand running up on sandbars, scratching over oyster bars, or being accidentally dropped at the boat launch. I look for durability in a boat and don't want something that needs babying.

For touring boats, consider storage capacity. Gear is usually stored in water-proof compartments with hatches. Look for watertight hatches that close safely and securely. The larger the boat, the more room you will have. This is a matter of personal preference. Today, not only are there single kayaks but also double kayaks and even triple kayaks. Most touring kayaks come with a foot pedal–based steering system using a rudder. Overall, kayakers need to be fussier when choosing their boats than do canoeists, as kayaks are more situation specific. Surf the internet and read reviews thoroughly to get an idea of what you want, then go to a store that sells kayaks and try them out. Rent one from an outfitter and go down their river. Look for "demo days" at outdoors stores. Borrow a friend's kayak. Outfitters often sell used canoes and kayaks. A well-informed, careful choice will result in many positive kayaking experiences.

Choosing a Canoe

Canoes and kayaks offer different venues for plying the waters of the two Virginias. When looking for a canoe, consider the type of water through which you will be paddling. Will it be through still bodies of water or moving rivers? Will you be on big lakes, mild whitewater, or sluggish streams? Canoes come in a wide array of oil-based materials and are molded for weight, performance, and durability. Do not waste your time or money with an aluminum canoe. They are extremely noisy and are more likely to get hung on underwater obstacles rather than slide over them. Consider material and design. Canoe materials can range from wood to fiberglass to composites such as Polylink 3, Royalex, Kevlar, and even graphite. I prefer more durable canoes and thus seek out the tougher composites, such as Royalex.

Canoe design comprises the following factors: length, width, depth, keel, and bottom curve, as well as flare and tumblehome.

- **Length.** Canoes should be at least 16 feet long for carrying loads and better tracking. Be apprised that shorter canoes are available and are often used in ponds, small lakes, and smaller streams for shorter trips.

- **Width.** Wider canoes are more stable and can carry more loads but are slower. Go for somewhere in the middle.

- **Depth.** Deeper canoes can carry more weight and shed water, but they can get heavy. Again, go for the middle ground.

- **Keel.** A keel helps for tracking in lakes but decreases maneuverability in moving water.

- **Bottom curve.** The more curved the canoe bottom, the less stable the boat. Seek a shallowly arched boat, as it is more efficient than a flat-bottom boat but not as tippy as a deeply curved boat.

- **Flare.** Flare, the outward curve of the sides of the boat, sheds water from the craft. How much flare you want depends upon how much whitewater you expect to encounter.

- **Tumblehome.** Tumblehome is the inward slope of the upper body of the canoe. A more curved tumble home allows paddlers to get their paddle into the water easier. Rocker, the curve of the keel line from bow to stern, is important. More rocker increases maneuverability at the expense of stability. Again, go for the middle ground.

Then there are situation-specific canoes, such as whitewater or portaging canoes. Whitewater boats will have heavy rocker and deeper flare but will be a zigzagging tub on flatwater. Portaging canoes are built with extremely light materials and will have a padded portage yoke for toting the boat on your shoulders. I recommend multipurpose touring/tripping tandem canoes, those with adequate maneuverability, so you will be able to adjust and react while shooting rapids. You want a boat that can navigate moderate whitewater, can handle loads, and can track decently through flatwater. If you are solo-paddling a tandem canoe, weight the front with gear to make it run true. However, if you have a solo boat, you cannot change it to a two-person boat.

Consider the Old Town Penobscot 16, long a favorite of mine. It is a great all-around boat that I have used on varied trips, from day paddles on rivers to multinight adventures, over years and years. Ultra-lightweight canoes, such as those built by Wenonah, are designed to be carried from lake to lake via portages but have their place throughout Virginia and West Virginia waterways. I highly recommend the 17-foot Wenonah Spirit II. At 42 pounds, this ultralight Kevlar boat can perform well in the water and not break your back between your vehicle and the water. I used it often while writing this book. Other times you may be going down rivers with significant stretches of whitewater where you will want a boat that can take bone-jarring hits from rocks in the mountains of the two Virginias. Finally, choose muted colors that blend with the land and water. It is easy on the eyes and easier to hide if you are executing a bike shuttle or going on a hike during your paddle.

Which Paddle Do I Use?

Wood is still holding on strong as a material for paddles, though plastics dominate the market, especially lower-end paddles, such as those used by outfitters, and also ultralight high-end paddles. Some cheap varieties combine a plastic blade with an aluminum handle. Bent-shaft paddles are popular as well, though I don't recommend them myself. They are efficient as far as trying to get from point A to point B, but while floating you are often drifting and turning, making constant small adjustments, turning the boat around, and doing all sorts of maneuvers other than straightforward paddling in a line. Bent-shaft paddles are poor when it comes to precision steering moves. How about a square vs. rounded blade? I prefer a rounded blade for precision strokes, whereas a power paddler, maybe the bow paddler, will desire a square blade. Paddles can vary in length as well, generally from 48 to 60 inches. I recommend a shorter paddle for the stern paddler, because that is the person who makes the small adjustments changing boat direction. A shorter paddle is easier to maneuver when making all these small adjustments, not only in the water but also when shifting the paddle from one side of the boat to the next.

Kayak paddles are double-bladed, that is they have a blade on both sides, resulting in more efficient stroking. Kayakers seem more willing to part with a lot of money to use an ultralight paddle. Almost all kayak paddles are two-piece, snapping in the middle. This makes them easier to haul around, but more importantly it allows paddlers to offset the blades for more efficient stroking. Four-piece blades are not unusual though. Kayak blades are generally 6 inches by 18 inches, with paddles averaging between 7 and 8 feet in length. Weight-wise, expensive paddles can go as low as 24 ounces or less, while average paddles are 30 to 40 ounces. Like anything, you get what you pay for. A paddle leash is a wise investment to prevent losing your paddle.

Whether in a canoe or kayak, an extra paddle is a smart idea. It is easy to stow an extra paddle in the canoe, but a kayak can be more troublesome. A four-piece paddle is easier for a kayaker to stow.

Paddling Accessories

Life Vest

Wearing a life vest is a good idea when paddling. Even if not wearing a life vest, I always have one with me. It's the law (you are also supposed to have a whistle, horn, or bell in Virginia). In the bad old days, I would use any life jacket that would meet Coast Guard standards just to get by. But now I carry a quality life vest, not only for safety but also for comfort. The better kinds, especially those designed for kayaking, allow for freedom of arm movement.

Chair Backs

These hook on to the canoe seat to provide support for your back. I recommend the plastic models that cover most of your back, especially giving lower lumbar support. The more elaborate metal and canvas chair backs get in the way of paddling. However, having no chair back on multiday trips can lead to "canoer's back." Kayaks have built-in backrests.

Dry Bags

Waterproof dry bags are one of those inventions that give modern paddlers an advantage of leaps and bounds over those of yesteryear. These dry bags, primarily made of rubber and/or plastic, have various means of closing themselves down that result in a watertight seal, keeping your gear dry as you travel waterways, whether they are lakes or rivers. Today's dry bags, which can range from tiny personal-size, clear bags in which you might throw things such as sunscreen, keys, bug dope, and a hat, to massive rubber "black holes" with built-in shoulder straps and waist belts designed not only to keep your stuff dry but also to be carried on portages. They come in various sizes and shapes, designed to fit in the tiny corners of a kayak or an open canoe. Long and thin bags can hold a tent, while wide bags will fit most anything. Kayakers should consider deck bags, which are attached to the top of the kayak just in front of the paddler for storing day-use items. You can also get small dry pouches specifically designed to carry your smartphone. Some are equipped with lanyards to go around your neck. Do not take unnecessary chances with your device—keep it dry.

Plastic Boxes

Plastic storage boxes, found at any mega-retailer, come in a variety of sizes and shapes. They are cheap, easily sit in the bottom of the canoe, and can double as a table. Store items in here such as bread that you don't want smashed. However, they are not nearly as waterproof as a rubber dry bag. Consider using these if you are on flatwater.

Paddlers' Checklist

- ❏ Canoe/kayak
- ❏ Paddles
- ❏ Spare paddle
- ❏ Personal flotation device
- ❏ Dry bags for gear storage
- ❏ Whistle
- ❏ Towline
- ❏ Bilge pump for kayak
- ❏ Spray skirt for kayak
- ❏ Paddle float/lanyard for kayak
- ❏ Maps
- ❏ Throw lines
- ❏ Boat sponge

Depending on your personal interests, you may also want to consider some other items: fishing gear, sunglasses (with strap), trash bag, GPS, weather radio, camera, watch, sunscreen, lip balm, extra batteries, binoculars, cooler, and wildlife identification books.

Traveling with Your Boat

Boats, whether they are canoes or kayaks, need to be carried atop your vehicle en route to the water, unless you are renting one from an outfitter. How you load your boat not only depends upon whether it is a canoe or kayak but what type of vehicle it is and also whether or not you have an aftermarket roof rack. No matter how you carry your boat, tie it down securely, for the sake of not only your boat but also your fellow drivers, who will be endangered if your boat comes loose. I have seen a canoe fly off the car in front of me, and have seen what a boat will do to a car after sliding off to the side of said car while still tied on! After cinching your boat down, drive a short distance, then pull over and recheck your tie job. I recommend using the flat straps with buckles, which are sold at any outdoor retailer and also big-box stores. Some strap buckles are encased in rubber and keep the buckle from scratching your boat or automobile.

A quality aftermarket roof rack installed atop your vehicle makes for a much safer way to transport boats. Invest in one of these if paddling frequently. I have one and cannot imagine carrying my canoes and kayaks without it. Roof racks can be customized to different types and numbers of boats as well. And don't skimp on tie-down straps either; this is what holds the boat to the rack.

Parking

In writing this book and other Virginia and West Virginia hiking, backpacking, and camping guidebooks, among over seventy outdoor guidebooks, I have parked all over the country, often for days and weeks at a time. Use your intuition when leaving your vehicle somewhere. It is always best to arrange with someone to look after your car, and a small fee is worth the peace of mind. National, state, and county parks with on-site rangers are a good choice for leaving your vehicle overnight. Also, check with fish camps and liveries, as many of these provide shuttle service and a safe place to park. Private businesses sometimes allow overnighters to park in their lots. Be sure to ask permission and offer to pay. When parking for day trips, it is better to leave the vehicle near the road in sight rather than back in the woods out of sight.

Shuttles

River trips require a shuttle. Setting up these shuttles is a pain, but the payoff is getting to explore continually new waters in an ever-changing outdoor panorama. The closer you are to home, the more likely you are to be self-shuttling. Always remember to go to the takeout point first, leaving a car there, with the put-in point car following. Leave no valuables in your car. Take your keys with you and store them securely while you are floating. I have seen many a person leave their shuttle vehicle then forget to take their keys with them on the paddle. Do not let this happen to you.

Outfitters can save you the hassle of shuttling and allow you to leave your car in a safe, secure setting. Of course, you will pay for this service. This especially helps on river trips that are far away from home. When inquiring, don't be afraid to ask about prices, distances, and reservations if you can't get this information from their website. It pays to make the phone call if you have questions, especially if the paddling destination is far from home. Also, ask about camping and potential crowds, especially during weekends. When outfitters are available, they are listed with each paddle in this book.

Paddling Safety

A safe paddler is a smart paddler. Be prepared before you get on the water and you will minimize the possibility of accidents. And if they do happen, you will be better prepared to deal with them.

Lightning

Lightning can strike a paddler. Play it smart. When you sense a storm coming, have a plan as to what you will do when it hits. Most plans will involve getting off the water as quickly as possible. Seek shelter in a low area or in a grove of trees, not against a single tree, and then wait it out.

Poisonous Plants

Yep, poisonous plants are growing out there. You know the adages, such as "leaves of three, leave it be." If you are highly allergic to poisonous plants, check ahead for the area in which you will be paddling, then take the appropriate action, such as having Benadryl-based creams.

Bugs

Sometimes when paddling we consider the possibility of death by blood loss from mosquitoes, but actually your chances of dying from a bug bite in the wild are less than your chances of dying on the car ride to the river. Watch out for black widow spiders, and ticks with Lyme disease (though you cannot tell the ones with Lyme disease until you get it). For those who are allergic, bee stings are a real danger. Be prepared if you are one of these people subject to bee stings.

Snakes

Paddlers will see snakes along rivers, especially on sunny streamside rocks. This is a preferred area for copperheads. I have seen other snakes swimming while floating by in a boat. Give them a wide berth and they will do the same for you.

Sun

When paddling Virginia and West Virginia, the sun can be your enemy and your friend. You welcome its light and warmth. Then it tries to burn your skin, penetrate your eyes, and kick up gusty winds. Finally you lament its departure every night as darkness falls. Sun can be a real threat no matter where you are. While boating, you will be on the water and thus open to the prowess of old Sol. Be prepared for sun. Have sunscreen, a hat, bandanna, long pants, and a long-sleeved shirt. Clothes are your best defense. Put on the sunscreen before you get in the sun. Consider covering your hands. I have personally seen several cases of sun poisoning on paddler's hands.

Heat

While paddling, take shade breaks and swim to cool off in the heat of summer.

Cold

In our eagerness to hit the river, especially after a string of nice March days, we take off for the nearest stream, disregarding the fact that twenty-one days of March are classified as winter, and the waterways can be really cold then. The possibility of hypothermia is very real if you take a tumble into the water. Try to stay dry if at all possible—it is easier to stay dry and warm, or even dry and not so warm, than to get wet and cold, then warm up. Same goes for paddling in late fall and winter.

Medical Kit

Today, medical kits have come a long way. Now you can find activity-specific medical kits that also come in different sizes for each activity, including paddling. Medical kits designed for water sports come in waterproof pouches. I recommend Adventure Medical Kits. They not only have a good variety of kits but also divide their kits into group-size units, so whether you are a solo paddler or on a multiple-boat multiple-day river trip, you will have not only the right kit but the right-size one.

Camping

Overnight camping can add to the Virginia and West Virginia paddling experience. Where camping is a possibility, I have noted it in the paddling narratives. Other places may have strict private property situations or other elements that prohibit camping. However, you may want to consider camping either before or after your paddle. Check out the plethora of Virginia and West Virginia state parks, national parks, national forests, and other public lands.

Final Note

Just remember, paddling the two Virginias is about having a good time, whether you are sea kayaking on a tidal river, winding along a remote Piedmont stream, or stroking a translucent mountain waterway. Now, get out there and make some memories!

Map Legend

81	Interstate Highway	Boat Launch	
23	US Highway	■ Building/Point of Interest	
20	State Highway	▲ Campground	
628	County/Local Road	▲ Campsite	
----------	Paddle Route	Gate	
----------	Trail	? Visitor Center/Information	
++++++++	Railroad	Picnic Area	
-·-·-·-	State Line	Bridge	
(12)	Paddle Location	⊛ Capital	
•—₂	Mileage Marker	○ Town/City	
➤	Put-In/Takeout	— Dam	
⬭	Body of Water	P Parking	
〜	River/Creek	Scenic View/Overlook	
～	Intermittent Stream	▲ Mountain/Peak	
Marsh		National Forest/Park	
//	Rapids	State/County Park	
≋	Waterfall	Recreation Area/Preserve	
		Small Park	

Virginia Paddles

Floating the South Fork Shenandoah River can be a relaxing summertime experience.

Virginia Mountain Paddles

1 North Fork of Pound Lake

Make a rewarding paddling circuit around this tapered mountain-rimmed reservoir that is a no-wake-motors impoundment throughout its entire length. The lake is great for camping, fishing, or just enjoying the pristine shoreline, all of which are protected public lands.

County: Wise
Start: Pound Launch, N37 7.402' / W82 38.142'
End: Pound Launch, N37 7.402' / W82 38.142'
Length: 6.9 miles, with additional mileage possibilities
Float time: 3.5 hours
Difficulty rating: Easy-moderate
Rapids: None
River/lake type: Flood and recreation reservoir
Current: Negligible
River gradient: None
Water gauge: North Fork Pound Lake (Water Management Huntingdon District)
Season: Apr–Aug

Land status: National forest; a little Army Corps of Engineers land
Fees and permits: Modest launch fee required
Nearest city/town: Pound
Maps: North Fork of Pound Lake; USGS: Flat Gap
Boats used: Kayaks, canoes, johnboats with trolling motors, motorboats leaving no wake
Organization: US Army Corps of Engineers, North Fork Pound Lake, 7530 Old North Fork Rd., Pound, VA 24279; (276) 796-5775; www.lrh.usace.army.mil
Contact/outfitter: George Washington & Jefferson National Forests, Clinch Ranger District, 1700 Park Ave. SW, Norton, VA 24273; (276) 679-8370; www.fs.usda.gov/gwj

Put-in/Takeout Information

To put-in/takeout: From Norton, take US 23 north to the second US 23 Business exit for Pound, the northern US 23 Business exit. Here, turn left on VA 630, Old North Fork Road and follow it for 0.6 mile, then keep straight for the boat ramp and continue for 0.3 mile farther to dead-end at the Jefferson National Forest boat ramp and parking area.

Paddle Summary

This aquatic adventure explores narrow and winding North Fork Pound Lake, surrounded by steep wooded hills, part of the Jefferson National Forest. In addition to being enveloped in nature, the entire lake is a no-wake zone, so although gasoline motors are allowed, they can only putter around. The slender nature of the lake makes it seem almost riverine as you wander up the shore of the impounded North Fork Pound River to the Wise boat ramp, looking for old homesites along the way. Your return route cruises down the opposite shore. Lakeside camping spots are available, adding to the recreation possibilities.

River/Lake Overview

The North Fork of Pound River had historically flooded the city of Pound and other communities downstream, therefore this lake and downstream Flannagan Reservoir were authorized. Construction began on the North Fork of Pound Dam in 1963 and was finished three years later. The dam stands 122 feet high and 600 feet long. The lake itself is set fast against the Kentucky border, where rises Pine Mountain, the imposing barrier dividing the Bluegrass State from the Old Dominion. Although the lake comes in at only 154 acres, the serpentine nature of the impoundment creates

Leave this dock to begin your adventure on the North Fork of Pound Lake.

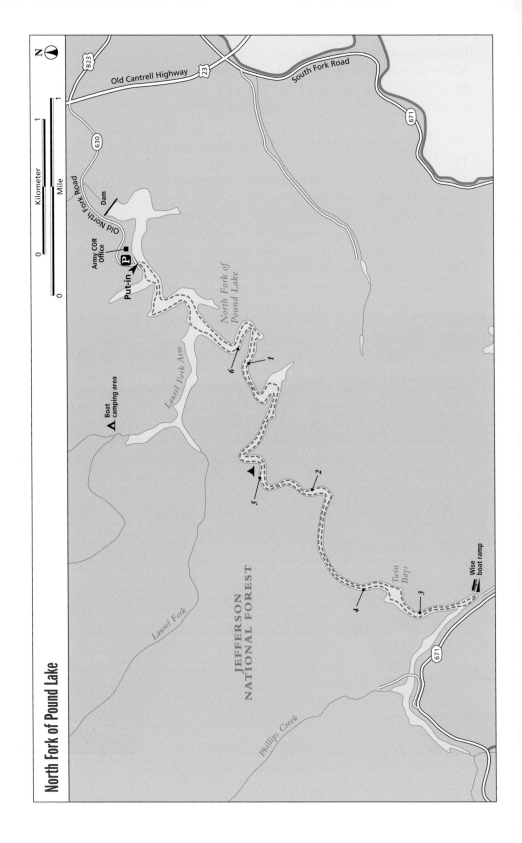

North Fork of Pound Lake

13.5 miles of shoreline. At full pool, the lake stands at 1,611 feet in elevation. The US Army Corps of Engineers manages the area around the dam, but the rest of the lake is part of the Jefferson National Forest, keeping the banks wild and scenic. A practiced eye will see many old roadbeds on the lakeside hills.

The Paddling

The boat ramp near the dam is concrete and large and has a floating dock, making it easy to unload and launch your craft. The lake dam is to your left and you can paddle that way for a short distance, but the balance of the lake is to your right, westerly. The blue-green water under normal conditions is extremely clear and you can easily see rocks 10 to 20 feet deep. Quickly pass the Hopkins Branch embayment to your right. The open water to your right clears a view of daunting Pine Mountain and the Virginia-Kentucky state line. Stay with the left bank, beginning one of the narrowest clockwise loops you will ever do. It does not take long to see that this lake more closely resembles a river—the valley is that narrow. In fact, in particularly slender spots, you may be able to detect current, but it is negligible from a paddler's point of view. Maple, hemlock, rhododendron, and a host of trees rise on steep hills above the water. Mountain laurel and oaks find their spots, while alder hugs the shore in thickets.

At 0.3 mile reach the spot where the two major arms of the lake split. Laurel Fork School was submerged here. To your right the Laurel Fork arm of the lake stretches almost due west and features a designated boat camping area that is completely primitive, just a shoreline spot. Our paddling adventure, however, stays left in the longer North Fork Pound River arm of the lake. Begin the circuitous shifting along the left shoreline. It is almost always best to stay along the shoreline, as you will see more interesting things, and in case the wind kicks up, you will be partly protected. Speaking of wind, this lake is so narrow that wind is less of a problem than in other impoundments.

You are fully in the left arm by 0.5 mile. At 0.7 mile curve around a slim point. It is almost as if you are hiking in the mountains, except on water. Watch for mountain laurel blooming in early June while the copious rhododendrons show their flowers in July. By the way, the US Army Corps of Engineers begins drawing down the lake in September, and it is a much less attractive prospect after that time. Therefore, spring through summer is the time to paddle here.

At 1.2 miles pass the only sizable bay in the lake on your left as you curve around another sharp point to your right. The clear waters will reveal fish galore, especially bass and bream. The water is almost like an aquarium if the rains have not fallen recently. Ahead, the lake surprisingly becomes still more slender. At 1.6 miles a campsite is on the far side of the water. This was an old homesite and even includes a concrete slab from the pre-lake days. Regal white oaks shade the spot. There has been a picnic table here in the past. I have camped here and enjoyed the experience.

Mountain laurel blooms add color to a foggy morn on North Fork of Pound Lake.

Our loop paddle continues on the opposite shore, however. At 2.1 miles a very obvious roadbed climbs out of the lake. This is but one of many old roads that you will begin to notice. After you spot one old roadbed, they will become easier to find, especially where rock was blasted along the old roadway. This was once heavily settled country, but when the dam came, the people were bought out using eminent domain, for better or worse. If you ask the people downstream, it was for the better, since the city of Pound was historically pounded by floodwaters on a regular basis.

At 2.9 miles the lake briefly widens to a spot known as Twin Bays. Here, two lookalike bays with grassy mouths occupy opposing shorelines. The creek up the left bay had many homes once. Continuing on, the main arm of the lake splits right at 3 miles, but you keep straight and eventually reach the Wise boat ramp at 3.3 miles. This is a good place to get out and stretch your legs if you want. The main waterway begins going along a road and makes it less pleasant. Therefore, I recommend circling back toward the dam, now on the left shoreline.

Looping back, you return to the Twin Bays at 3.9 miles. Look for evidence of beavers gnawing down trees in the woods. Look also for old stone fences and rock piles when these hills were tilled. On some segments of shoreline, you will notice a lesser understory, as well as burned bases of trees. Here, the Forest Service has used prescribed burning to keep the forest in its historical state. Wildflowers are prevalent along the north-facing slopes here. At 4.7 miles paddle by the campsite/homesite with the stone slab. I highly recommend the overnight experience here. You can always add exploring the Laurel Fork arm of the lake the next day to your paddle as well. Pass the Laurel Fork arm at 6.3 miles, and finally return to the boat ramp at 6.9 miles, ending your loop paddle on one of the narrowest lakes in the Old Dominion.

2 Flannagan Reservoir

This deep mountain lake in far-Southwest Virginia presents a lake-paddling opportunity on a reservoir with protected natural shoreline.

County: Dickenson
Start: Junction Marina, N37 12.885' / W82 22.237'
End: Junction Marina, N37 12.885' / W82 22.237'
Length: 7.9 miles, with additional mileage possibilities
Float time: 4.5 hours
Difficulty rating: Moderate
Rapids: None
River/lake type: Flood and recreation reservoir
Current: None
River gradient: None
Water gauge: J. W. Flannagan Dam (Water Management Huntingdon District)

Season: Apr-Sept
Land status: Army Corps of Engineers land
Fees and permits: Launch fee required
Nearest city/town: Haysi
Maps: J. W. Flannagan Reservoir; USGS: Haysi, Clintwood
Boats used: Kayaks, canoes, fishing boats, pontoon boats
Organization: US Army Corps of Engineers, John W. Flannagan Dam, 192 White Water Rd., Haysi, VA 24256; (276) 835-9544; www.lrh.usace.army.mil
Contact/outfitter: Breaks Interstate Park, 627 Commission Circle, Breaks, VA 24607; (276) 865-4413; www.breakspark.com

Put-in/Takeout Information

To put-in/takeout: From Haysi, take VA 63 north, Big Ridge Road. Follow VA 63 for 3.4 miles, then keep straight, joining VA 614. Drive a half mile then veer left, staying with VA 614. Drive for 1.2 more miles, then turn right, staying with VA 614 for 0.9 mile farther, then turn right onto VA 755 (a sign here says "Marina"). Descend for 0.4 mile to dead-end at the Junction boat ramp.

Paddle Summary

Known for its clarity, Flannagan Reservoir and surrounding uplands will present paddlers with opportunities to explore alluring terrain rising from its blue-green waters. You will start at Junction Marina, leaving a small cove and opening onto the confluence of Cranes Nest River and the Pound River, now stilled as part of Flannagan Reservoir. Our paddle makes a very slender loop, heading up the embayment of Cranes Nest River, replete with wooded shoreline, rising bluffs, and plenty of tributaries creating small arms of their own. You will paddle up to Tarpon Branch before returning on the opposite shoreline. Along the way, visit a few low-flow waterfalls that in springtime add moving water to the adventure.

Flannagan Reservoir

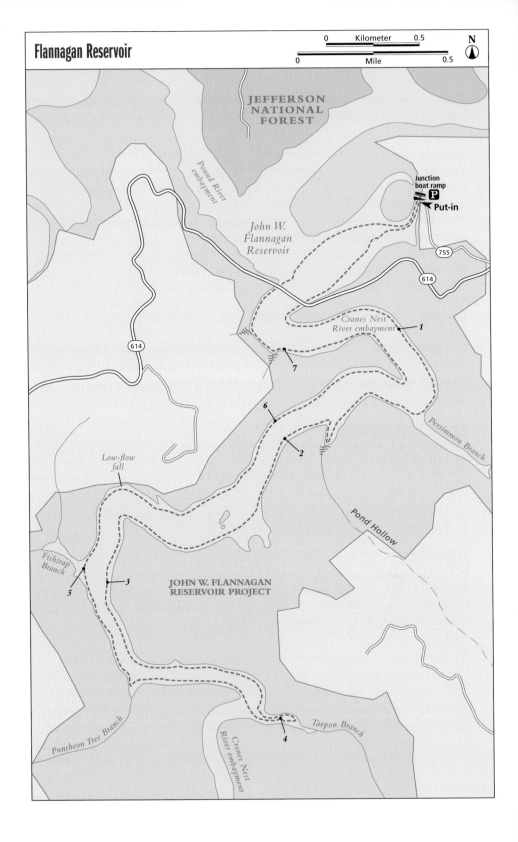

0   Kilometer   0.5

0   Mile   0.5

N

JEFFERSON
NATIONAL
FOREST

Pound River embayment

John W.
Flannagan
Reservoir

Junction
boat ramp
P
Put-in

755

614

614

Cranes Nest
River embayment

1

7

Persimmon Branch

6

2

Low-flow
fall

Pond Hollow

Fishtrap
Branch

5

3

JOHN W. FLANNAGAN
RESERVOIR PROJECT

Puncheon Tree Branch

Cranes Nest
River embayment

Tarpon Branch

4

River/Lake Overview

Flannagan Reservoir is a flood-control project undertaken by the Army Corps of Engineers, set deep in the folded intertwined hills of Southwest Virginia. The primary tributary backed up is the Pound River, a waterway historically prone to violent floods. The other main stream is the Cranes Nest River (and it is the lake arm up which we travel). Part of the greater Big Sandy River basin and in turn part of the Ohio River basin, Flannagan Reservoir slows downstream floods. The dam was authorized as part of the Flood Control Act of 1938, but construction on the dam did not begin until 1960. It was completed in 1964, creating a 1,145-acre lake blessed with nearly 40 miles of shoreline for our paddling pleasure. At full pool, Flannagan Reservoir stands in just short of 1,400 feet elevation. However, every October the lake is lowered the full 16 feet in order to store winter and spring runoff, doing its main job of preventing floods. The lake has several recreation areas that are used primarily during the summertime, including campgrounds, picnic areas, and boat launches.

The Paddling

The paddle leaves the Junction boat ramp area, passing houseboats and a small marina store before opening onto the main body of Flannagan Reservoir. This is among the widest portions of the lake, and even it is not wide at all. The watery preserve is completely enveloped in forest. To your right, the embayment of the Pound River splits

A slide cascade adds its flow to Flannagan Reservoir.

The embayment of Tarpon Branch narrows ahead.

right, as does the main body of the lake heading toward Flannagan Reservoir Dam, adding miles of paddling potential. Our route heads up the Cranes Nest River arm of the lake, and finding it is as simple as paddling toward the VA 614 bridge crossing the reservoir. It is the only bridge in sight.

Paddle under the bridge at 0.5 mile, sticking on the left shoreline as the route makes a sharp bend around a peninsula. Look back toward the main body of the lake to admire sheer tan bluffs as well as Pine Mountain rising to form the border between Kentucky and Virginia. The Cranes Nest River embayment narrows considerably as wooded, ferny hills, broken with hidden rock protrusions, rise sharply from the often rocky shoreline. Watch for floating logs and submerged trees. Overhanging trees are common, too, providing a corridor of shade in spots. As summer progresses, the clarity of the water sharpens until the reservoir can be aquarium-like.

Pass the deep embayment of Persimmon Branch at 1.3 miles. The twists and turns are such that you can rarely see down-lake very far. At 1.8 miles look for a rock sentinel standing left on the shore. Here, paddle up a small bay to find a low-flow 25-foot slide cascade accompanied by an overhanging rock house. Continue curving up the narrowing Cranes Nest arm to paddle by Fishtrap Branch at 2.9 miles. Here, watch for buoys indicating a no-wake area, obviously applying to the motorized-boating set—we paddlers need not worry about paddling so fast as to create a disturbing wake.

The waterway bends and narrows yet more. Find signed Puncheon Tree Branch on your right at 3.3 miles, allowing you to locate yourself with certainty. At 3.8 miles come to some bluffs and turn left into the slender Tarpon Branch bay. The narrowing and dark cove can be perceptibly cooler in summertime. This is a good place to turn around, but if you want to extend your paddle, it is 2.3 miles one-way to Cranes Nest boat launch.

CHECK OUT THE BREAKS

Breaks Interstate Park is just a few short but winding miles from Flannagan Reservoir. Here Russell Fork cuts such a deep valley through Pine Mountain that this chasm is dubbed the "Grand Canyon of the South," the breaks for which the park is named. View the Towers, a large rock prominence around which Russell Fork flows. Enjoy more vistas from the Overlook Trail. Take your vehicle on Nature Drive, a one-way scenic road for those less inclined to walk. Breaks Interstate Park has a large 138-site campground with a mix of good and less-than-good sites. The campground is open through October and presents a mix of tent and RV sites as well as both electric and nonelectric sites. Your best bet is to come here and choose your site in person.

During October weekends Flannagan Reservoir is lowered, filling Russell Fork and turning it into frothy whitewater for expert boaters. Crowds line the river to watch the action. The 3 miles from Bartlick Bridge to Garden Hole drop 28 feet per mile, presenting Class II–III water. Garden Hole is the last chance to get out before entering the Russell Fork gorge. The 4-mile section from Garden Hole to Ratliff Hole is what makes the Russell Fork the stuff of legend. Here, the river drops markedly under steep sandstone walls, making its way in a giant semicircular loop cutting through Pine Mountain. River gradients reach an astounding 190 feet per mile. Paddlers are taking on rapids named Triple Drop and El Horrendo, among others. This section, full of continuous, complex rapids, is for top-notch paddlers only. Enter Kentucky just before the takeout at Ratliff Hole, where paddlers gather to swap tales of tackling Russell Fork. For more information about Breaks Interstate Park and the Russell Fork, please visit www.breakspark.com.

However, our loop paddle begins working along the left shore as we return to Junction Marina, paddling by Puncheon Tree Branch a second time at 4.6 miles. And we reverse the process, with the lake widening. Come near Fishtrap Branch at 5 miles. Ahead, listen left for a low-flow waterfall dropping about 40 feet from a bluff at 5.3 miles. By 7 miles the VA 614 bridge comes into view. Hereabouts is another low-flow slide cascade that will completely dry up by August. Pass a final minor sliding spiller before paddling under the bridge at 7.3 miles. Ahead, aim for the bluffs across the open water, admiring them before turning toward Junction Marina, which is in plain sight. Work your way among the docks of the marina to reach the boat ramp, ending your paddle at 7.9 miles.

By the way, despite the shoreline being all natural and public property, camping is allowed only at designated campgrounds around the reservoir. Also, consider camping at nearby Breaks Interstate Park, a fantastic destination that is perched on the gorge of the Russell Fork and is where the waters of this lake empty.

3 Clinch River

Take a trip back in time on this relaxing float through a pastoral mountain valley, bending your way past fields and hills on one of the most biologically diverse rivers in the United States.

Counties: Russell; Wise
Start: Carterton Access, N36 54.875' / W82 13.276'
End: Saint Paul Access, N36 54.190' / W82 18.454'
Length: 8.9 miles
Float time: 4.5 hours
Difficulty rating: Easy
Rapids: Class I riffles
River/lake type: Medium pastoral river
Current: Moderate
River gradient: 2.5 feet per mile
Water gauge: Clinch River at Cleveland, no minimum runnable level
Season: Apr–Oct
Land status: Private

Fees and permits: None
Nearest city/town: Saint Paul
Maps: Virginia VGDIF: Carterton to Saint Paul; USGS: Carbo, Saint Paul
Boats used: Kayaks, canoes, a few johnboats, tubes near Saint Paul
Organization: Virginia Department of Game and Inland Fisheries, 7870 Villa Park Dr., Ste. 400 (Villa Park 3), Henrico, VA 23228; (804) 367-1000; www.dgif.virginia.gov
Contact/outfitter: Clinch River Adventures, 16642 E. Riverside Dr., Saint Paul, VA 24283; (276) 275-4154; www.clinchriveradventures .com. This friendly operation rents boats and runs shuttles for this very trip. Highly recommended!

Put-in/Takeout Information

To the takeout: From exit 17 on I-81 at Abingdon, take US 58 Alt west for 30 miles to the bridge over the Clinch River and immediately enter Saint Paul. Take your first right on VA 270 / Fourth Avenue at a traffic light and follow it briefly, then turn right again on VA 225 to reach Riverside Park and a small-craft boat launch on your right, just after the park's red caboose.

To the put-in from the takeout: Backtrack from the park to VA 270 / Fourth Avenue, then turn right and drive 0.2 mile to turn right on Wise Street and follow it for 0.7 mile. Then turn right on VA 628 and follow it for 1.6 miles to turn left on VA 615 / VA 628 at a T intersection. Stay with VA 628 for 4 miles, then turn right on VA 614, near the Springfield Baptist Church. Follow it for a mile to cross the bridge over the Clinch River. Continue for 0.3 mile farther, then sharply turn right onto Carterton Place Road. Follow this road for 0.2 mile, then turn right at Riverside Inn Drive to quickly dead-end at the VGDIF Carterton boat ramp.

Paddle Summary

This adventure travels along one of my favorite rivers in the Old Dominion. The section of this paddle, from Carterton to St. Paul, is a classic float through a pastoral valley enveloped by mountains. The serene valley takes you back to a simpler, more relaxing time. Leave your cares behind as the waterway leaves Carterton and begins winding its way southwesterly. Though having a current, this section of the Clinch has but a few rapids and all of them are easily negotiable even by the least capable paddlers, allowing you to focus on the scenery where rustic barns stand on hillsides below wooded ridges. Overhanging trees provide shade much of the way. A little civilization creeps in just before entering Saint Paul and paddle's end.

River/Lake Overview

The Clinch River continues to gain momentum as a paddler's river, especially with the establishment of Virginia's Clinch River State Park, still under development. The Clinch River is born near Tazewell, where the South Fork and North Fork converge a little south of the Old Dominion's border with West Virginia. The Clinch then begins its southwesterly journey, absorbing tributaries as it flows some 70 miles for Tennessee. It is quite a paddler's river in Old Virginny, winding in repeated beds. Its bluffs, banks, and bottoms harbor rare flora. Generally considered floatable by the time it reaches Richlands, Virginia, the Clinch avails some Class II+ waters before settling down to more pedestrian rapids. The river enters Tennessee in the midst of a long straightaway, hemmed in by Copper Ridge and Big Ridge. It finally leaves the mountainous straitjacket above Kyles Ford, curving a bit, then resumes its nearly

Take a trip back in time on this relaxing float through a pastoral mountain valley.

Clinch River

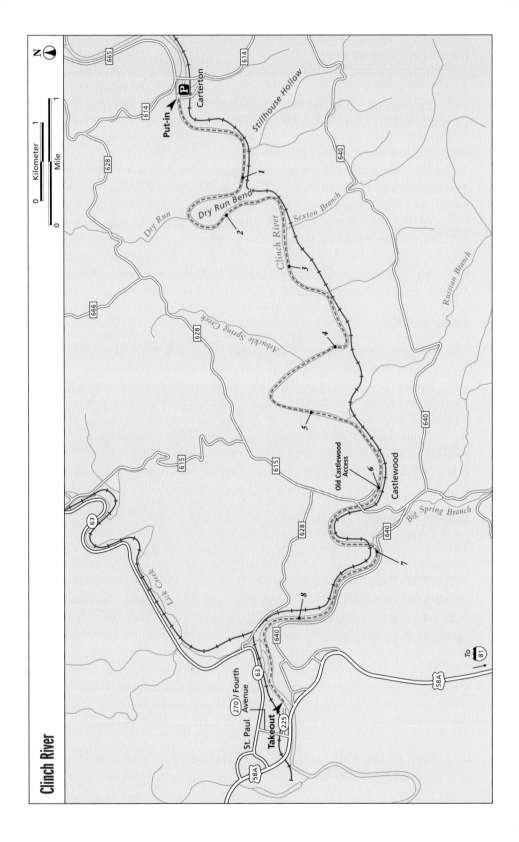

linear track until about 5 miles below Sneedville. From here on, the Clinch winds and works its way through rising mountains before being slowed at Norris Lake, then is dammed again near the city of Oak Ridge as Melton Hill Lake. Below Melton Hill Dam, the Clinch is briefly freed one last time before meeting the Tennessee River under the waters of Watts Bar Lake.

The Paddling

Leave the quiet Carterton boat ramp. The Clinch stretches about 100 feet wide here, bordered with overhanging ash and sycamore trees. Stone and mud banks rise about 10 feet high. The waterway speeds around gravel bars, where you will see exposed mussel shells. Although the Norfolk Southern Railroad is to your left, the Clinch occasionally winds away from the tracks. Furthermore, rail traffic on this line is way down from days gone by. In fact, I have made this paddling run without a single train passing while I was on the river. Soon jigger through a small shoal where Stillhouse Hollow comes in on your left. Enter Dry Run Bend as it makes a 180-degree-plus curve. Watch for small bluffs ahead. Dry Run comes in on the right at 1.6 miles, at a riffle. Gravel bars will typically be found on the inside of bends. Craggy hills rise to your right.

Leave Dry Run Bend at 2.4 miles, and leisurely float southwesterly. Sexton Branch comes in on your left at 2.9 miles. Sometimes, when the rail line is close, creeks such

MUSSEL MANIA

I bet you didn't know that the Clinch River is the number-one spot in the United States for rare and imperiled mussel species. The Clinch River harbors an impressive concentration of freshwater mussels, over forty in all. The names might not mean much, but they do sound like they were coined by mountaineers that settled this country: birdwing pearlymussel, rough rabbitsfoot, shiny pigtoe.

Concerning river health, mussels are the veritable canary in the coalmine. See, mussels are sedentary feeders, filtering the river to obtain nutrients. Thus, when toxins enter the river, the mussels absorb them. Today, we have an ever-increasing awareness of how our practices affect rivers. Now, you will see more protection of the land along the rivers, as in keeping banks vegetated and feeder streams shaded, and simply awareness that dumping something in the river does have consequences. On the Clinch groups such as the Nature Conservancy have purchased land and islands along the river to preserve mussel habitat. The group has helped set aside over 1,000 acres in the greater Cleveland, Virginia, area to preserve not only the mussel habitats but also dolomite barrens on bluffs overlooking the river. They also have an 850-acre tract near Kyles Ford, Tennessee, among others in their greater Clinch Valley Program, designed to help preserve this great Appalachian waterway.

Trees overhang parts of the Clinch River.

as Sexton Branch flow through culverts under the rail line just before merging with the Clinch. Begin another major river bend at 3.9 miles, turning north. A light, noisy shoal runs here. Arbuckle Spring Creek enters on river right at 4.2 miles. Pass a narrow little island at 4.4 miles. The current speeds at this point.

At 5.2 miles you have completed the second major bend. The current speeds here, too, and Russian Branch enters on your left. It is common for shoals to be found near the mouths of tributary streams, for the side creek often pushes rocks into the main river, making the water of the main stream speed up around the rocks, thus creating shoals.

Float through a slow, lazy section before reaching the newer Old Castlewood access on river right at 6 miles. A boat slide and steps make entering the river a breeze for self-propelled craft. This newer access is part of the continued development to increase the paddling possibilities on this scenic and botanically rich waterway. I have tripped down this waterway 60-plus miles from Cleveland, Virginia, to the Tennessee state line. Paddle beneath the Castlewood Bridge at 6.2 miles. Float under the Norfolk Southern Railway Bridge at 6.9 miles. Big Spring Branch enters on river left just after the rail span.

Hurry through a rapid at 7.3 miles. Ahead on your right, big boulders line the river's edge, leftover rock after a cliff was blasted to put in the rail line. Begin passing a few houses along the river as you near Saint Paul. At 8.3 miles Lick Creek comes in on your right as the Clinch divides around some islands as fast shoals. Stay left, as the route to the right is passable only at high water. Just ahead you come alongside Riverside Park. The boat slide and steps of the ramp are on the lower end of the park, on river right, a little before the US 58 Alt bridge crossing the Clinch.

4 Hungry Mother State Park

Explore the mountain-rimmed small lake at one of Virginia's venerated state parks. Not only can you paddle this scenic, "no gas motors allowed" impoundment, you can also engage in all manner of other outdoor activities.

County: Smyth
Start: Hungry Mother State Park ramp, N36 52.356' / W81 30.819'
End: Hungry Mother State Park ramp, N36 52.356' / W81 30.819'
Length: 3.7 miles
Float time: 2.0 hours
Difficulty rating: Easy
Rapids: None
River/lake type: Small mountain lake
Current: None
River gradient: None
Water gauge: None
Season: Apr–Oct

Land status: State park
Fees and permits: Daily parking pass required
Nearest city/town: Marion
Maps: Hungry Mother State Park; USGS: Marion, Chatham Hill
Boats used: Kayaks, canoes, paddleboats, johnboats
Organization: Hungry Mother State Park, 2854 Park Blvd., Marion, VA 24354; (276) 781-7400; www.dcr.virginia.gov/state-parks
Contact/outfitter: Friends of Hungry Mother State Park, PO Box 362, Marion, VA 24354; www.hungrymotherparkfriends.com

Put-in/Takeout Information

To put-in/takeout: From exit 45 on I-81 near Marion, take VA 16 west for 2.5 miles as it winds through the town of Marion, then split right on VA 617, reached before you come to the main state park facilities. Take VA 617 for 1 mile then veer left onto West Lakeview Lane, and continue driving for 0.6 mile to reach the park boat ramp after entering the park.

Paddle Summary

Conveniently located off I-81 near Marion, Hungry Mother State Park is a Virginia classic. And located within the bounds of this historic state park is a fine impoundment located in mountainous terrain between Little Brushy Mountain, Brushy Mountain, and Walker Mountain. Here, you start in the embayment of Mitchell Valley at the park boat launch and work your way into the main part of a narrow reservoir, where Hungry Mother Creek was dammed back in the 1930s, when the state park was established. Stroke your way north toward the imposing rampart of nearly 4,000-foot-high Walker Mountain. Along the shore, park facilities from trails to fishing docks to the park swim beach are visible. Head to the uppermost part of the lake to meet Hungry Mother Creek. From here you work your way back around the lake,

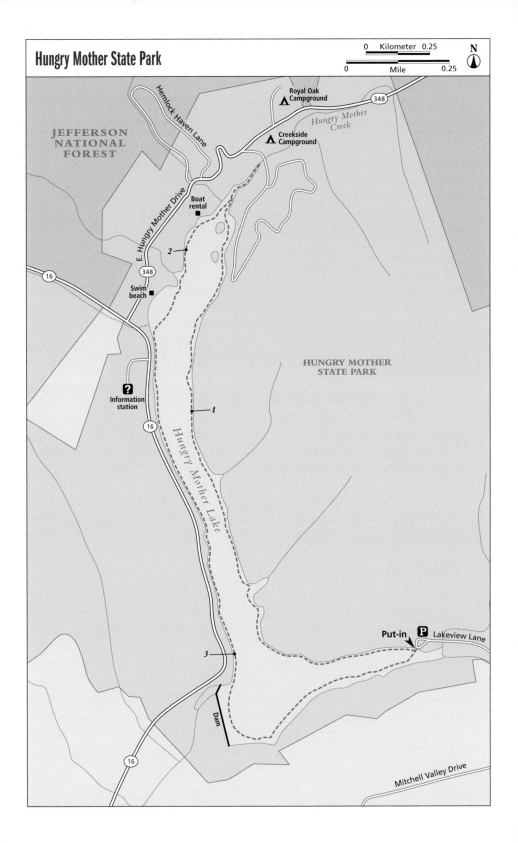

Hungry Mother State Park

Kilometer 0.25

Mile 0.25

N

JEFFERSON
NATIONAL
FOREST

Hemlock Haven Lane

Royal Oak
Campground

Hungry Mother
Creek

348

Creekside
Campground

Boat
rental

E. Hungry Mother Drive

348

2

16

Swim
beach

Hungry Mother Lake

HUNGRY MOTHER
STATE PARK

Information
station

16

1

Put-in

Lakeview Lane

3

Dam

16

Mitchell Valley Drive

passing more facilities that will leave you wishing to expand your Hungry Mother State Park adventure beyond paddling.

River/Lake Overview

Hungry Mother Lake is a linear impoundment that forms the centerpiece of Hungry Mother State Park. The lake comes in at 108 acres and is popular for not only paddling but also fishing and swimming. Hungry Mother Creek is the primary tributary, draining Little Brushy Mountain and Walker Mountain. The strange name was derived from an incident early in Southwest Virginia settler history. Area Indians had attacked settlements in the nearby New River Valley, taking some settlers prisoner. A lady by the name of Molly Marley and her unnamed child eventually escaped, fleeing down the valley between Little Brushy Mountain and Walker Mountain. Molly collapsed but her child continued down the creek still looking for help. The youngster ran into a fellow settler, and all she could utter were the words "hungry" and "mother." In the meantime Molly Marley passed away, but her surviving child left the name on this creek and what became the state park. Molly Knob, rising directly above the lake, was named for the mother.

The Paddling

Note the picnic tables and hiking trails at the boat launch. It is a special treat to make the 5.7-mile hiking circuit around Hungry Mother Lake. Consider this trek after your paddle. The park also has many other shorter trails if you are so inclined. The no-motors lake has a small concrete ramp along with a floating dock that paddlers find helpful. Additionally, since no one will be unloading big motorboats, there is normally no rush to get on or off the ramp. However, make sure to park your vehicle in the designated lot located a short distance from the ramp. The paddle begins in the largest embayment of Hungry Mother Lake, created by an unnamed stream flowing out of Mitchell Valley. As you begin heading westerly, the lake dam will come into view. Begin cruising along the right shoreline, beginning a counterclockwise loop of mountain tarn. The lake here is a couple of hundred feet wide, bordered by heavily vegetated shores.

At 0.3 mile enter the main body of the lake. Steep piney shores dotted with mountain laurel and rock outcrops rise along the west-facing shoreline. The hills rise directly from the water here. Unobstructed views of Walker Mountain open to the north. Paddle past a deep little inlet at 0.6 mile. By now you will have noticed designated bank-fishing spots along the opposite shoreline. These wooden landings also have lantern posts for night fishing. Hungry Mother Lake is a popular fishing venue for nearby residents of Marion. Largemouth and smallmouth bass, sunfish, crappie, and catfish are the preferred species, although muskellunge and walleye are stocked annually and are prized fish, unusual for these parts.

Walker Mountain rises majestically above Hungry Mother Lake.

Our paddle takes us past likely fishing destinations, an advantage that paddlers have over bank fishermen. At 1.1 miles the paddle curves northeasterly, aiming for the upper lake. Walker Mountain looms larger in the background. At 1.4 miles paddle beside an island used for interpretive programs. It is connected to the mainland by a pedestrian bridge. Near here, one of the park's rental cabins overlooks these upper waters, not quite lake and not quite creek, sort of a mountain marshland. In summer you may feel the water cool under your feet while working your way into the clear waters of Hungry Mother Creek. Rhododendron lines the stream and a small picnic area stands to your left. Ahead you will come to a small road bridge that is about the limit of paddleability of the stream, as it becomes too shallow and rocky. Creekside Campground, part of the park facilities, is just on the other side of the bridge.

After turning around work your way under the pedestrian bridge linking to the island on the right-hand shore, paddling by the park boat-rental facility at 1.9 miles. You will see they offer kayaks, canoes, paddleboats, and johnboats for rent. If renting a boat from the park, you will have to start your trip here; this will be no inconvenience. Ahead, paddle by the park swim beach. During the summer this is a popular

Canoes and kayaks reflect off the still waters of Hungry Mother Lake.

place for kids to frolic the waters watched over by lifeguards. Even though Hungry Mother Lake stands a little below 2,200 feet, it can still get warm enough for a cooling swim.

At this point the paddle comes along the west bank of the impoundment. Here stands a concentration of bank fishing platforms. You are also close to VA 16, but it provides little nuisance. How can paddling on this picturesque state park lake be a nuisance? At 3.1 miles the park dam comes into view again. Do not get too close, especially to the spillway. Finally, you enter the embayment of Mitchell Cove. Upon nearing the boat ramp notice the willowy wetland that lies where the lake and the stream of Mitchell Cove come together. Feel free to inspect this wetland before ending your paddle at 3.7 miles. However, do not run off from Hungry Mother State Park—there is too much to do and see. Dine in the park restaurant or overnight in a historic cabin. Pitch your tent or park your RV in the campground. Hike some of the 17 miles of hiking and biking trails. Learn about the flora and fauna of the park at the Discovery Center. Picnic at one of the shelters. Face it, Hungry Mother State Park is worth at least a day of your life, and it presents plenty of add-ons to your paddling experience.

5 New River: Eggleston to Pembroke

This Virginia stretch of the New combines majestic bluffs, mountain panoramas, and perky rapids on a king-size waterway.

County: Giles
Start: Eggleston River Road, N37 16.60' / W80 36.75'
End: Snidow Park Landing, N37 18.89' / W80 38.55'
Length: 6.7 miles
Float time: 3.1 hours
Difficulty rating: Moderate
Rapids: Class I–II
River/lake type: Mountain river
Current: Moderate
River gradient: 4.2 feet per mile
Water gauge: New River at Radford, no minimum runnable level, exercise caution above 5,000 cfs

Season: Apr–Oct
Land status: Private
Fees and permits: None
Nearest city/town: Pembroke
Maps: National Geographic Trails Illustrated map #787–Blacksburg/New River Valley; USGS: Eggleston, Pearisburg
Boats used: Kayaks, canoes, rafts, tubes, dories
Organization: New River Conservancy, 1 N. Jefferson Ave., West Jefferson, NC 28694, www.newriverconservancy.org
Contact/outfitter: Tangent Outfitters, 201 Cascade Dr., Pembroke, VA 24136; (540) 626-4567; www.newrivertrail.com

Put-in/Takeout Information

To the takeout: From exit 118 on I-81 near Christiansburg, take US 460 west for 27 miles to Pembroke and Cascade Drive. Tangent Outfitters will be on your right. Here, turn left and follow Cascade Drive 1 block to turn left on Snidow Street. Drive just a short distance on Snidow Street, then make a hard right on River Road, VA 623. Follow River Road for 0.3 mile, crossing the railroad tracks just before bridging the New River, then veer left into Snidow Park and the boat ramp at road's end.

To the put-in from the takeout: Return to River Road, VA 623, from Snidow Park Landing and turn left, bridging the New River. Stay with VA 623 for 2.7 miles, then turn left on VA 622, Guinea Mountain Road, and follow it 1.6 miles to turn right on VA 815 in Eggleston. Follow VA 815 for 0.2 mile, then turn right on VA 730, Eggleston River Road, and follow it 0.1 mile to turn left on Eggleston River Road. Follow Eggleston River Road for 1 mile and put in on your left.

Paddle Summary

This is a majestic paddle on a huge mountain river, complete with some exciting rapids to hone your paddling skills. Figure out a way to waterproof your phone or camera as you will want to capture the river scenes. The waterway leaves Eggleston and bends past the Palisades, the first of many tall riverside bluffs. Paddle past islands and riverside dwellings as Sinking Creek adds its flow. Some Class II rapids are interspersed throughout the trip. More bluffs await as you make a 180-degree bend. Your final attraction is Castle Rock, located near the takeout. Novice paddlers need not sweat the Class II shoals as they are mostly simple read-and-run rapids. The potential troubles come at higher flows when big waves can form on the rapids, potentially swamping your boat. Just be cautious at higher flows, avoid the big waves, and you will be fine.

River/Lake Overview

The New River is one of America's great waterways, and it travels through the mountains of three states. Born in the North Carolina highlands near the Blue Ridge town of Boone, the New River winds north and east through the Tarheel State, where it makes for a mostly gentle yet attractive paddling venture. The New enters Virginia at Independence. By then it has gained steam and has become a medium-size river. Dammed at Fries, the New pushes forth past Mount Rogers National Recreation Area and beyond to Foster Falls, a long Class III rapid. Hereabouts the 57-mile New River Trail—a rail trail—parallels the river. Slowed again at Claytor Lake, the New pushes west, brawling through high ridges where this paddle takes place. After breaking through the pass between East River Mountain and Peters Mountain, the now burly New enters West Virginia. A truly massive mountain waterway, the New is

The New River is known for its floating and fishing.

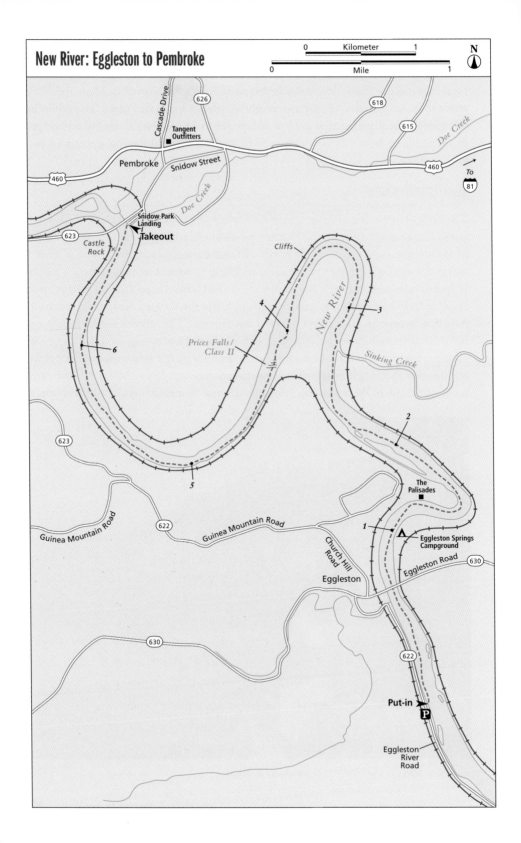

New River: Eggleston to Pembroke

0   Kilometer   1

0   Mile   1

N

626

618

615

Doe Creek

Cascade Drive

Tangent
Outfitters

Pembroke

Snidow Street

460

460

To

81

Doe Creek

Snidow Park
Landing

Takeout

623

Castle
Rock

Cliffs

New River

4

3

Sinking Creek

Prices Falls /
Class II

6

2

623

5

The Palisades

1

Eggleston Springs
Campground

Guinea Mountain Road

622

Guinea Mountain Road

Church Hill
Road

Eggleston Road

630

Eggleston

630

622

Put-in

P

Eggleston
River Road

dammed again at Bluestone Lake then enters the New River Gorge National River, with abundant recreation opportunities. Here, the entire New crashes over incomparable Sandstone Falls, then cuts deeper into the Appalachian Plateau. The scenery and history of the New River Gorge is the setting (and where another paddle in this guide takes place) until the New is dammed at Hawks Nest State Lake Park, yet another paddle included in this guide. From there, the New pushes a few more miles to meet the Gauley River, and together they form the Kanawha River. Overall, the New offers 250 plus or minus miles of paddling opportunity, from mild Class I floats to raucous whitewater for helmeted kayakers and rafters. It is truly a first-rate American paddling resource flowing through both Virginia and West Virginia.

The Paddling

You will notice several potential accesses along Eggleston River Road, as gravel bars and impromptu put-ins are located along the road. This is a popular access area, and on weekends vehicles will be lined up along Eggleston River Road. You can extend your trip by driving farther up Eggleston River Road. The paddle begins serenely on the 300-foot-wide New River, heading northbound. Heavily vegetated banks rise to hills and mountain beyond. The river flows clear green, opening to the rocks below. No matter what direction you look, mountains rise in the distance. Rail lines run along both sides of the waterway. A couple of small, warm-up rapids push you under the Eggleston Bridge at 0.6 mile. The New flows calm and slow for a bit, allowing you to gather yourself and truly appreciate the scenery. Although riverside houses

VISIT CASCADES WATERFALL

One of Virginia's most acclaimed cataracts is located very near the takeout for this paddle, Cascade Waterfall. It is 2 miles one-way to 60-foot Cascade Waterfall, the centerpiece of a nicely developed Jefferson National Forest day-use/picnic area on Little Stony Creek. A network of interconnected trails visiting rock walls, boulders, pools, and rapids leads up to Cascade Falls. No matter your route, you climb 700 feet from the trailhead to the cataract and its massive plunge pool, popular with swimmers. The trails range from challenging, narrow, and undulating to a well-graded wide track. I recommend taking the scenic and exciting Lower Trail first. Carved-stone signs located at trail intersections keep you on track. Using stone steps and rock walkways integrated into the incredible landscape, the waterside trails literally explore the heart of the Little Stony Creek valley. Boulder gardens, cliffs, and cataracts fashion an everywhere-you-look beauty that cannot be denied. To reach the Cascade Waterfall trailhead from Snidow boat ramp, simply return to US 460 and continue north on Cascade Drive to dead-end at the parking area.

Castle Rock looms large above a New River paddler. Keri Anne Molloy

are commonplace, they do not detract from the overall experience. Eggleston Springs Campground stretches along the right bank. It offers an alternate boat launch for a fee as well as campsites and cabins. At 1.3 miles the New curves right as the Palisades rise to your left. These are craggy pillar-like bluffs that have been a Virginia landmark for eons.

At 1.7 miles an island forms on river left, but the vast majority of flow stays to the right of the island, as do most paddlers. Downstream, a few rapids pick up. Often they are a mixture of even-gradient shoals as well as ledges on one side or another of the waterway. Therefore, you can make the rapid as challenging or easy as you please. At 2.4 miles the river bends right (north), and a host of mountains, led by 4,200-foot Butt Mountain, stand imposing before you. It is sight enough to distract you from the nearby riverside bluffs as well as the rapids ahead at 2.6 miles. Sinking Creek enters on river right at 2.7 miles.

Begin your 180-degree turn to the south, passing additional impressive cliffs. The New widens. At 4.1 miles enter a long set of Class II rapids known as Prices Falls. Watch for boat-stopping shallows as you work down the shoal. The river begins a long curve back to the north. Shoot through some mild rapids at 5.6 miles. Mountain views rise near and far. The stately bluff on river left is known as Castle Rock. Here, you float in its shadow before moving over to river right, reaching the Snidow Park landing, with a ramp and gravel bar, just where Doe Creek adds its flow to the New River.

6 Emberson Falls at Philpott Lake

Paddle a winding lake embayment to view an exciting cataract spilling into Philpott Lake.

Counties: Patrick; Franklin
Start: Ryans Branch Recreation Area, N36 50.958' / W80 6.076'
End: Ryans Branch Recreation Area, N36 50.958' / W80 6.076'
Length: 5.0 miles
Float time: 3.5 hours
Difficulty rating: Easy–moderate
Rapids: None
River/lake type: Hill-rimmed impoundment
Current: None
River gradient: None
Water gauge: Philpott Lake, 974 feet full pool
Season: Mar–June for best waterfall viewing

Land status: Army Corps of Engineers impoundment
Fees and permits: None
Nearest city/town: Martinsville
Maps: Philpott Lake Blueway; USGS: Philpott Lake
Boats used: Kayaks, canoes
Organization: US Army Corps of Engineers, 1058 Philpott Dam Rd., Bassett, VA 24055; (276) 629.2703; www.saw.usace.army.mil/Locations/District-Lakes-and-Dams/Philpott/
Contact/outfitter: Dan River Basin Association, 308 Craghead St., Ste. 104, Danville, VA 24541; (434) 792-3700, ext. 233; www.danriver.org

Put-in/Takeout Information

To put-in/takeout: From the town of Bassett, take VA 57 west, Fairy Stone Park Highway, for 10 miles to VA 346. Turn right on VA 346 north, Fairy Stone Lake Road, and follow it 0.4 mile to VA 623, Union Bridge Road. Turn left on Union Bridge Road and follow it 5.2 miles to the Ryans Branch boat ramp, on your right just after bridging both Philpott Lake and Ryans Branch.

Paddle Summary

This paddle takes you up the bluff-rimmed embayment of the Smith River where it is impounded as part of Philpott Lake, itself a US Army Corps of Engineers reservoir situated along the eastern base of Virginia's Blue Ridge. From the Ryans Branch boat ramp, you will emerge into the narrow hill-bordered upper lake, then snake your way up the Smith River embayment, where stony bluffs divide lesser seasonal drainages spilling into the lake. After twisting up the embayment, you will reach Emberson Falls, a 22-foot spiller tumbling over a rock face, framed in rhododendrons. You will return via the same route, enjoying more of this riverine segment of Philpott Lake.

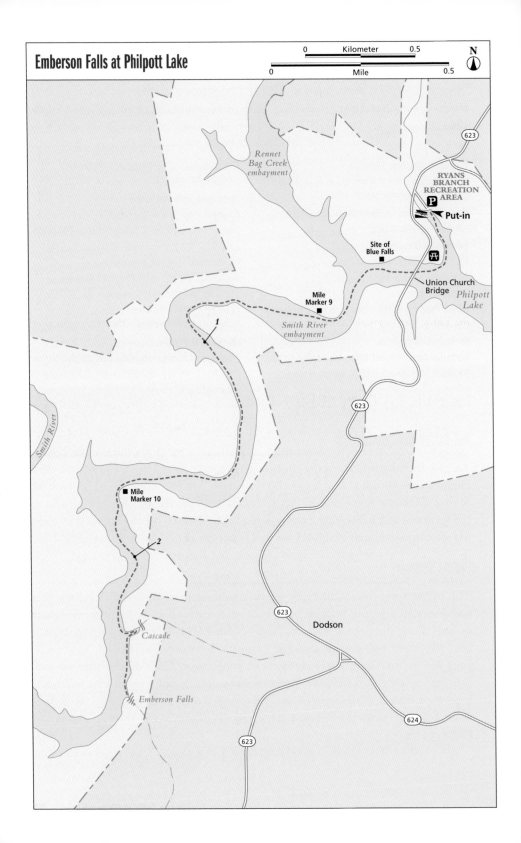

Emberson Falls at Philpott Lake

Kilometer
0   0.5

Mile
0   0.5

N

623

Rennet Bag Creek embayment

RYANS BRANCH RECREATION AREA

P

Put-in

Site of Blue Falls

Mile Marker 9

Union Church Bridge

Philpott Lake

Smith River embayment

1

623

Smith River

Mile Marker 10

2

623

Dodson

Cascade

624

Emberson Falls

623

River/Lake Overview

Philpott Lake was created back in 1952 as a flood-control and hydroelectric-power-producing impoundment. Stretching over three counties at the eastern base of the Blue Ridge—Franklin, Patrick, and Henry—the reservoir primarily backs up the Smith River, itself draining the highlands of the Blue Ridge. Over 3,000 acres of land in the Smith River basin were inundated after the dam was built, creating 100 miles of shoreline managed by the US Army Corps of Engineers, now a wooded scenic shoreline dotted with recreation areas, including Ryans Branch, where this paddle starts, as well as Virginia's famed Fairy Stone State Park.

The Paddling

The Ryans Branch boat ramp is tucked away in a hilly little hollow just north of the Union Church Bridge. The relatively quiet launch offers several parking spots and one ramp, as well as a floating dock, allowing paddlers to enter their boat away from the ramp. The normally blue-green water greets you upon leaving the widening cove of Ryans Branch, whereupon you are passing the Ryans Branch picnic area and a popular bank-fishing point in the main lake. Pines and hardwoods rise from the shore.

WHAT IS THE FAIRY STONE?

As if Philpott Lake is not enough to entice you to this part of the Old Dominion, Fairy Stone State Park is but a few miles distant. Originally developed by the Civilian Conservation Corps, Fairy Stone was one of Virginia's very first state parks.

How does a state park get a name like Fairy Stone? Within its boundaries lie some unusual crystals that are made of iron aluminum and silicate. These six-sided crystals connect at right angles, often forming crosses. Legend has it that fairies once roamed this land in the shadow of the Blue Ridge. When the fairies learned of Jesus's death, their tears crystallized when they hit the ground. The fairies have since moved on, but the fairy stones mark the sorrowful spot where they were when Jesus died. These fairy stones were one attraction that led to this locale becoming one of Virginia's original six state parks.

Fairy Stone offers a 168-acre lake of its own, complete with a swim beach, watched over by lifeguards in season. This lake is adjacent to Philpott Lake. No gasoline motors are allowed at Fairy Stone Lake, making it a serene destination. Rowboats, paddleboats, stand-up paddleboards, kayaks, and canoes may be rented during summer. The park has hiker-only, mountain-bike, and equestrian trails. The park also offers rustic cabins and yurts as well as a modern campground for tents and RVs. Enhance your visit to Philpott Lake with a trip to Ferry Stone State Park.

Emberson Falls flow boldly after a spring storm muddies Philpott Lake.

Here, head west, quickly paddling under two-lane Union Church Bridge, stretching across a narrow span of Philpott Lake. Truth be known, few wide sections exist anywhere along this lake and that is part of what makes it such a scenic impoundment and an ideal place for paddlers who do not mind a few motorboats here and there. In fact, this upper stretch of the lake is so narrow that waterskiing is not allowed above Union Church Bridge, where this paddle takes place.

After a quarter mile the impoundment splits into two arms. To your right the strangely named Rennet Bag Creek embayment splits right (northwest) while we stay left (southerly) with the Smith River arm of the lake. Interestingly, the confluence of Rennet Bag Creek and the Smith River was once the site of Blue Falls and the head of navigation for boats traveling upriver on the Smith. However, Blue Falls was inundated when Philpott Lake was dammed; all that remains is an outcrop rising from the water.

Turn south into the Smith River arm. The waterway is not more than 100 yards wide at this point. Natural shoreline circles Philpott Lake, since the public lands around the water are managed by the US Army Corps of Engineers. This creates an eye-pleasing atmosphere on both land and water. Pass channel marker number 9 on your right at 0.7 mile. These mile markers indicate how far you are from the Philpott Lake dam. During spring, the time when Emberson Falls will best be flowing, you will hear other streams flowing into Philpott Lake. However, many of these tributaries dry up later in the year. The sloped, wooded shores make for difficult stopping spots, but look on points where other visitors have pulled up to the land, such as the point on lake left at 0.9 mile.

Pass a rising bluff ahead. The narrow lake arm lessens wind problems. Pass channel marker number 10 at 1.7 miles. The waterway continues to narrow, and at 2.2 miles you will hear a cascade falling in a little cove. This is not Emberson Falls but a rather modest spiller dashing under cover of rhododendron and other growth. However, keep up the lake arm and stay on the left shoreline, then the sound of Emberson Falls will soon be ringing into your ears. And at 2.5 miles you discover the cataract. Here, an unnamed creek flows off the ridgeline above to make a final tumble over a craggy rock face framed in evergreens. The 22-foot spiller splashes into the still lake, creating an endless wave reverberation extending outward. Emberson Falls will be most bold in spring and can reduce to but a trickle in autumn. It is fun for paddlers to guide their boats to the edge of the cataract, enjoying the natural shower. No easy landing spots are near the falls. If you want to extend this paddle, you can backtrack to Rennet Bag Creek and paddle up it to view the bluff known as Calico Rock, adding about 4 miles to the paddle (2 miles each way).

If you like this undertaking on Philpott Lake, other adventurous lake paddles await you, all part of the greater Philpott Lake Blueway. Other destinations include Bowens Creek Falls, Fairy Stone Falls, and Deer Island—it offers boat-in camping. Multiple access points can be used to visit these lake features.

7 Roanoke River Blueway

Paddle your way through the heart of Salem on the Roanoke River, enjoying Class I–I+ rapids, plus one Class II. A parallel greenway most of the way allows for an easy bike shuttle.

County: Salem City
Start: Green Hill Park Access, N37 16.546' / W80 6.801'
End: Salem Rotary Park Access, N37 16.015' / W80 2.252'
Length: 5.4 miles
Float time: 2.5 hours
Difficulty rating: Moderate
Rapids: Class I–I+ rapids, one Class II
River/lake type: Small river
Current: Moderate–swift
River gradient: 6.8 feet per mile
Water gauge: Roanoke River at Glenvar, minimum runnable level 150 cfs

Season: Dec–June for adequate water levels
Land status: Private; greenway; and parkland
Fees and permits: None
Nearest city/town: Salem
Maps: Roanoke River Blueway; USGS: Salem
Boats used: Kayaks, canoes
Organization: Roanoke River Blueway, 313 Luck Ave. SW, Roanoke, VA 24016; www .roanokeriverblueway.org; roanokeriverblueway@ gmail.com
Contact/outfitter: Back Country Ski & Sport, 1931 Apperson Dr., Salem, VA 24153; (540) 389-8602; www.bcski.com

Put-in/Takeout Information

To the takeout: From exit 141 on I-81 just west of Roanoke, take 419 south / Electric Road for 2.6 miles, then stay left. Continue on Electric Road for 1.7 more miles, coming to the right turn into Salem Rotary Park on the right, just after crossing US 11, Apperson Drive.

To the put-in from the takeout: From Salem Rotary Park, turn left on Electric Road and quickly reach US 11 / Apperson Road and turn left. Follow US 11 for 0.9 mile, then turn left on Riverland Drive, continue a short piece to Bethel Baptist Church, then immediately turn right on Bowman Avenue. Follow Bowman Avenue for 0.7 mile to turn left on Eddy Avenue and follow it for 0.1 mile to turn right on Piedmont Avenue. Trace Piedmont Avenue as it becomes Riverside Drive, driving a total of 2.6 miles, to turn left on VA 760. Follow VA 760 a moment then turn right into Green Hill Park. Go for 0.1 mile, then turn right again for "River Access." After 0.4 mile you will see a picnic pavilion on your right and the stream access.

Paddle Summary

This is one different paddling trip, mostly for its setting, as you float the Roanoke River through the heart of Salem. The urban paddle starts at Green Hill Park then dances its way through a ribbon of green, bordered by the Roanoke River Greenway—a hiking/biking trail. Trail users will be watching you in action. The Roanoke, small-ish in this stretch, runs mostly clear over a rocky bed, presenting shoals and mostly Class I+ rapids, likely a tougher run when the water is up. You will pass under no fewer than five bridges, roads crossing the river, en route to your destination at Salem Rotary Park. The Roanoke River Greenway is your conduit back to the put-in for a fun bike shuttle.

River/Lake Overview

The Roanoke River is born in the highlands near Blacksburg, where the forks of the Roanoke merge to form the main stem not far from Salem and this paddle's begin-ning. The Roanoke then flows through its namesake town before cutting through the Blue Ridge, where it is next dammed as Smith Mountain Lake. The Roanoke then enters the Piedmont and is dammed as Leesville Lake. However, when the Roanoke River emerges from Leesville Dam, it has magically become the Staunton River, as it was named back in the 1700s for Lady Rebecca Staunton, the wife of colonial Virginia governor William Gooch. For 80 miles down to the confluence with the Dan River, the name remains Staunton River. Here, the 51 miles from Long Island, Virginia, to the US 360 Bridge—where this paddle ends—the (Roanoke) Staunton is a Virginia State Scenic River. Below the confluence with the Dan, the river once again becomes the Roanoke, and here it is dammed as Buggs Island Lake and then Lake Gaston. The river name remains the Roanoke throughout its remaining mileage to Albemarle Sound and its end at the North Carolina coast.

This stretch of the Roanoke River can be swift, shallow, and fun.

Roanoke River Blueway

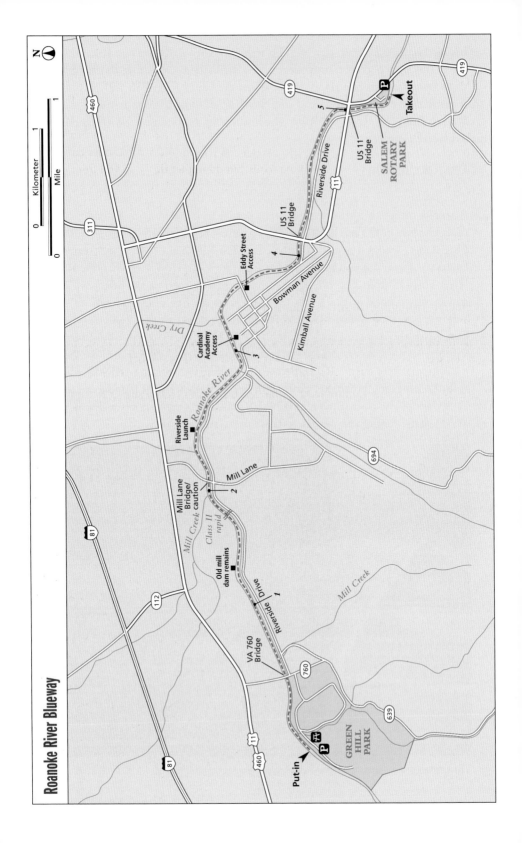

The Paddling

Get ready for some fun and some "performance paddling," since you will be running rapids alongside the Roanoke River Greenway, where walkers and bicyclists will inevitably stop and watch you dance through a shoal, or make a turn around a bend, or even just stare in unabashed envy, wishing they could be in your shoes—or river sandals. Do know that the greenway in its current incarnation does have a few lapses where you must use adjoining roads, but do not let that stop you from making a bike shuttle. It adds to the fun. I have done it myself. There is even a bike parking area at Salem Rotary Park, your takeout. And on the way back you can pedal along the Roanoke River, reveling in the glory of a successful paddle as you look down on the watercourse—and up at the mountains. For despite flowing through the heart of Salem, you will gain stellar montane views in places, as well as plenty of urban and suburban scenes. Want to know the downsides of this paddle? Well, there is a little more trash around the river than your average rural waterway. You will see urbanity all around—buildings, roads, cars, railroad tracks, and businesses. Yet the Roanoke River Blueway and the Roanoke River Greenway, along with the waterside parks that run along them, provide a ribbon of green and blue amidst the backdrop of Salem. I have even seen a deer while paddling this very stretch of the Roanoke!

The river makes for a fun run—at the proper levels. This stretch of the Roanoke tends to run below minimum runnable levels by mid- to late summer. Early spring through June is the normal season, but summer storms can raise the water. Speaking of that, be very careful about being on here in rainy times. Being in a city, this stretch of the Roanoke can rise in a heartbeat, though you can get out just about anywhere if troubles come up. Do exercise caution when passing under the Mill Lane Bridge. It is quite low and at flows of 1000 cfs or more, you cannot make it under the bridge.

Now to the paddling fun. A picnic shelter stands at the put-in, a sandy riverside beach. At this point the Roanoke is around 30 to 40 feet wide, flowing fast and clear, eastbound for the heart of Salem and the city of Roanoke. Pass a fishing pier on river right. Despite being an urban float, the waterway is bordered by vegetation and trees most of the way, with occasional grassy spots when passing along parklands and the greenway.

A pair of rapids greets you in the first 0.3 mile. Typical of this stretch of the Roanoke, they offer lively standing waves with a clear channel and some rock obstructions, which should be avoided. Be careful about getting going too fast so you can be ready for whatever lies downriver. Gravel bars and small islands narrow the waterway. Pass under the VA 760 bridge at 0.5 mile. The river remains shallow. At 1.3 miles pass the remains of an old milldam in the midst of a shoal, as the waterway bends right. At 1.6 miles the river splits around an island. This is the most substantial drop of the paddle and is a Class II rapid with rocks in its midst. If you do not want to tackle this, go left around the island, then walk your boat through.

Rapids and mountain views make this paddle a double delight.

Mill Creek comes in on your left just before dancing through a rock garden and passing under the low Mill Lane Bridge at 2 miles, in the midst of a continuing shoal. If the water is up, approach this bridge with caution, and if you have any doubts about getting under, don't wait until you are at the bridge. Remember, at flows of 1,000 cfs or higher, you must portage (I would not be on the river at all at 1,000 cfs). Look for the West Riverside Drive concrete ramp access on the river at 2.3 miles. The Roanoke River widens in spots here.

At 2.8 miles the Roanoke curves left, with a bluff to your right. Shoot a couple of short drops. Some of these drops are caused by concrete-encased pipelines crossing the bottom of the river, resulting in a shoal. Pass the Cardinal Academy access (concrete ramp) on river right at 3.1 miles, and float under Eddy Street Bridge at 3.5 miles. Just after the bridge you come to the Eddy Street access (concrete ramp) on river right. The river widens here in rocky shallows. Mill Mountain rises ahead, and more mountain views open behind you. Stay on guard as fun shoals keep you going but do demand attention.

Float under the US 11 bridge at 4.1 miles. Keep east, then paddle under US 11 a second time at 5 miles. This is your signal—bridge number 5. Keep floating and keep left as the Roanoke makes a bend to the left. Here you will find a big gravel bar / water play area at Salem Rotary Park. The gravel bar makes for easy landing, and it is but a short carry to the parking area. Perhaps you may have left your bike here and are ready to pick up the greenway and make the fun pedaling shuttle. You could also do it by foot, or jog. Paddle or not, the Roanoke River Greenway is almost as fun as the Roanoke River Blueway.

8 Carvins Cove Reservoir

Paddle to the head of this mountain-rimmed lake with continuous views. The drinking-water basin for Roanoke, Carvins Cove Reservoir presents gorgeous natural mountain shores rising to the Appalachian Trail, ringing the impoundment.

County: Botetourt
Start: Carvins Cove Reservoir ramp, N37 23.046' / W79 56.805'
End: Carvins Cove Reservoir ramp, N37 23.046' / W79 56.805'
Length: 6.0 miles, with additional mileage possibilities
Float time: 3.6 hours
Difficulty rating: Moderate
Rapids: None
River/lake type: Drinking-water reservoir
Current: None
River gradient: None
Water gauge: Carvins Cove Reservoir—Western Virginia Water Authority
Season: Mid-Mar through early Nov

Land status: Water authority property; city park above 1,200-foot elevation line
Fees and permits: Daily boat pass; annual passes available
Nearest city/town: Roanoke
Maps: Carvins Cove Natural Reserve; USGS: Daleville
Boats used: Kayaks, canoes, paddleboats, motorboats with 10 or less horsepower
Organization: Carvins Cove Reservoir / Boat Landing, 644 Reservoir Rd., Roanoke, VA 24019; (540) 362-1757; www.westernvawater .org/carvinscove
Contact/outfitter: Roanoke City Parks, 215 Church Ave. SW, Room 303, Roanoke, VA 24011; (540) 853-2236; www.playroanoke.com

Put-in/Takeout Information

To put-in/takeout: From exit 150A on I-81 just north of Roanoke, take US 220A south for just a short distance, then turn right onto US 11 south / Lee Highway and follow it for 2.9 miles. Turn right onto VA 648 / Reservoir Road and follow it 2.4 miles to reach the reservoir launch and parking area.

Paddle Summary

This lake paddle in the mountains just beyond Roanoke is a feast for the eyes. Here, you will paddle a tree-lined reservoir from which rise mountains atop which runs the Appalachian Trail. The scenery is all natural since the lake was established for holding drinking water and the lands above it are managed as a preserve. From the lone civilized outpost on the lake, you will leave the boat ramp and head up the east shore of Carvins Cove Reservoir, intermittently carved with intimate watery coves begging exploration. Continue up the reservoir to its uppermost reaches, where you can paddle up to Carvin Creek, then work your way back down the steeper south and west banks of the impoundment, where more coves lure you in. Despite the mountainous terrain, occasional stopping spots are available.

River/Lake Overview

Carvins Cove Reservoir occupies 630 acres tucked away beneath Tinker Mountain and Brushy Mountain in the Appalachians just west of Roanoke. Back in the 1920s a stable water supply was needed for Roanoke and its neighboring towns. The land in Carvins Cove was purchased, but it was not until 1946 that Carvin Creek was finally backed up and the impoundment, elevation 1,170 feet, as we know it today came to be, holding 6.42 billion gallons of water at full pool. The area surrounding the lake covers 12,700 acres and is managed by the city of Roanoke as Carvins Cove Natural Reserve, the second-largest municipal park in the United States. It offers over 60 miles of trails for hikers, mountain bikes, and equestrians. Horse Pen Branch, Angell Branch, Sawmill Branch, and Rocky Branch are other major tributaries feeding Carvins Cove Reservoir.

The Paddling

Note: The marina rents single and double kayaks, johnboats, and paddleboats. Leave the boat ramp and head north, quickly passing the lake picnic area on your right. Mountain views are immediate as Tinker Mountain forms a rampart to your north. The Appalachian Trail runs atop it. Creek coves are continually carved into the shoreline, each one a draw unto its own. Most paddlers heading up the lake go from point to point rather than curving into each cove, but even at that, it is a full 6 miles to the headwaters and back. The lake does allow motorboats but only up to 10 horsepower. Other than that and some power lines, the atmosphere remains wild. Bears are regularly seen here. Pass under a power line at 0.6 mile.

At 1 mile pass the embayment of Angell Branch on your right. Note the bridge deep in the cove. While paddling you will undoubtedly notice the very clean waters and shores of this spectacular paddling destination. Spring and autumn are excellent times to visit, as you can see the greens of spring climbing the mountains and the colors of fall spreading over the land above. The contours of the mountains contrast with the flat lake. You cannot help but wonder what the lake looks like from the top of the mountains, and the Appalachian Trail can be your conduit to enjoy such vistas. In fact, a signed overlook is located near the headwaters of Angell Branch.

The lake is becoming more slender and the mountains are crowding higher above as you bend westerly, following the curves of Tinker Mountain and Brushy Mountain. Look for rock outcrops on the slopes above. By 2.2 miles reach a point where the lake splits into three arms. Sawmill Branch arm stretches to your right, there's an unnamed creek on your left, and the Carvin Creek arm is dead ahead. Keep straight for the Carvin Creek arm. Tinker Mountain rises steeply in front of you as you are now going west. The embayment continues to narrow. Look on the right for a patch of pines that is a popular stopping spot, should you need to get out of the boat. By 2.9 miles the upper reaches of Carvin Creek become more of a marshland from which rise thickets of willows. Sycamores tower over the creek and

Carvins Cove Reservoir

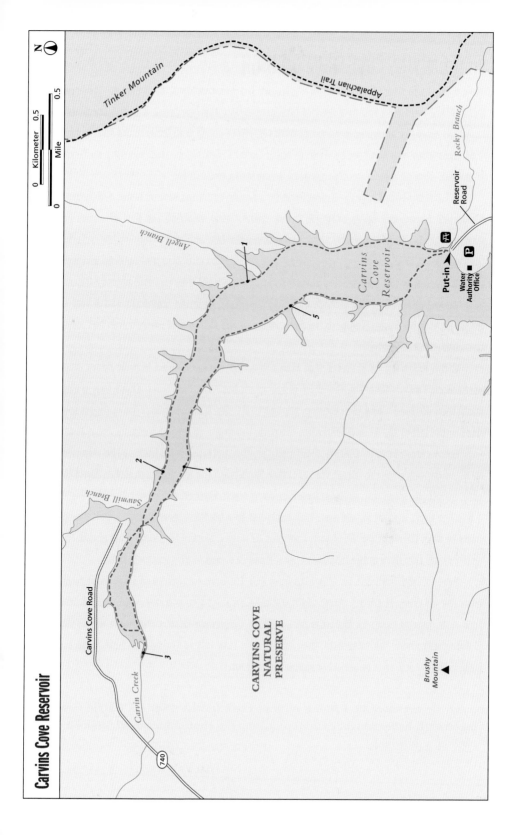

VIEW CARVINS COVE FROM ON HIGH

Want a top-down view of Carvins Cove Reservoir? The granddaddy of all pathways—the Appalachian Trail—will lead you to a host of lake panoramas. This gorgeous 9.2-mile there-and-back hike starts at a commuter parking lot off I-81. Here a spur trail leads to the Appalachian Trail, whereupon you head southbound to reach Tinker Creek. Soon, start climbing up Tinker Mountain, winding among boulder gardens, stone walls, and bluffs.

At 1.8 miles the AT takes you directly under a power-line transmission tower and through a clearing. Ahead, the valley of Angell Creek opens below, allowing the first of numerous views of Carvins Cove Reservoir. Sand, pines, and pale, tan, and gray outcrops characterize the ridge here. More views continue ahead. At 2.5 miles an unobstructed outcrop and high point to the left of the trail delivers a westerly prospect across the reservoir, across I-81, and into the Roanoke Valley. The balance of Tinker Mountain, Catawba Mountain, and a host of ridges stretches onward. The path becomes rocky to the extreme, slowing travel, but elevation changes are minimal.

At 3.6 miles the AT makes a "Fat Man's Squeeze" between chest-high boulders. Keep north along Tinker Mountain, the crest dropping off both east and west. Climb over a little knob, then descend along the ridgetop, coming to Hay Rock at 3.9 miles. The upthrust rock rises to the left of the AT and overhangs the path, forming a shelter of sorts.

There's more beyond. Quickly come along another upthrust rock, then saddle alongside an upthrust rock wall, the "Great Wall of Tinker Mountain." The barricade stretches along the path, eventually gives way, and you meander stony track. Emerge at a power-line clearing at 4.6 miles. Here, a short signed spur trail leads left to a bouldery view. Below, Angell Branch flows to meet Carvins Cove Reservoir, encircled by ridges. Brushy Mountain rises ahead. This vista reveals the glory of the lake below, enveloped in a nest of Virginia highlands.

To reach the trailhead for this hike from exit 150B on I-81 north of Roanoke, emerge from the off-ramp at US 11. Head south 0.2 mile on US 11 to a traffic light and US 220. Turn right (northbound) for Daleville on US 220 / Cloverdale Road. Drive north on US 220 / Cloverdale under the interstate, then at 0.2 mile turn left to Tinker Mountain Road and immediately reach an interstate commuter parking lot.

you may be serenaded by a chorus of frogs. Look for the mouth of Carvin Creek. If the water is high enough, you can paddle up the clear mountain stream for a bit flanked by a little bluff.

Looking down at Carvins Cove Reservoir from the Appalachian Trail

After going as far up as you can, begin your return journey down the impound-ment, with the declivitous slopes of Brushy Mountain rising to your right. Stopping spots are less frequent here. Mountain views remain spectacular and continuous. Turn southeast at 4.7 miles, and keep southerly. Stay with the shoreline until you are almost across from the boat landing, then make the less-than-a-half-mile lake crossing to reach the ramp after 6 miles. And if you feel like circling the whole lake, including the Horse Pen Branch arm of the reservoir, add about 4 miles to the paddle, not including any side trips up coves.

$\textstyle\bigcirc$ James River: Horseshoe Bend to Buchanan

Float past fun rapids complemented by mountain views on the upper James.

County: Botetourt
Start: Horseshoe Bend boat ramp, N37 35.343' / W79 43.666'
End: Buchanan boat ramp, N37 31.792' / W79 40.756'
Length: 8.6 miles
Float time: 4.2 hours
Difficulty rating: Moderate
Rapids: Class I–II
River/lake type: Mountain river
Current: Moderate
River gradient: 5.4 feet per mile
Water gauge: James River at Buchanan, recommended level 2-4 feet is ideal, stay off above 6 feet

Season: Apr–Oct
Land status: Private
Fees and permits: None
Nearest city/town: Buchanan
Maps: James River Water Trail; USGS: Buchanan
Boats used: Kayaks, canoes
Organization: James River Association, 4833 Old Main St., Richmond, VA 23231; (804) 788-8811; www.jamesriverassociation.org
Contact/outfitter: Twin River Outfitters, 640 Lowe St., Buchanan, VA 24066; (540) 254-8012; https://canoevirginia.net

Put-in/Takeout Information

To the takeout: From exit 168 on I-81 near Buchanan, take US 11 south, Lee Highway, for 1.4 miles, bridging the James River in Buchanan, then immediately turning right onto Lowe Street. Drive just a short distance on Lowe Street, then turn right into the Buchanan boat ramp, just across the street from Twin River Outfitters.

To the put-in from the takeout: Backtrack to Lee Highway, US 11, and head north, bridging the James again to turn left on VA 43 after 0.2 mile. Follow VA 43 for 6.7 miles, then turn left into the Horseshoe Bend boat ramp on your left.

Paddle Summary

This paddle offers a lot: mountain scenery, alluring water, fun rapids—and an easy shuttle. The boat landings on both ends of the paddle are clearly marked and well maintained. Start your adventure at the Horseshoe Bend boat ramp, immediately launching into a rapid. Cruise downstream, then come to the biggest rapid of the trip—Ritchie's Falls, a Class II endeavor. From there you will alternate pools and shoals past the Springwood boat ramp. From here, the shoals ease for a while as you relaxingly float toward the Blue Ridge and views of the Blue Ridge Parkway. The rapids resume while closing in on Buchanan, ending your paddling adventure in the heart of the classic Southern small town. Overall, easy access from the interstate, an outfitter on-site, and a shuttle make this a must-do paddle, especially if driving down

A paddler flotilla relaxes on the upper James River.

I-81. Finally, the 8.6-mile distance is just right, considering how the beginning of the paddle is fast, the middle a little slow, and the end fast also.

River/Lake Overview

The James River is Virginia's contribution to great rivers of the world and is Virginia's largest watercourse, flowing across the entire state from the mountains in the west to the Atlantic Ocean in the east. The James is born in the upper reaches of the Appalachians, fast against the West Virginia border in appropriately named Highland County, where the Cowpasture River and the Jackson River converge to form the James at a water pass between ridges known as the Iron Gate. Here in Botetourt County, the James officially begins its 340-mile journey to Chesapeake Bay, making it one of the longest rivers in the United States that begins and ends in the same state, passing through the Piedmont and Tidewater, as well as through Virginia's capital city of Richmond along the way. The James's watershed encompasses 25 percent of Virginia, around 10,000 square miles, draining the heart of the Old Dominion.

The Paddling

The Horseshoe Bend boat ramp can be busy on summer weekends with self-shuttlers and the local outfitter. Be cautious when taking off, since you are in the middle of a mild but fast rapid. Make sure your boat is secure while loading or it might float off on you. Begin working south after the put-in rapid. By 0.9 mile the CSX Railroad

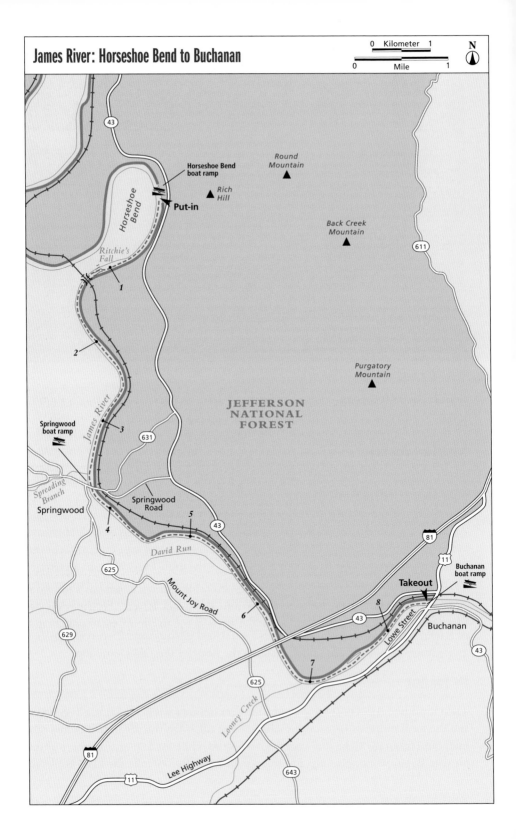

James River: Horseshoe Bend to Buchanan

0   Kilometer   1

0   Mile   1

N

43

Horseshoe Bend
boat ramp

*Round
Mountain* ▲

▲ *Rich
Hill*

Put-in

*Back Creek
Mountain* ▲

611

*Horseshoe
Bend*

*Ritchie's
Fall*

1

*Purgatory
Mountain* ▲

2

**JEFFERSON
NATIONAL
FOREST**

James River

Springwood
boat ramp

3

631

*Spreading
Branch*

Springwood
Road

Springwood

5

43

81

4

David Run

11

Buchanan
boat ramp

625

Takeout

8

Mount Joy Road

6

43

Buchanan

629

Lowe Street

43

7

625

Looney Creek

81

Lee Highway

11

643

A kayaker enters Class II Ritchie's Falls.

bridge comes into view. This is your cue to head over river left, in anticipation of Class II Ritchie's Falls. This shoal consists of ledges, with the best route far left, very close to the left bank. It is a fun, splashy ride, and you can scout on river left, but it is not necessary. Most paddlers on this section have heard of Ritchie's Falls before they get on and are often a little nervous at the put-in. However, the name sounds scarier than the reality. It is not a waterfall in any sense of the word, merely a Class II rapid. And if you can make it down Ritchie's Falls, you have got it made all the way to Buchanan. Float under the CSX bridge at 1.3 miles, then veer left. Ash, river birch, and sycamore line the banks. Hills rise in the near, with mountains in the far.

Pass a private boat ramp on river right at 3.3 miles. The public Springwood boat ramp is located just before the Springwood bridge at 3.7 miles. Notice Spreading Branch entering on river-right at the bridge. Spreading Branch fashions a sonorous waterfall just before delivering its waters into the James River. The James divides around small islands near the bridge. At 4.1 miles come to a long, entertaining rapid that lasts almost a third of a mile. Long shoals such as these are fun to run and navigate, and they really keep you moving along. A bluff on river right awaits at the base of this rapid. You also have a dead-on view of Purgatory Mountain rising from the river.

Look for striations in the riverbed as you drift through a long slow section, eventually turning southeast. Here is where long-reaching panoramas of the Blue Ridge open. A keen eye will spot the cleared, straight lines of the Blue Ridge Parkway. Before or after your paddle, consider an adventure on the parkway that includes a trip to Apple Orchard Falls (see sidebar below) or the Peaks of Otter. The slow, easy section continues as you float under the twin bridges of I-81 at 6.5 miles. At 6.9 miles bend left as big Looney Creek enters on river right. A long set of easy yet almost continuous riffles and shoals speed you past abandoned bridge abutments. You are going northeast. Tubers join the fray in this segment, sometimes giving the river a carnival atmosphere. By 8.1 miles the habitations of Buchanan come into view. You know you are almost there when the US 11 bridge appears. Take note of a parallel pedestrian bridge located here. It is fun to walk the pedestrian bridge and look down on your fellow paddlers, especially on a busy summer weekend. The Buchanan boat ramp is on river right just before the bridges at 8.6 miles.

VIEWS AND FALLS ON THE PARKWAY

On this paddle you will be looking up directly at the Blue Ridge and the Blue Ridge Parkway. From there enjoy a rewarding walk from Sunset Fields Overlook on the parkway to visit 200-foot Apple Orchard Falls, adding another aquatic feature to complement your paddle. Interestingly, the waters of Apple Orchard Falls flow into the James River. A worthwhile loop allows you to see the falls as well as hike part of the famed Appalachian Trail. To get there from Buchanan, take VA 43 east 5 miles to the parkway, then turn left and follow it to milepost 78.4, Sunset Fields Overlook, where you can view the James River Valley. The 5-mile loop leaves Sunset Fields on the paved Apple Orchard Falls Trail. Join a natural-surface path, reaching the long cataract after 1.3 miles. Here, a bridge crossing at the base of Apple Orchard Falls creates for an ideal viewing platform. Look up—from the bridge you can see the cataract spill over an open ledge then slide down an angled chute. From there the foam encounters a huge midcataract boulder, where water disperses into multiple spills, then filters into a rock jumble as it passes underneath the bridge. There is a little bit of everything in this waterfall. Backtrack to join Apple Orchard Road (a trail), then head left on the Cornelius Creek Trail. Close the loop with a walk on the Appalachian Trail, seeing more wonders of the James River Valley.

10 Lake Moomaw

This big lake deep in the mountains offers big-time views while you make a big-time 9-mile still-water paddle, with overnighting possibilities and additional padding mileages, deep within the George Washington National Forest.

County: Bath
Start: Bolar Flat boat ramp, N37 59.573' / W79 56.868'
End: Bolar Flat boat ramp, N37 59.573' / W79 56.868'
Length: 8.9 miles
Float time: 4.2 hours
Difficulty rating: Moderate-difficult
Rapids: None
River/lake type: National forest mountain lake
Current: None
River gradient: None
Water gauge: None
Season: Apr-Oct

Land status: National forest
Fees and permits: Launch fee required
Nearest city/town: Warm Springs
Maps: National Geographic #788 Covington/ Allegheny Highlands; USGS: Falling Spring
Boats used: Kayaks, canoes, motorboats
Organization: George Washington National Forest, 422 Forestry Rd., Hot Springs, VA 24445; (540) 839-2521; www.fs.fed.us
Contact/outfitter: Virginia Department of Game and Inland Fisheries, 7870 Villa Park Dr., Ste. 400 (Villa Park 3), Henrico, VA 23228; (804) 367-1000; www.dgif.virginia.gov

Put-in/Takeout Information

To put-in/takeout: From the intersection of VA 39 and US 220 in Warm Springs, take VA 39 west for 10.5 miles to VA 600. Turn left on VA 600 and follow it 7 miles to the intersection with Twin Ridge Drive. VA 600 bears left and becomes VA 603. Stay left here, now on VA 603, going toward Bolar Flat and McClintic Point, drive for 1.6 more miles, and turn right into Bolar Flat and the Lake Moomaw marina. The boat launch is at the lower end of the marina.

Paddle Summary

This big mountain lake, an impoundment of the Jackson River, sits enveloped in the splendor of the George Washington National Forest. Allegheny Mountain to the west and Coles Mountain to the east form twin ramparts lording over the waters from above. The paddle leaves the narrows of Lake Moomaw near Bolar Flat (also known as the Lake Moomaw marina), then heads south, opening onto a wider stretch of water, bordered by bluffs and open to first-rate panoramas in all directions. Come to a tall man-made stone bluff, then cross over to the west side of the impoundment, circling past coves, including the one where you find Greenwood Point Campground, accessible only by foot or boat. The circuit paddle continues along the shoreline, where you find campsites, picnic areas, and swim beaches before returning to the narrows

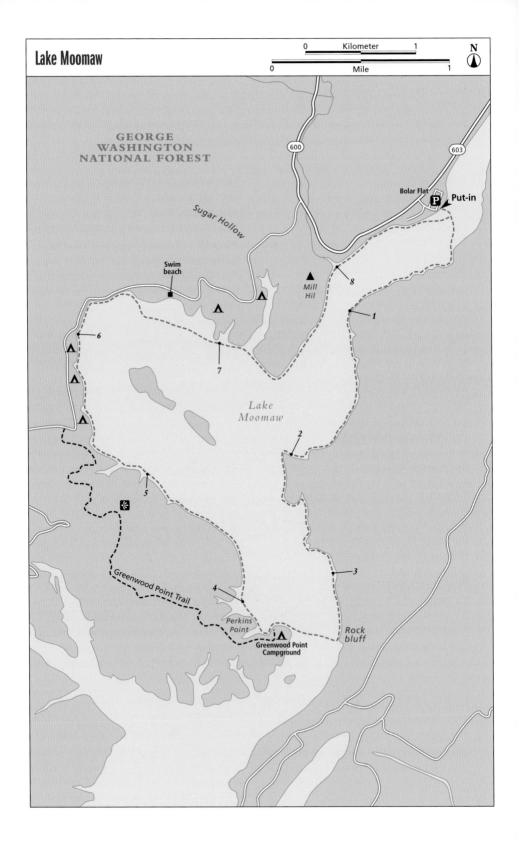

Lake Moomaw

0 Kilometer 1

0 Mile 1

N

GEORGE
WASHINGTON
NATIONAL FOREST

600

603

Sugar Hollow

Bolar Flat

P Put-in

Swim
beach

Mill
Hil

8

1

Lake
Moomaw

6

7

2

5

3

Greenwood Point Trail

4

Perkins
Point

Greenwood Point
Campground

Rock
bluff

and Bolar Flat. The paddle can easily be lengthened or shortened depending on weather and your whim. Do be apprised that the lake is large enough to be problematic in strong winds.

River/Lake Overview

Talk about a long time coming! Lake Moomaw was authorized by Congress in 1946 to dam the Jackson River, one of the major headwaters of the James River, for flood control. The project was later deferred, then put back on the burner in 1967. The dam was completed in 1981, and the 2,530-acre impoundment was filled, creating 43 panoramic miles of shoreline deep in the Allegheny Mountains of western Virginia. The surrounding terrain is managed by the George Washington National Forest as well as the Virginia Department of Game and Inland Fisheries. The Forest Service has installed campgrounds, picnic areas, and other recreational facilities to enhance the already alluring lake, which is among Virginia's finest reservoirs.

A kayaker runs the shore of Lake Moomaw.

Although motorboats have unrestricted horsepower and unrestricted access (except for the immediate vicinity of the swim beaches), the entire lake is more than suitable for paddling adventures. This particular trip circles the heart of Lake Moomaw, but another major trip could be paddled up the narrows of the lake where it emerges from Richardson Gorge, as well as the lower part of the lake near the dam, where two major embayments are created by the Big Lick Creek and Hughes Draft. Therefore, if you like this paddle, there is plenty more to explore here at Lake Moomaw. Moreover, several drive-up campgrounds can be your overnighting quarters between paddling adventures.

Bolar Flat offers a standard boat ramp, plus an additional "hand launch craft only" dock. That way you will not be stuck waiting for motorboats to launch or caught half-loaded when a motor boater backs in their trailer. Leave the dock and paddle by the small marina, aiming for the opposite shoreline, which you reach at 0.3 mile, beginning a clockwise circuit. The ultra-clear mountain water is eclipsed only by rewarding mountain panoramas. Head south along the shore, aiming for a narrow neck of the reservoir. The waters are bordered by rising forests.

Reach a neck at 1 mile, paddling by a small, tawny-gravel beach. The lake opens and views get even better, if that is possible. Low, water-washed bluffs rise from the shore in places. Curve around a second point at 2.1 miles. It also has a gravel beach.

BACKCOUNTRY CAMP AT LAKE MOOMAW

Want to get away from it all? Lake Moomaw is a great escape, especially Greenwood Point Campground, accessible by boat or foot. This is a first-come, first-served fee camping area, so upon arriving at Bolar Mountain Recreation Area, let recreation personnel know you are heading for Greenwood Point Campground. Then you can pay your fee and get parking instructions (overnight parking areas differ whether you are hiking or paddling in).

Greenwood Point Campground, where the Greenwood Point Trail ends, has six sites available. The primitive camp is set on a grassy, tree-bordered hill in a cove of Lake Moomaw. Backpackers will find the campground views of the lake and mountains rewarding. Boaters and backpackers keep Greenwood Point hopping during summer, especially weekends.

The hike to Greenwood Point is a good break-in trip for novice backpackers. The trek features ample hills to challenge but is not far distance-wise—it's only 3.1 miles each way. Potable water is not available, therefore you must treat your water from the lake or bring your own.

Trees border the large, grassy area. Picnic tables are scattered about, delineating the 6 campsites. A small beach lies at water's edge. Pick your spot and enjoy lakeside camping at Lake Moomaw, backcountry-style.

A view of Lake Moomaw from the Greenwood Point Trail

The two big islands of Lake Moomaw stand directly west. These are ridges that once separated Mud Run from the Jackson River. At 2.3 miles curve around yet another point. Your impossible-to-miss marker rises 200 feet from shore—a man-made, layered rock bluff created when stone was quarried to build the dam for Lake Moomaw. Paddle to the impressive layered stone wall, then cut due west across the reservoir, keeping a lone island to your south.

Reach the west shore of the lake at 3.6 miles. Begin curving along the banks. Turn into a deep cove, reaching Greenwood Point Campground at 3.8 miles. This is a fine destination. Read the sidebar for more information about camping here.

Continuing the paddle, work your way along scenic coves, paddling past signed Perkins Point. Make sure to scope north, as the long ridge of Allegheny Mountain stretches to the horizon, while simultaneously delineating the boundary of Virginia and West Virginia. You are now angling northwesterly with a lot of open water to your right. Watch as the islands to your right become more clearly defined. Come alongside Bolar Mountain Campground 3. Begin a segment of paddling by recreation-area facilities. Marshy, willowy banks characterize much of the shoreline hereabouts.

Turn easterly with the contours of the lake at 6.5 miles. Soon come to the swim beach area. Paddling or boating through it is strictly forbidden. Buoys delineate the swim beach with a second line of buoys marking the no-boating zone. Work around the buoys and return to the shoreline, paddling by a picnic shelter and more camping areas. If you still have energy, the slender embayment of Sugar Hollow beckons. Otherwise soon turn north and work your way up the reservoir. You can see the marina in the distance ahead. Paddle by the slender small embayment of Mill Creek at 8.1 miles. Now it is a simple matter of keeping the paddle going, passing a smaller swim beach, and you are back at Bolar Flat and paddle's end at 8.9 miles.

11 South Fork Shenandoah River near Elkton

Paddle a smaller, more intimate section of South Fork Shenandoah River. Despite the smallish size, this adventure still offers big mountain views as well as alternating shoals and pools throughout the trip.

County: Rockingham
Start: Island Fork ramp, N38 21.271' / W78 41.735'
End: Elkton ramp, N38 24.555' / W78 38.127'
Length: 7.2 miles
Float time: 3.4 hours
Difficulty rating: Easy–moderate
Rapids: Class I–I+
River/lake type: Mountain-rimmed valley river
Current: Moderate
River gradient: 5.0 feet per mile
Water gauge: South Fork Shenandoah River near Lynnwood, 2.2 feet minimum runnable level, stay off the river above 5.0

Season: Mar–Oct
Land status: Private
Fees and permits: None
Nearest city/town: Elkton
Maps: VDGIF Island Ford to Elkton; USGS: McGaheysville, Elkton West, Elkton East
Boats used: Kayaks, canoes, tubes, rafts
Organization: Friends of the Shenandoah River, 1460 University Dr. / Gregory Hall, Winchester, VA 22601; (540) 665-1286; www.fosr.org
Contact/outfitter: Shenandoah River Adventures, 415 Long Ave., Shenandoah, VA 22849; (888) 309-7222; www.shenandoahriver adventures.com

Put-in/Takeout Information

To the takeout: From exit 247 off I-81 take US 33 east and follow it for 14 miles, then turn left onto US 33 Business east and follow it for 0.8 mile. Just after crossing the South Fork Shenandoah River, turn right into a combination park / recycling center, then quickly turn right again to reach the Elkton boat ramp.

To the put-in from the takeout: Leave the Elkton ramp and drive east on US 33 Business for 0.9 mile, then turn right at the traffic light, joining US 340 south, and follow it for 5.9 miles to turn right on VA 649, Island Ford Road. Follow Island Ford Road for 0.4 mile, then turn left onto Captain Yancy Road, and briefly follow it to turn right into the Island Ford ramp.

Paddle Summary

This paddle in the upper Shenandoah Valley is on a smaller waterway, where the freshly born South Fork Shenandoah River bounces and pushes north, freshly fed by no fewer than four streams flowing from Shenandoah National Park, as well as other waterways from the southern tip of Massanutten Mountain. It is a little quieter than the lower, busier downstream sections of the waterway. You will start at the confluence of the South Fork and Twomile Run, rolling through the "Upper Valley,"

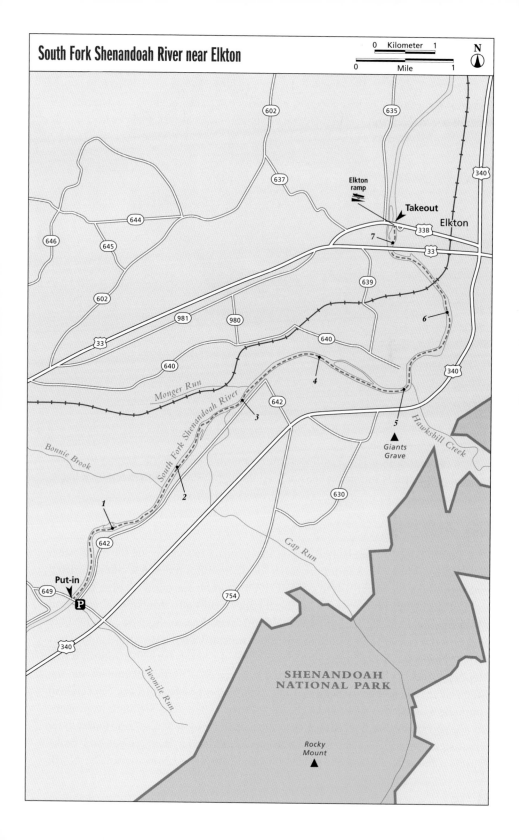

South Fork Shenandoah River near Elkton

0   Kilometer   1

0   Mile   1

N

Elkton
ramp

Takeout

Elkton

33B

7

33

602

635

340

637

644

646

645

602

639

981

980

640

33

640

640

642

6

340

3

4

5

Monger Run

South Fork Shenandoah River

Bonnie Brook

2

642

Hawksbill Creek

Giants
Grave

630

1

Gap Run

649

Put-in

P

754

340

Twomile Run

SHENANDOAH
NATIONAL PARK

Rocky
Mount

The author paddles the South Fork into the morning light. KERI ANNE MOLLOY

pushed on by sonorous rapids, stilled in other spots by slower pools, perfect for relaxing. Enjoyable rapids and shoals are scattered throughout the paddle, keeping it lively. Views open in places where the waterway twists and turns.

River/Lake Overview

The South Fork Shenandoah River is the primary waterway of the main stem Shenandoah River. The South Fork flows for 97 beautiful miles in a valley bordered by Shenandoah National Park to the east and the mountains of the George Washington National Forest to the west. The South Fork's headwaters flow from Shenandoah Mountain, forming the Virginia–West Virginia state line to the west and the Blue Ridge to the east. It is here in the upper Shenandoah Valley where the South River and the North River meet near Grottoes, forming the South Fork Shenandoah River. Here the waterway heads north, squeezing between Massanutten Mountain and the Blue Ridge, where this particular paddle takes place. The South Fork Shenandoah continues gaining tributaries from the Blue Ridge while demonstrating its propensity for repeatedly bending. Massanutten Mountain being lower, it contributes lesser tributaries. Nevertheless, the river continues north under these ridges and peaks. Finally, at Front Royal, the South Fork Shenandoah River meets the smaller North

VISIT SHENANDOAH NATIONAL PARK

During this paddle you will gain views of Shenandoah National Park as waters from its heights propel you downstream. Have you ever visited this special preserve? When mentioning Shenandoah National Park, visitors often get that faraway look in their eye, fondly recalling the sights, sounds, and smells of previous adventures at this scenic mountain jewel rising high atop Virginia's Appalachians. Whether it is a tawny deer bounding through the grasses, a rousing panorama from a roadside overlook, a vista from a backcountry crag, or a side trip to a cooling waterfall, a trip to fabled Shenandoah will enhance your paddling adventure.

And there is so much to do—auto-tour Skyline Drive, hike to sights historical, natural, and cultural, waterfalls, overlooks, and pioneer homesites. Set up your camper at a campground under the stars while mountain breezes sing you to sleep, dine and overnight at a lodge after enjoying an informative ranger program. Delve deep into the backcountry, pitching your tent near a clear stream in solitude. Picnic under budding oak trees. Try to identify the plethora of wildflowers and trees that inhabit this special piece of the Old Dominion.

Cobbled together along the Blue Ridge from Front Royal to Waynesboro, the long, narrow preserve divides the proud Shenandoah Valley from the rolling Piedmont to the east. The park contains a wide array of flora and fauna as it rises from a mere 550 feet at its lowest elevation to over 4,000 feet atop Hawksbill. Here, you can absorb panoramic views from overlooks scattered on lofty Skyline Drive, which runs the length of the 300-square-mile sanctuary. Beyond Skyline Drive lies another Shenandoah, where bears furtively roam the hollows and brook trout ply the tumbling streams. Trailside flowers color the woods. Quartz, granite, and greenstone outcrops jut above the diverse forest, allowing far-flung views of the Blue Ridge and surrounding Shenandoah Valley. It is this beauty found up close on the trail and in distant views that creates the special Shenandoah experience. Check it out for yourself.

Fork Shenandoah River to then form the main-stem Shenandoah River. Here, the Shenandoah River leaves the Old Dominion and enters West Virginia before flowing a few more miles to give its waters to the Potomac River at historic Harpers Ferry. However, take note that the South Fork Shenandoah River is often simply referred to as the Shenandoah River, even though the actual Shenandoah River flows for just a short distance in Virginia and not much more in West Virginia before emptying into the Potomac.

The Paddling

Leave the gravel bar and ramp of the Island Ford landing, then float beneath the Island Ford Road bridge. The river opens before you downstream, stretching about 110 feet from bank to bank, lined with trees, predominantly sycamore. Start in a slow section, allowing you to gather yourself before tackling any fast-moving water. At 0.6 mile the waterway helps a little bit, speeding over rock in a riffle. The clear water reveals sand and rocks at the bottom. The smaller waterway certainly delivers a more intimate aura than the wide, lower South Fork Shenandoah. By 0.8 mile you reach a bona fide rapid splitting around a small island. Stay on the right side of the isle. The exciting, Class I+ run has a nice little drop followed by lesser shoals and extends for 0.3 mile. Along the way the river has turned northeasterly. Occasional breaks in the shoreline tree screen allow views of the rich agricultural tradition for which the Shenandoah Valley is known, and of course the mountains that envelop the valley and enhance its splendor.

The river remains shallow, with neither white rapids nor deep doldrums, just a steady current. Bonnie Brook adds its flow from river left at 1.7 miles. At 2.4 miles the South Fork Shenandoah splits around a skinny island, where you will stay left. On the right Gap Run flows in. More small islands follow, effectively narrowing the main channel to 40 to 50 feet wide. At 2.6 miles shoot a simple straightforward rapid. Pass another island and lesser shoal at 2.8 miles. Relax a bit, then pass another mild shoal at 3.1 miles, where Monger Run enters on river left. From there, the South Fork Shenandoah slows like the passage of a lazy afternoon in summertime (a great time to be floating the South Fork).

At 3.8 miles you have turned east and have a dead-on look at the heights of Shenandoah National Park and Hightop Mountain. The doldrums end at 4.1 miles, as the river speeds past a sycamore-covered gravelly island for 100 yards or more. At 4.6 miles the island to your left ends. At 4.7 miles an unnamed creek enters on river right. At 5 miles the waterway turns north and Hawksbill Creek enters on river right at a rapid. Pass some low rock bluffs, then run yet another shoal. Ahead, enjoy a series of riffles and rapids, primarily with straightforward drops.

At 6.1 miles rapids lead you under the Norfolk Southern railroad bridge. You are now turned northwest with a view of Massanutten Mountain. At 6.9 miles the river narrows at a shoal and pushes into a bluff at the point where US 33 bridges the South Fork Shenandoah River. Note how the bridge is perched atop this sturdy bluff. Continue downriver, and big Elk Creek (for which Elkton was named) delivers its clear waters at 7 miles. At this point get over river right as the Elkton ramp is in moving water directly under the US 33 Business bridge. Reach the ramp and complete your paddle at 7.2 miles.

12 South Fork Shenandoah River near Luray

Enjoy an easy, delightful, and beauty-filled run on the middle South Fork Shenandoah River in the shadow of Shenandoah National Park.

County: Page
Start: Bixlers Ferry (Inskeep) ramp, N38 42.10' / W78 29.51'
End: Bealers Ferry ramp, N38 44.910' / W78 26.200'
Length: 7.3 miles
Float time: 3.5 hours
Difficulty rating: Easy
Rapids: Class I-I+
River/lake type: Mountain-rimmed valley river
Current: Moderate
River gradient: 5.4 feet per mile
Water gauge: South Fork Shenandoah River near Luray, 2.0 feet minimum runnable level, 2.5-3.5 ideal, 3.5-5.5 experienced paddlers only—use caution, stay off the river above 5.5

Season: Mar-Nov
Land status: Private; takeout in national forest
Fees and permits: None
Nearest city/town: Luray
Maps: National Geographic #792 Massanutten and Great North Mountain; USGS: Luray
Boats used: Kayaks, canoes, tubes
Organization: Friends of the Shenandoah River, 1460 University Dr. / Gregory Hall, Winchester, VA 22601; (540) 665-1286; www.fosr.org
Contact/outfitter: Shenandoah River Outfitters, 6502 S. Page Valley Rd., Luray, VA 22835; (540) 743-4159; www.shenandoah-river.com

Put-in/Takeout Information

To the takeout: From the intersection of Main Street / US 211 Business and Broad Street / US 340 Business in the heart of downtown Luray, take Broad Street / US 340 Business north for 0.2 mile, then turn left on Mechanic Street and follow it for 1.7 miles. Then turn left on VA 675 / Bixlers Ferry Road and follow it for 1.8 miles, crossing the South Fork Shenandoah River. Turn right here (passing the put-in at Bixlers Ferry) on Page Valley Road / VA 684 and follow it for 5.8 miles to turn right onto gravel but well-used Bealers Ferry Road. Be watchful as this road may be poorly marked. Turn right and descend 0.2 mile to reach the Bealers Ferry ramp.

To the put-in from the takeout: Backtrack on Page Valley Road / VA 684 for 5.8 miles and turn left into the Bixlers Ferry (Inskeep) ramp on your left.

Paddle Summary

This section of the South Fork Shenandoah complements a visit to adjacent Shenandoah National Park. And with the town of Luray between the park and the river, you can fashion a complete vacation package. The paddling part leads you on a winding course in the shadow of Massanutten Mountain and the Blue Ridge. The wide waterway makes long loping bends scattered with easy shoals. These bends invariably lead you on a collision course with long ridgelike Massanutten Mountain, only to turn away at the base of the peak. Then you once again are pointed toward the Blue Ridge, where the protected highlands of Shenandoah National Park form the backdrop for your river experience. The shoals are simple Class I, making the paddle doable by anyone. The put-in and takeout are in good shape, too.

River/Lake Overview

The South Fork Shenandoah River is the primary waterway of the main-stem Shenandoah River. The South Fork flows for 97 beautiful miles in a valley bordered by Shenandoah National Park to the east and the mountains of the George Washington National Forest to the west. The South Fork's headwaters flow from Shenandoah Mountain, forming the Virginia–West Virginia state line to the west and the Blue Ridge to the east. It is here in the upper Shenandoah Valley where the South River and the North River meet near Grottoes, forming the South Fork Shenandoah River. Here the waterway heads north, squeezing between Massanutten Mountain and the Blue Ridge. The South Fork Shenandoah continues gaining tributaries from the Blue Ridge while demonstrating its propensity for repeatedly bending. Massanutten Mountain being lower, it contributes lesser tributaries. Nevertheless, the river continues north in these ridges and peaks. Finally, at Front Royal the South Fork Shenandoah River meets the smaller North Fork Shenandoah River to then form the main-stem Shenandoah River. Here, the Shenandoah River leaves the Old Dominion and enters West Virginia before flowing a few more miles to give its waters to the Potomac River at historic Harpers Ferry. However, take note that the South Fork Shenandoah River is often simply referred to as the Shenandoah River, even though the actual main-stem Shenandoah River flows for just a short distance in Virginia and not much more in West Virginia before emptying into the Potomac.

The Paddling

Bixlers Ferry, the put-in location, has been a river crossing for a long time. Where once was a simple ford, then the site of a ferry operation, then a low-water bridge, we now have the fine high span in use today. Contemplate the historical nature of this spot as you enter the river. A boat ramp leads you down to the water, just downstream of the old low-water bridge. The river moves fast here, snaking amongst some small isles, with the main flow of the river away from the Virginia Department of Game and Inland Fisheries ramp. By the way, this ramp is also referred to as the Inskeep ramp. Push out into the moving water and you are immediately rushing downstream, so be prepared. This section of South Fork Shenandoah River appropriately starts with a bend, then settles down. The slower parts of the river offer an assortment of submerged stone, ranging from small pebbles to big boulders, as well as long striations of rock. Shallows will keep you moving, though you have to be on guard for running aground or follow a not-deep channel that devolves to a fanlike sweep of water barely

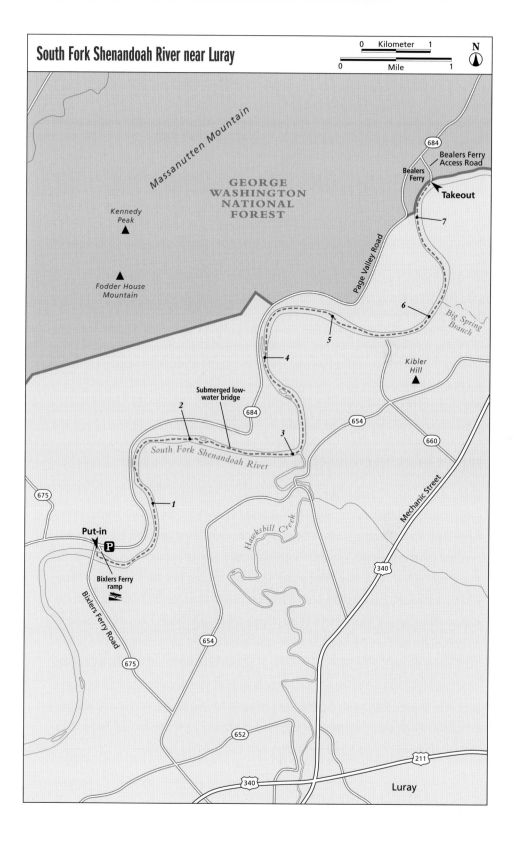

South Fork Shenandoah River near Luray

0   Kilometer   1

0   Mile   1

N

Massanutten Mountain

GEORGE
WASHINGTON
NATIONAL
FOREST

684

Bealers Ferry
Access Road

Bealers
Ferry

Takeout

Kennedy
Peak

7

Fodder House
Mountain

Page Valley Road

6

*Big Spring
Branch*

5

Kibler
Hill

4

Submerged low-
water bridge

684

3

660

2

South Fork Shenandoah River

654

675

1

Hauksbill Creek

Put-in

P

Bixlers Ferry
ramp

340

Mechanic Street

Bixlers Ferry Road

654

675

652

211

340

Luray

covering a gravel bar. The river turns north and you are looking dead-on at Kennedy Peak, standing just short of 2,600 feet on greater Massanutten Mountain. This is the first of many mountain views you will enjoy on this paddle. Do not forget to look down on the river! The elevation of the banks runs around 700 feet.

Slip over some minor shoals at 0.7 mile. By 1.6 miles you are heading east over another easy shoal, passing sporadic river camps, but the overall area is quiet. Your views now are of Shenandoah National Park, the crest of which is just less than 7 miles distant as the crow flies. At 2.1 miles a Class I+ river-wide shelf will keep you on your toes. Far right is the best route. Shoals continue. At 2.4 miles float over a now-submerged low-water bridge. The underwater concrete forms a shelf of its own and this marks the end of the long section of fast-moving water.

At 3.1 miles big Hawksbill Creek enters on your right, draining the highlands of the Blue Ridge, with its fresh, cool, and authentic mountain water. Interestingly, not only does the stream drain Shenandoah National Park's high point of Hawksbill at 4,050 feet, but also Hawksbill Creek flows through the town of Luray en route to South Fork Shenandoah River.

The river slows below Hawksbill Creek. Speed up in rapids at 4.1 miles, then you once again turn away from Massanutten Mountain. Bounce through an easy shoal at 4.6 miles. Now you are into a long shallow section, rife with riffles. Knob Mountain rises in the distance. It is hard to become tired of viewing mountains while floating down a scenic waterway. The long riffles end at 5.3 miles, but you hit a fun V-shaped rapid at 5.6 miles that may have been an old Indian fish trap.

MARYS ROCK HAS THE VIEWS

Marys Rock is located almost due east of this paddle, in Shenandoah National Park, and presents fantastic panoramas of the South Fork Shenandoah River and the lands below, including Luray, the town that stands between the park and the river. Marys Rock is a huge open outcrop, and views range—well, just about everywhere. Choose your overlook spot. To the north, easy views open of many Blue Ridge peaks. The town of Luray and the Shenandoah Valley stretch to the west, including the South Fork Shenandoah River. The Thornton Gap entrance station of Shenandoah National Park stands clearly below. Agile hikers can walk to the highest rock of the outcrop, due south from the main overlook. The top is marked with a pair of USGS survey markers. From there, you can see in all four cardinal directions. It is undeniably one of the best vistas in Virginia and a personal favorite of mine. A good route to reach Marys Rock is to take the Meadow Spring Trail from milepost 33.4 of Skyline Drive. It will lead you 0.7 mile to the legendary Appalachian Trail. From there, turn right (northbound) and you are at Marys Rock in 0.7 more mile. Enjoy lording over your paddling domain.

Massanutten Mountain frames Shenandoah paddlers.

Lowermost Kibler Hill rises from the river at 5.9 miles, and the waterway bends again. The South Fork Shenandoah River slows. At 6.2 miles Big Spring Branch enters on river right. At 6.5 miles the waterway widens, shallows, and aims dead-on for Massanutten Mountain. A few final river-wide shoals stretch across the river at 6.9 miles. Ease over to river left and you will reach the Bealers Ferry takeout at 7.3 miles, next to a pair of very small islands. It pays to scout this takeout from the land before you make your float.

13 South Fork Shenandoah River near Front Royal

Make a scenic run with views and rapids on the iconic South Fork Shenandoah near Front Royal, the self-styled Canoe Capital of Virginia.

County: Warren
Start: Bentonville Landing, N38 50.399' / W78 19.807'
End: Karo Landing, N38 52.290' / W78 15.165'
Length: 8.7 miles
Float time: 4.1 hours
Difficulty rating: Easy
Rapids: Class I
River/lake type: Mountain-rimmed valley river
Current: Moderate
River gradient: 5.2 feet per mile
Water gauge: South Fork Shenandoah River at Front Royal, 1.1 feet minimum runnable level, use caution above 4.0 feet, stay off river above 5.0 feet

Season: Mar–Nov
Land status: Private; some state park; a little national forest
Fees and permits: None
Nearest city/town: Front Royal
Maps: National Geographic #792 Massanutten and Great North Mountain; USGS: Bentonville, Strasburg
Boats used: Kayaks, canoes, tubes
Organization: Friends of the Shenandoah River, 1460 University Dr. / Gregory Hall, Winchester, VA 22601; (540) 665-1286; www.fosr.org
Contact/outfitter: Downriver Canoe, 884 Indian Hollow Rd., Bentonville, VA 22610; (800) 338-1963; www.downriver.com

Put-in/Takeout Information

To the takeout: From exit 6 on I-66 near Front Royal, take US 340 south / Stonewall Jackson Highway to and through Front Royal for a total of 13 miles to Bentonville. Turn right on VA 613 / Indian Hollow Road and follow it for 1 mile, crossing the South Fork Shenandoah River. Turn right into the Bentonville Landing access immediately after bridging the river.

To the put-in from the takeout: Backtrack to US 340 / Stonewall Jackson Highway, turn left (north), and follow it for 4.7 miles to turn left onto Chapman Farm Road. Immediately pass Gooney Creek Campground and stay straight to drive under railroad tracks, then reach Karo Landing at 0.2 mile. This landing can get busy. Be considerate and smart when parking here.

Paddle Summary

This eye-pleasing and worthy river trip explores the lowermost South Fork Shenandoah River before it meets the North Fork Shenandoah River at Front Royal. Here, you will be treated to nearly continuous mountain views while traversing a series of bends that aim alternately toward Massanutten Mountain and the Blue Ridge. The South Fork Shenandoah is big here, and wide in places, increasing the panoramas.

Alternating shoals and slow sections sweep you downriver from Bentonville Landing to eventually pass Shenandoah River Raymond R. "Andy" Guest Jr. State Park, adding natural shoreline—and camping possibilities. After swinging around The Point, paddle down a particularly wide stretch before pulling into Karo Landing. Check the water levels before you go. At lower water levels, often found in late summer, you will often have to pick and pull your way through wide shallows.

River/Lake Overview

The South Fork Shenandoah River is the primary waterway of the main-stem Shenandoah River. The South Fork flows for 97 beautiful miles in a valley bordered by Shenandoah National Park to the east and the mountains of the George Washington National Forest to the west. The South Fork's headwaters flow from Shenandoah Mountain, forming the Virginia–West Virginia state line to the west and the Blue Ridge to the east. It is here in the upper Shenandoah Valley where the South River and the North River meet near Grottoes, forming the South Fork Shenandoah River. Here the waterway heads north, squeezing between Massanutten Mountain and the Blue Ridge. The South Fork Shenandoah continues gaining tributaries from the Blue Ridge while demonstrating its propensity for bending time and again. Massanutten Mountain being lower, it contributes lesser tributaries. Nevertheless, the river continues north between these ridges and peaks. Finally, at Front Royal, the South Fork

Bridge view of author paddling the South Fork KERI ANNE MOLLOY

South Fork Shenandoah River near Front Royal

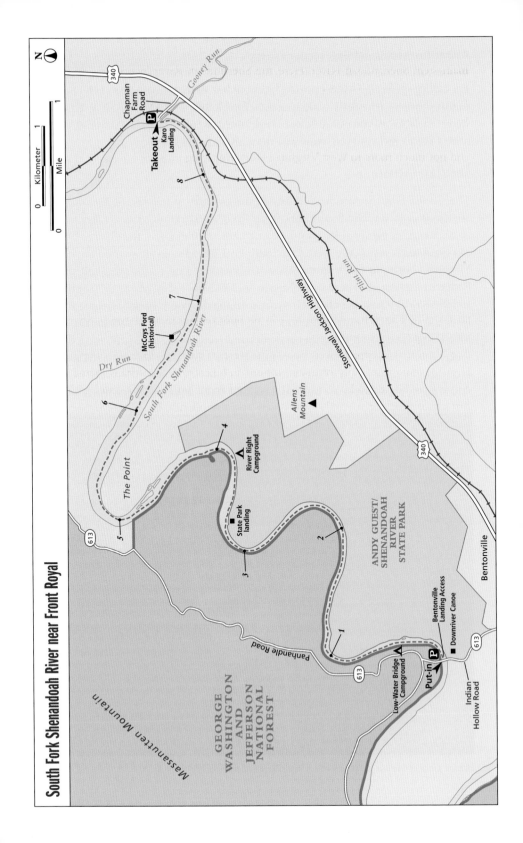

Shenandoah River meets the smaller North Fork Shenandoah River to then form the main-stem Shenandoah River. Here, the Shenandoah River leaves the Old Dominion and enters West Virginia before flowing a few more miles to give its waters to the Potomac River at historic Harpers Ferry, West Virginia. However, take note that the South Fork Shenandoah River is often simply referred to as the Shenandoah River, even though the actual Shenandoah River flows for just a short distance in Virginia and not much more in West Virginia before emptying into the Potomac.

The Paddling

Leave the Bentonville Landing access, bending northbound, your primary direction. The river is about 200 feet wide and normally running clear/green over a boulder, rock, and gravel bottom. An outfitter operates across the river from the put-in, in case you want last-minute supplies or need a shuttle or boat rental. Massanutten Mountain rises to your left and will stay in view for much of the paddle. It is not long before the river speeds and you are passing Low-Water Bridge Campground on river left at 0.4 mile. This private operation can be busy on summer weekends. Shenandoah River Raymond R. "Andy" Guest Jr. State Park (the longest state park name in the two Virginias) occupies river right. The preserve offers a drive-up campground; a riverside tent camp; trails for hikers, mountain bikers, and equestrians; picnic shelters; and cabins. For us paddlers it offers a natural shoreline with amenities. Enjoy your first set of shoals at 0.6 mile. The shoals here are often ledges mixed in with riffles and even-gradient rapids. On some of the longer shoals such as this, you will have

MAKE ELIZABETH FURNACE YOUR SHENANDOAH BASE CAMP

Elizabeth Furnace, a George Washington National Forest campground and recreation area, is located near this paddle and makes for a great base camp for paddling the Shenandoah River and exploring the Shenandoah Valley. Located a few miles west of Front Royal, the camp is located along the banks of Passage Creek nestled between Massanutten Mountain and Green Mountain in an area known as Fort Valley. The shady campsites have leveled tent pads, a lantern post, fire ring, and picnic table. Hot showers and running water enhance the camping here. Furthermore, the campground is conveniently located next to a first-rate picnic area, trout fishing, and the historic Elizabeth Furnace. Here, you can explore interconnected nature trails that present a splendid overview of the charcoal- and iron-making industries in 1800s Virginia. The short walk is long on interpretive information and you get to see the iron-furnace remains up close, as well as a cabin from the 1830s. Walk the swinging bridge over Passage Creek, too. Plan to add picnicking, trout fishing, and car camping to your South Fork Shenandoah River paddle—it is all here at Elizabeth Furnace.

Summertime is a great time to be on the South Fork Shenandoah River.

to route-find, especially at lower water levels. Avoid shallows as much as possible and look for longer, deeper channels. At 1 mile the river seemingly bounces off the base of Massanutten Mountain and the river bends right, heading through a long set of easy rapids. The shore remains heavily wooded with lots of shoreline willows, although parts of the state park are in fields back from the river.

Depths of the river vary from deep pools to extensive shallows. An unnamed creek enters on river right at 2 miles. Bend left, then navigate a 100-yard stretch of rapids at 2.5 miles. You are now face-on with 2,000-foot-high Massanutten Mountain, a long, narrow ridge that parallels nearly the entire length of the South Fork Shenandoah River. At 3.4 miles you are bending east and the state park landing on your right is in the near and Dickey Hill in the far. Dickey Hill is one of the prominent peaks in the North District of Shenandoah National Park, just a few miles away as the crow flies.

Beyond the state park landing, begin working over a series of easy ledges that make the paddling fun. Since you are now within the developed area of the state park, expect to see shoreline anglers and others playing in the water or tubing. Float by River Right Campground, for tenters, at the state park at 3.9 miles. Experience yet another bend, leaving the state park behind but now looking again at Massanutten Mountain, rising from the river itself. Enjoy some buoyant shoals near a small island at 4.6 miles. The South Fork Shenandoah makes a particularly sharp bend at 5 miles, as it works around "The Point," a peninsula. The river widens to upwards of 300 feet, opening a rousing view to the east of Shenandoah National Park and Skyline Drive. Float over some small ledges. Be wary of getting stuck in shallows. Sometimes-dry Dry Run comes in on river left at 6.3 miles, and you continue in wide river with shallows and small ledges. These shallows were the reason for McCoy's Ford, a historical river crossing, being there at 6.7 miles. The South Fork Shenandoah narrows a bit and deepens at 7.4 miles. Continue in deeper, slower water with light shoals. At 8.2 miles Flint Run enters on river right. Start curving north and stay over on river right, as the takeout is not obvious from the water. However, you will see and hear Class II Karo Rapids below the takeout. Look for Karo Landing on river right, ending your paddling adventure at 8.7 miles.

Virginia Piedmont and Coastal Paddles

14 Potomac River near Leesburg

This big river paddle presents some Class I rapids while winding through attractive island-studded scenery.

County: Loudon
Start: Point of Rocks (McKimmey) ramp, N39 16.352' / W77 32.820'
End: White's Ford Regional Park, N39 11.220' / W77 29.006'
Length: 9.4 miles
Float time: 4.4 hours
Difficulty rating: Easy
Rapids: Class I
River/lake type: Big river
Current: Steady
River gradient: 1.8 feet per mile
Water gauge: Potomac River at Point of Rocks, MD, no minimum runnable level
Season: Year-round

Land status: National park on Maryland bank; mostly private on VA bank; some other parkland
Fees and permits: None
Nearest city/town: Leesburg
Maps: Potomac River Guide; USGS: Point of Rocks, Buckeystown, Poolesville
Boats used: Kayaks, canoes, tubes, johnboats
Organization: Chesapeake & Ohio Canal National Historical Park, 1850 Dual Hwy., Ste. 100, Hagerstown, MD 21740; (301) 739-4200; www.nps.gov/choh
Contact/outfitter: White's Ford Regional Park, 43646 Hibler Rd., Leesburg, VA 20176; (703) 779-9372; www.novaparks.com

Put-in/Takeout Information

To the takeout: From the intersection of US 15 Business and VA 7 in downtown Leesburg, take US 15 Business north for 1.8 miles, then join US 15/501 north, James Monroe Highway, for 2.5 miles. Turn right on VA 661 / Limestone School Road. Follow VA 661 / Limestone School Road for 2.2 miles, then turn right onto VA 656 / Hibler Road and drive for 2.2 miles to turn right into White's Ford Regional Park and follow the signs to the paddler access. Next, get out and walk down to the river's edge, as this takeout is not obvious from the river. Additionally, be sure not to mistake this with nearby White's Ferry, which also has a Potomac River access.

   To the put-in from the takeout: From White's Ford Regional Park, backtrack on VA 656 to turn right on VA 661 / Limestone School Road, and follow it for 1.3 miles to turn left on VA 657 / Spinks Ferry Road. Follow this for 1.5 miles to turn right onto US 15/501 north, James Monroe Highway. Stay with US 15/501 north for 5 miles, then turn left on Lovettsville Road just before bridging the Potomac at

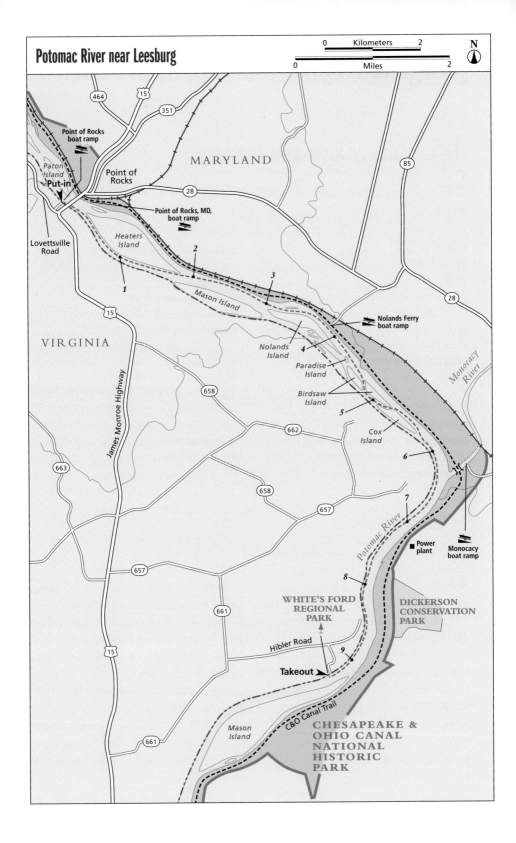

Potomac River near Leesburg

Kilometers 0 — 2

Miles 0 — 2

N

464
15
351

Point of Rocks
boat ramp

MARYLAND

85

Point of Rocks

Paton Island
Put-in

28

Point of Rocks, MD,
boat ramp

Lovettsville
Road

Heaters
Island

2

3

28

Nolands Ferry
boat ramp

VIRGINIA

Mason Island

1

Nolands
Island

4

Paradise
Island

Monocacy River

658

Birdsaw
Island

5

663

662

Cox
Island

6

658

657

7

Power
plant

Monocacy
boat ramp

657

8

661

WHITE'S FORD
REGIONAL
PARK

DICKERSON
CONSERVATION
PARK

15

Hibler Road

9

Takeout

Potomac River

James Monroe Highway

661

Mason
Island

C&O Canal Trail

CHESAPEAKE &
OHIO CANAL
NATIONAL
HISTORIC
PARK

Paddlers take a shoreline break on the Potomac.

Point of Rocks. Follow Lovettsville Road just a short distance, then take an immediate right into the Point of Rocks (McKimmey) ramp.

Paddle Summary

This aquatic adventure starts scenic and stays scenic. It departs at Point of Rocks, a stony bluff rising from the water, then immediately enters a nest of attractive wooded isles, dividing the river into channels. The Maryland bank is protected as national park land, part of the Chesapeake & Ohio Canal National Historical Park. Class I rapids move you along while working among the isles. The Potomac becomes a single great channel again upstream of the inflow of Maryland's Monocacy River, and you bend south in big water before coming to the primitive landing at White's Ford Regional Park, just as another group of islands once again divides the Potomac into channels. Since it is a big river, the paddle can be subject to winds, but that is not the only reason for winding among the isles—it is the most attractive and interesting route. Among the isles you will see wildlife, find shade in summer, and your paddle will vary by paddling waters from 30 to 300 feet wide.

River/Lake Overview

The Potomac River is one of America's great waterways and an integral aquatic element in the history of our country. Its headwaters are found in Virginia and West Virginia, as well as Maryland and Pennsylvania. However, the Potomac's ultimate headwater is said to be near a place called the Fairfax Stone, a marker settling a boundary dispute in colonial lands that ultimately divided Maryland from what became West Virginia. Here, spring waters form the North Branch Potomac River. Yet other, higher feeder branches of the river are found in the two Virginias, on its two other tributaries, namely the South Branch Potomac River draining Virginia's Highland

County as well as West Virginia mountains. The Shenandoah River, another significant tributary, drains the high peaks of Shenandoah National Park. The river's official start is where the South Branch and North Branch merge near Green Spring, West Virginia. Gathering steam, the Potomac also takes in West Virginia's Cacapon River. The Monocacy, a river you will pass by during this paddle, is Maryland's largest tributary feeding the Potomac. All Pennsylvania tributaries enter Maryland before giving their waters up to the Potomac. Downriver, the Potomac enters its famed gorge at Great Falls, a site of incredible whitewater, before settling down and becoming a wide, tidal waterway flowing by Washington, DC, and into Chesapeake Bay. The river forms state boundaries for much of its 405-mile length, while draining 14,700 square miles of land.

The Paddling

The boat ramp sits below the US 15/501 bridge and across from Point of Rocks, the iconic bluff and major physical feature of this segment of the Potomac River. However, downstream, you will encounter many other physical features in the form of teardrop-shaped islands. With these big islands, you have to choose your route and live with it, as many of the isles are sizable. First float under the James Monroe Highway bridge and come to the head of Heaters Island at 0.2 mile. The Point of Rocks, Maryland, boat ramp is on the northern shore. Heaters Island is part of a protected wildlife management area. Cruise a narrower channel along the densely forested island. Pass the foot of the island at 1.8 miles. Mason Island begins on the Virginia side just as you pass the end of Heaters Island. Where no islands are present, the Potomac is upwards of 400 feet wide. Reach the head of Nolands Island at 3 miles. Here, the Potomac breaks into channels again. Start a series of long, narrow teardrop-shaped islands. You have a choice of routes among these channels. Most will be passable at normal flows, especially for kayakers and canoeists. The channels give you a chance to see the Potomac as both a broad, powerful river and an intimate waterway. The river shallows and speeds along Nolands Island.

Paddle by an old waterworks building at 3.8 miles, on the Maryland side of the river. The C&O Canal Trail is a little back from the river. This is part of the Nolands Ferry area, and you pass the Nolands Ferry boat ramp at 4 miles. Soon leave Nolands Island and pass small Paradise Island, a popular camping isle, at 4.4 miles. Now it is time to have a little fun weaving your way down the Potomac. Cut between the two portions of Birdsaw Island, then come alongside Cox Island. These smaller channels are generally shallower than the main river. Small sandbars along the channels allow for stopping.

Return to wide-open river at 5.7 miles. You are bending south. The Monocacy River comes in on river left at 6.3 miles. It also has a boat ramp. Note the picturesque bridge over the waterway. The Potomac widens more with the influx of the Monocacy River. The Little Monocacy River enters on river left at 6.6 miles, adding still more volume. Enter a slower section, passing a power plant on the Maryland side at

7.3 miles. At this point consider heading over to the Virginia side of the river. Paddle by a rock bluff at 8.4 miles and soon begin paddling alongside land of White's Ford Regional Park. Scan downriver and spot the head of big Mason Island (same name as an upstream island you pass). You should be on the right bank by now. Hang close to shore and look for the steps and boat slide of White's Ford Regional Park. This is easily missed. Reach the access at 9.4 miles, completing the paddle.

THE GREAT FALLS OF THE POTOMAC

Downriver of this paddle, within easy striking distance, stand the Great Falls of the Potomac, undeniably the single-greatest feature of this big river, awash in both natural beauty and American history. The crashing whitewater wonder will shock and impress first-time visitors. The history of Great Falls' past is nearly as impressive. George Washington himself commissioned a system of canals and locks to allow barge traffic to navigate around this extensive whitewater froth crashing through Mather Gorge. Today, you can visit the Great Falls, the locks, canals, and even the ghost town of Matildaville, built for the men and families tending the lock-and-canal system.

The Great Falls Park Visitor Center is a good starting point. Here, you can learn all about the Great Falls and all that has transpired at this point where the Potomac River cuts through rock while descending to the Atlantic coastal plain. The preserve is laced with trails that offer views of the gorge, the river, the canal, and more.

Young George Washington, as he traveled the Potomac and surveyed interior lands of the Ohio River valley, saw this crashing cascade, admiring its beauty yet deciding the Potomac River could be a trade corridor if only the Great Falls and other, lesser rapids could be bypassed. An idea was born: create a canal system on the Potomac River.

What became the Patowmack Canal took a long time to build. Washington's dream, this canal system linking the Potomac River valley with its access to the Atlantic Ocean and the Ohio River valley to the west, would bind these two regions economically, strengthening a fragile yet expanding United States. Along this point, the Potomac descends 70 feet in a mile, dropping from the Piedmont to the Atlantic coastal plain through a rugged gorge of exposed bedrock. Explore Great Falls and learn the story behind this Potomac River icon. For more information, visit www.nps.gov/grfa.

15 Pohick Bay

Make a scenic still-water paddle in a park-rimmed bay of the lower Potomac River.

County: Fairfax
Start: Pohick Bay Shore Launch,
N38 40.622' / W77 10.140'
End: Pohick Bay Shore Launch,
N38 40.622' / W77 10.140'
Length: 5.3 miles
Float time: 3.0 hours
Difficulty rating: Moderate
Rapids: None
River/lake type: Slightly tidal bay
Current: None
River gradient: None
Water gauge: None
Season: Year-round

Land status: Regional park; military reservation
Fees and permits: Park entrance fee required
Nearest city/town: Woodbridge
Maps: Pohick Bay Regional Park; USGS: Fort Belvoir
Boats used: Kayaks, canoes, motorboats
Organization: Pohick Bay Regional Park, 6501 Pohick Bay Dr., Lorton, VA 22079; (703) 339-6104; www.novaparks.com
Contact/outfitter: Potomac Conservancy, 8403 Colesville Rd., Ste. 805, Silver Spring, MD 20910; (301) 608-1188; www.potomac.org

Put-in/Takeout Information

To put-in/takeout: From exit 161 on I-95 near Woodbridge, join US 1 north and follow it for 2.5 miles to turn right on Gunston Road / VA 242 / VA 600 and follow it 3.2 miles to turn left into Pohick Bay Regional Park. Follow the signs for the marina, then continue to the nonmotorized-boat launch.

Paddle Summary

This paddle explores the waters of Pohick Bay, an offshoot of the Potomac River. You will execute a loop around mostly parklands as well as a natural portion of Fort Belvoir Military Reservation, making it a scenic experience. Leave the nonmotorized launch and head westerly along the shore, exploring the estuarine waters of Pohick Creek where it enters Pohick Bay. Skirt north past heron nests and the mouth of Accotink Creek. From here paddle near a recreation area at Fort Belvoir, skirting an island. After rambling along the shore, reach a point of land where it is time to head south, crossing Pohick Bay, with historic Gunston Hall Plantation standing proudly in the distance. Return to Pohick Bay Regional Park, floating by some bluffs before returning to the launch. Take note that Pohick Bay can be subject to winds, and the open water crossing of Pohick Bay is about 0.7 mile long. Additionally, the park rents kayaks, canoes, and stand-up paddleboards, should you need something to paddle.

Top: Paddling the shallows of Pohick Bay
Bottom: The boat-rental facility at Pohick Bay Regional Park

Pohick Bay

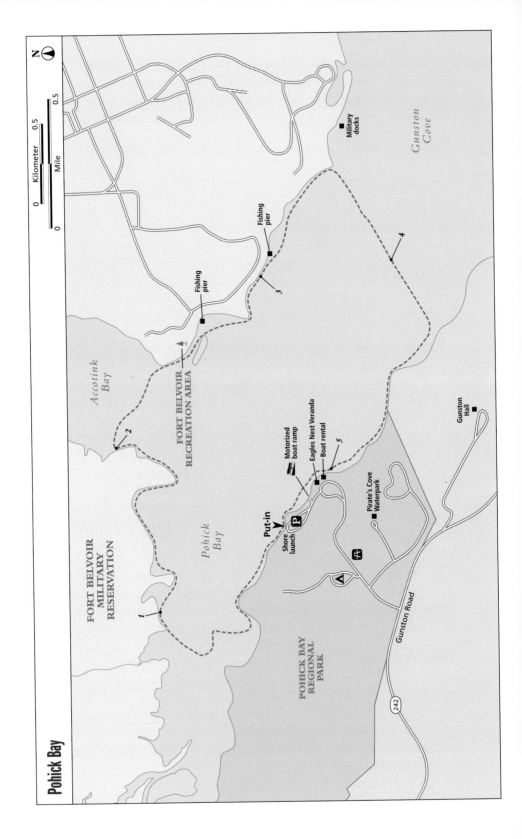

FORT BELVOIR MILITARY RESERVATION

Accotink Bay

Pohick Bay

FORT BELVOIR RECREATION AREA

Fishing pier

Fishing pier

Gunston Cove

Military docks

Put-in

Shore launch

Motorized boat ramp

Eagles Nest Veranda

Boat rental

Pirate's Cove Waterpark

POHICK BAY REGIONAL PARK

Gunston Road

Gunston Hall

242

N

Kilometer   0   0.5
Mile   0   0.5

1   2   3   4   5

River/Lake Overview

Part of the watery northern boundary of Mason Neck, a peninsula of land, Pohick Bay is part of the greater Potomac River watershed as the Potomac River opens into Chesapeake Bay. Pohick Creek enters from hills to the west in Fairfax County. Accotink Creek enters Pohick Bay from the north, also draining lands of Fairfax County to the north and west. Together, these two streams pour their waters into Pohick Bay.

The Paddling

This is a fun place to paddle, and on summer weekends you will see paddlers of all abilities trying their hand at kayaking, canoeing, and manning stand-up paddleboards. That is because Pohick Bay Regional Park offers a wide array of self-propelled watercraft for rent. It can get comical at times watching someone try to stand up on and paddle a paddleboard for the first time, or a pair of novice canoers zigzagging all over the bay. But face it, we were all there once, trying out this sport of paddling and getting into the boat for the first time, likely making fools of ourselves. Yet that is how it works—we learn by doing. Of course, you will also see the experienced pros streaking across the bay in a straight line, poetry in motion, still others embarking from their own boats, leisurely paddling along the shore, soaking in the sights and the freedom that comes with floating a canoe or kayak across the water.

Our Pohick Bay paddle leaves west from the shore launch, a gravel bar in a little cove, aiming for the mouth of Pohick Creek, away from the park facilities. The bulk of Pohick Bay is to your right while skirting the wooded shore after passing two houses. As you near Pohick Bay, beware of the waters being quite shallow, especially on an outgoing tide. Though Pohick Bay is all freshwater, it is still under mild tidal influence. If the tide is in, you will not have to worry about the water depth as much. Explore as you please in the estuarine zone where the Pohick Creek meets the bay, among waterweeds and mudflats. Bird life is rich—look for bald eagles, ospreys, and herons.

Reach the northern shoreline of Pohick Bay at 0.9 mile, beyond the mouth of Pohick Creek. You are on the property of Fort Belvoir Military reservation, yet this shore is managed as a 1,200-acre wildlife refuge within the base. Occasional gravel points make for stopping spots. Work around a point a 1.7 miles. Heron nests have been spotted here before and may be here on your trip. These colonies of heron nests are often called a rookery, but the more specific term is a "heronry." These nests are usually over 100 feet off the ground. Nesting materials are gathered by the males, then the females weave together a nest platform of sticks and line it with softer materials such as pine needles or grass. An egg clutch averages two to six eggs and takes about a month to incubate. Seeing these nests can be a highlight of the paddle.

After working around the point, you soon turn into the mouth of Accotink Creek and Accotink Bay. This mouth is larger than the mouth of Pohick Creek, and discerning the actual outflow of the creek can be difficult later in the summer as waterweeds may have spread. However, the far-west and far-east channels of the creek are open should you want to explore up that creek. Look for snags in the water to help determine creek depth. Come to the eastern end of Accotink Bay at 2.4 miles. Now you are paddling by a recreation area on the reservation, where military personnel can camp, fish, and enjoy the great outdoors. At 2.5 miles squeeze between the mainland and an island. Here you will see a popular fishing pier jutting into the water from the mainland. Hills rise behind the shoreline.

At 2.8 miles work around another point, still within the military recreation area. The shoreline remains wooded. Ahead, paddle by a second fishing pier, then the gravelly mouth of a small creek, before reaching yet another point of land at 3.5 miles. It is time to cross the bay. In addition, some off-limits military docks are around the corner from this point. Begin paddling southwest across the open water. From here you will see the white hilltop manse that is Gunston Hall, the home of founding father George Mason. It can be your beacon. Stay to the right of the home and aim for the south shore. If the winds are moderate, it will be simple crossing. To the left, easterly, you can see the main Potomac River and Maryland on the far shore.

Return to the shoreline at 4.3 miles. Head northeast, with parkland rising to your left. View sheer bluffs rising from the shore that eventually reduce to wooded hills. Enjoy the paddle before reaching the park boat-rental area, located in a gravelly cove. This can be quite a scene in summertime, with paddlers of all abilities renting kayaks, canoes, stand-up paddleboards, and even pedal boats, going in every direction with varying degrees of success, with park boat-rental personnel trying to help as best they can. Finally, curve around the point where the Eagles Nest Veranda stands (a great spot for viewing paddlers in Pohick Bay) and then reach the marina, passing the motorized-boat launch before returning to the shore launch at 5.3 miles, completing the paddling adventure.

VISIT GUNSTON HALL

Located on property adjacent to Pohick Bay Regional Park stands Gunston Hall, the home of one of our founding fathers and distinguished Virginian George Mason. The former 5,500-acre tobacco plantation owner wrote *The Virginia Declaration of Rights*, in which he stated, "That all men are by nature equally free and independent, and have certain inherent rights . . .," a statement that profoundly affected the American Declaration of Independence. Start your Gunston Hall tour at the visitor center to learn about George Mason and his mansion and times, then move on to Gunston Hall itself. Tour the grounds, where you can enjoy the gardens and replica farm buildings that have been constructed, depicting life in the 1700s. Also, take a look down on Pohick Bay, recalling your paddling experience in this part of the world. For more information about Gunston Hall, visit www.gunstonhall.org.

16 Accokeek Creek

This out-and-back paddling adventure on a tidal waterway traces one of Virginia's newer state nature preserves.

County: Stafford
Start: Crow's Nest State Nature Preserve Canoe & Kayak Access, N38 22.164' / W77 19.968'
End: Crow's Nest State Nature Preserve Canoe & Kayak Access, N38 22.164' / W77 19.968'
Length: 8.0 miles there and back
Float time: 4.5 hours
Difficulty rating: Easy to moderate, winds could be problematic
Rapids: None
River/lake type: Creek, tidal bay
Current: Moderately tidal
River gradient: None
Water gauge: None

Season: Year-round, winter could be cold and windy
Land status: State natural area preserve; private
Fees and permits: None
Nearest city/town: Brooke
Maps: Crow's Nest Natural Area Preserve Hiking & Water Trails; USGS: Passapatanzy
Boats used: Kayaks, canoes
Organization: Virginia Department of Conservation and Recreation, 600 E. Main St., Richmond, VA 23219; (804) 786-6124
Contact/outfitter: Friends of the Rappahannock, PO Box 1459, Tappahannock, VA 22560; (540) 373-3448, ext. 210; www.riverfriends .org

Put-in/Takeout Information

To the put-in/takeout: From exit 140 on I-95 near Stafford, south of DC, take Courthouse Road east, passing through Stafford, and driving for 3.5 miles to turn right onto Andrew Chapel Road. Follow Andrew Chapel Road for 1 mile into Brooke, then turn left onto Brooke Road and follow it for 2.9 miles to the Brooke Road Access at Crow's Nest Natural Area Preserve on your right.

Paddle Summary

No shuttle is required on this out-and-back adventure on a tidal tributary of the Potomac River. On this trip you will carry your boat out to Accokeek Creek, located within the confines of the newer Crow's Nest Natural Area Preserve. Follow widening Accokeek Creek along the shores of the peninsular preserve to meet the larger Potomac Creek. Here you will stay along the edge of the hilly and scenic shoreline to reach Boykins Landing, an elevated point where you can gaze easterly to the Potomac River and beyond to Maryland. The preserve is also fine for hiking. Consider combining hiking and paddling at this preserve.

River/Lake Overview

Accokeek Creek is a short stream flowing easterly from central Stafford County, located between Fredericksburg and the DC Metroplex. Accokeek Creek flows easterly under I-95 and through the hamlet of Brooke. Upon nearing its end, the stream flattens out and enters a marsh, widening with only a water channel passing between surface growth of lily pads and grasses. The waterway continues to widen and bends past hills before turning south to meet wide and tidal Potomac Creek. Potomac Creek is larger than Accokeek Creek yet also starts in central Stafford County, where it is dammed as Stafford County Reservoir before continuing east to become a marshy stream, then an open-wide tidal creek forming part of the boundary of Crow's Nest Natural Area Preserve. Finally, Potomac Creek gives its wide waters up to the Potomac River, just east of this paddle. In fact, the Potomac River is within easy striking distance and could be added to this adventure also.

The Paddling

Crow's Nest Natural Area Preserve is becoming one of the more popular Virginia state natural areas and not just for paddling. The hiking-trail system was dedicated in 2017. The park first had the ADA-accessible dock and kayak ramp that we use for this paddle. It is no secret that the greater DC area is growing rapidly and the acquisition of 2,872 acres that comprise the preserve were very important. Stafford County is

Upper Accokeek Creek is bordered by aquatic vegetation.

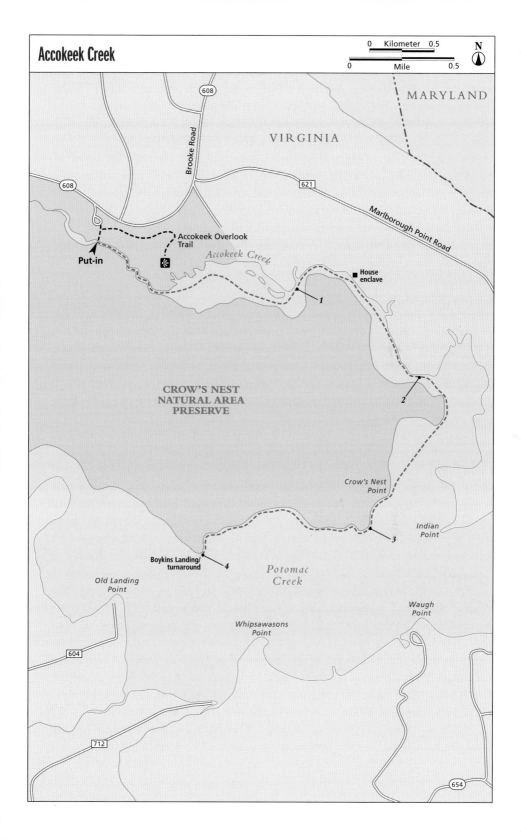

Accokeek Creek

608

Brooke Road

MARYLAND

VIRGINIA

608

621

Marlborough Point Road

Accokeek Overlook
Trail

Accokeek Creek

Put-in

House
enclave

1

CROW'S NEST
NATURAL AREA
PRESERVE

2

Crow's Nest
Point

Indian
Point

3

Boykins Landing/
turnaround   4

Potomac
Creek

Old Landing
Point

Waugh
Point

604

Whipsawasons
Point

712

654

0   Kilometer   0.5

0   Mile   0.5

N

under growth pressure and efforts by multiple entities resulted in the purchase of over 1,700 acres in 2008 followed by a second purchase in 2009. It took several years to get the park ready for opening, despite it mostly being passive recreation. Over 7 miles of hiking trails have been developed, some using old roads and others created to best reveal the natural attributes of the preserve. One such trail is the Accokeek Overlook Trail beginning at the same parking lot from which this paddle begins.

Crow's Nest Natural Area Preserve is a hilly peninsula bounded by Accokeek Creek and Potomac Creek. The preserve also includes 750 acres of tidal and nontidal wetlands, including some of the best preserved wetland habitats in the Potomac River drainage. Over 2,200 acres of hardwood forests thrive on the peninsula. Between the wetlands and hilly woods, raptors, waterfowl, and migratory songbirds have a place to utilize. The peninsula rises 160 feet above the waters that surround it. Seasonal streambeds cut steep ravines, adding more habitat. Along the banks, calcium-rich soils support imperiled plant communities.

Take note of the hours at the preserve. For starters, the Brooke Road Access, where our paddle begins, is open seven days a week. However, the Raven Road Access, where almost all the hiking trails begin, is open Thursday through Sunday and is closed Monday through Wednesday. Furthermore, both areas are open from 8 a.m. to 8 p.m. from March 15 through October 31. From November 1 through March 14, the preserve is open from 8 a.m. to 5:30 p.m. The gates are opened and closed promptly, so do not take a chance on getting locked in, which will happen if you leave your car there after hours.

From the parking area it is a full 300-foot carry, first through the woods then on a long, wide, and elaborate boardwalk over marsh to reach the first-rate canoe-and-kayak launch. Then you start in the heart of the eye-catching wetland with a central channel through which you will paddle. Head east (though you can paddle west a ways into the upper marsh) and begin following a lily-pad-bordered, modestly tidal creek. The effective paddling area is but 20 or 30 feet since surface vegetation covers most of the marsh. Look for beaver dams in the margin. Stationary hunt blinds border the channel in places. Also spot minor channels linking to the primary channel of Accokeek Creek.

The current will be minor whether coming in or going out. By 0.5 mile the channel has taken you by the rising hilly peninsula that comprises the terra firma portion of the preserve. Bird life is rampant whether on land or above the water, from red-winged blackbirds to waterfowl to bald eagles. Wind through the marsh, curving to its north side and paddling beside a house enclave at 1.5 miles. The channel has widened some. Beyond here turn south into increasingly open waters. Accokeek Creek becomes an expansive estuarine body of water. Stick with the right shoreline, the preserve shoreline. Houses stand on the far side of Accokeek Creek.

Paddle by Crow's Nest Point at 2.8 miles. A hiking trail leads to this vista. You can now glance far in the distance up and down Potomac Creek, revealing the openness of the water that could be subject to wind. An early morning paddler will stand less

The paddler launch at Crows Nest Natural Area Preserve

chance of catching the afternoon breezes. Indian Point is to your east-southeast, and beyond it a half mile of open water takes you to the Potomac River and the Maryland state line. However, our adventure continues tracing the shoreline of Crow's Nest Natural Area Preserve, where wildlife-viewing opportunities open on land and water. The far side of Potomac Creek is a half mile or more distant. Continue to stay with the preserve shoreline—it is a safer proposition and more interesting than paddling in open water.

Ahead, Boykins Landing stands in the distance. This is your destination. Continue working along the shoreline as it often rises sheer from the waters of Potomac Creek. Upon coming closer you begin to see the fence guarding the overlook at Boykins Landing. At 4.0 miles you are upon the point. A small beach provides a landing spot below the overlook. Clamber up the hill and reach a bench and the oak-, pine-, and locust-bordered overlook about 20 feet above the water. A hiking trail comes in from the landward side. Here, you can gaze east and south across Potomac Creek, soaking in the view. Massive Potomac River lies in the far distance, while the lands of the preserve extend to your left. If the hiking trails are open, you could secure your watercraft and take a walk or simply complete the paddle then go take a hike. However, first comes the backtrack, as you get to view Crow's Nest Natural Area Preserve a second time, reentering the marshy closing waters of Accokeek Creek, another Virginia paddle under your belt.

17 Belle Isle State Park Paddle

Paddle the big Rappahannock River along the scenic shores of Belle Isle State Park.

County: Lancaster
Start: Belle Isle State Park Canoe/Kayak Launch, N37 46.949' / W76 36.265'
End: Belle Isle State Park Canoe/Kayak Launch, N37 46.949' / W76 36.265'
Length: 7.0 miles
Float time: 3.5 hours
Difficulty rating: Easy to moderate, potential waves in Rappahannock River
Rapids: None
River/lake type: Massive tidal river, plus smaller bodies of water
Current: Tidal
River gradient: None

Water gauge: None
Season: Mar–Oct
Land status: State park
Fees and permits: Park entrance fee
Nearest city/town: Warsaw
Maps: Belle Isle State Park; USGS: Lively
Boats used: Kayaks, canoes
Organization: Belle Isle State Park, 1632 Belle Isle Rd., Lancaster, VA 22503; (804) 462-5030; www.dcr.virginia.gov/state-parks
Contact/outfitter: Friends of the Rappahannock, PO Box 1459, Tappahannock, VA 22560; (540) 373-3448, ext. 210; www.riverfriends .org

Put-in/Takeout Information

To put-in/takeout: From the north side of Warsaw at the intersection of US 360 and VA 3, take VA 3 east for 14.5 miles, then turn right on River Road, VA 354 south. Follow it for 3 miles, then turn right on Belle Isle Road and follow it 0.7 mile to enter the state park. Continue straight beyond the entrance station, then turn right toward the campground/car top launch, continuing to dead-end at the canoe/kayak launch after 0.6 mile. Be sure to park in the adjacent lot and not at the launch point itself.

Paddle Summary

This paddling adventure takes place on the lower, regal Rappahannock River where it passes alongside the banks of Belle Isle State Park, a picturesque yet underused Virginia state park that presents multiple opportunities for outdoor recreation enthusiasts. The paddle first starts on Mulberry Creek, then curves past Brewers Point, where stands a backcountry campsite, and then the adventure opens onto the massive tidal Rappahannock River. Here, you paddle along the park shoreline, enjoying sights near and far. Little inlets invite exploration before you turn into Deep Creek and reach the state park's boat ramp. Now, you can either do a foot/bike shuttle for a 3.5-mile one-way paddle, or simply paddle back to the canoe/kayak launch on Mulberry Creek for a 7-mile endeavor.

River/Lake Overview

Mulberry Creek is a small yet wide tributary of the Rappahannock River, draining a small portion of uplands in the Northern Neck. The Rappahannock River is one of the Old Dominion's larger waterways and is free-flowing from its headwaters to Chesapeake Bay. Born on the slopes of the Blue Ridge at famed Shenandoah National Park, the Rappahannock winds its way easterly, picking up other Blue Ridge tributaries and forming county boundaries through most of its journey. It picks up a major tributary in the Rapidan River just west of Fredericksburg, the major city through which the Rappahannock flows and where the river drops off the fall line. From that town the river widens, becomes tidal, and forms the southern boundary of the rural and beautiful Northern Neck, finally emptying into Chesapeake Bay after a 184-mile journey. Deep Creek is another tributary of the Rappahannock that you will paddle. It is also a wide, tidally influenced creek with many arms, yet drains just a small portion of land.

Paddling the massive lower Rappahannock River

Belle Isle State Park Paddle

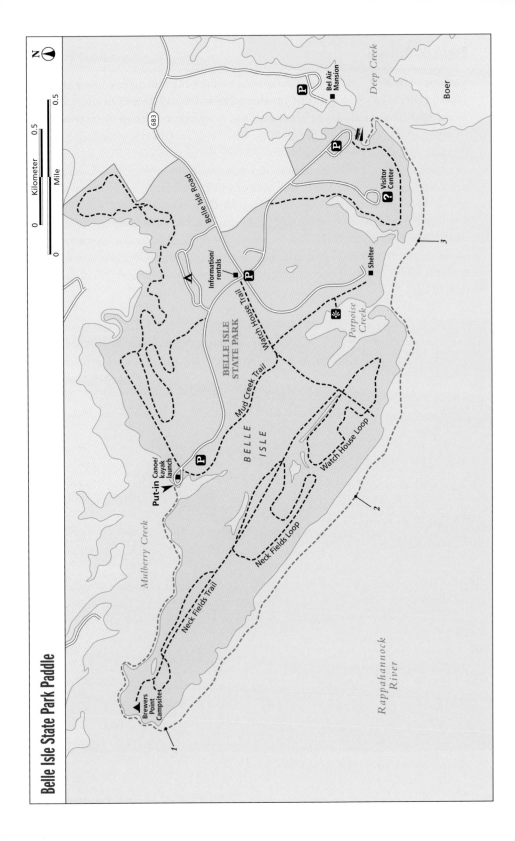

N

Kilometer
0   0.5

Mile
0   0.5

Deep Creek

Boer

P Bel Air Mansion

683

Belle Isle Road

P

? Visitor Center

3

Information/rentals

P

BELLE ISLE STATE PARK

Shelter

Watch House Trail

Mud Creek Trail

Porpoise Creek

BELLE ISLE

Watch House Loop

P

Put-in Canoe/kayak launch

Neck Fields Loop

Mulberry Creek

2

Neck Fields Trail

Rappahannock River

Brewers Point Campsite

1

The Paddling

Ensconced on the Northern Neck, the picturesque peninsula in far-eastern mainland Virginia, Belle Isle State Park is a menagerie of water and land, of fields and woods, of marshes and meadows, rich with hiking, paddling, and camping opportunities. The paddle here is a good one and offers opportunities to stroke your way along the protected shoreline of a big tidal river, with the added possibility of doing a one-way easy paddle with a foot/bike shuttle or a simple yet longer there-and-back paddle. Additionally, you have the option of overnighting at Brewers Point campsite, accessible only by paddle or foot.

You can embark from either a small beach or a dock exclusively for paddlers. The park's rental boats are located here. Set off into Mulberry Creek, a wide, bay-like stream. Houses are located across the water. Head west, keeping along the shoreline of the park. Immediately pass an enticing tidal creek on your left. Clear waters reveal a sand bottom, dotted with scattered shells. Much of the shoreline is grassy marsh interspersed with forests of cedar, pine, sweetgum, and other hardwoods.

At 0.8 mile swing around a point populated by wind-pruned cedar and low grasses. The massive Rappahannock River stretches before you beyond the point. Parts of the far riverbank are in excess of 3 miles distant. That is why you are best served to stick along the banks of the state park. Moreover, there is an additional reason to hang close to the shoreline, for just ahead you reach the beach and grassy landing for Brewers Point backcountry campsite. This is your paddler access for overnighting here.

The paddle continues as you fully enter the Rappahannock at 1 mile. Turn southeasterly here. The shoreline is grassy and backed by woods. Begin a cruise along the Rappahannock, likely under your own power here, since the tides are not strong this far upriver. The water is all fresh. If you have troubles, it will be from a strong south wind blowing across the extent of the river that could be bothersome. Contrastingly, a west wind will be your friend. By 1.7 miles pines have inched their way to the edge of the water. Fallen, sun-bleached skeletons of trees add a picturesque dimension to the meeting place of land and water. Downriver views of the Rappahannock extend for miles and miles. Curve around a point at 2.6 miles and you soon come to the sandy mouth of Porpoise Creek. This shallow inlet invites exploration should you want to extend your paddle. Note the trail-accessible waterfowl blind overlooking Porpoise Creek.

Just ahead reach a small beach and bluff. Stairs lead up to a picnic shelter. This is where boatless park visitors access the Rappahannock River. This is also the best beach in the park. The paddle passes a small, sandy inlet and the hill where the park visitor center stands before turning into Deep Creek. You will find the waters along the shoreline not deep at all. Houses occupy the far shore. Stay with the left bank, and Bel Air Mansion and Guest House (part of the state park) come into view, as does the park boat ramp. This is a full double-lane ramp with dock. A nearby shelter offers a

CAMP AT BREWERS POINT

Belle Isle State Park presents an opportunity to enjoy backcountry camping along the Rappahannock. Belle Isle has established backcountry campsites at Brewers Point, accessible by a 1-mile paddle or a 2-mile hike. And if you just feel like car camping, Belle Isle serves up a thirty-site drive-up campground will full amenities.

Brewers Point is alluring. A small beach is located near the campground, with four individual sites. The camping area shares a common fire ring. A raised gravel tent pad and picnic table are provided for each camping party. A vault toilet is located nearby. Bring your own drinking water. A self-pay station is located at the Brewers Point campsite. However, I recommend heading to the ranger station or visitor center to register and pay there. That way the rangers will know about your vehicle being left there overnight. The self-pay station at Brewers Point is for boat-in campers launching from outside the park.

Should you choose to access Brewers Point by foot, the trail system at Belle Isle State Park is well signed and maintained. Start at a picnic shelter overlooking the Rappahannock River. Join the Porpoise Creek Trail, traveling the margin between woods bordering Porpoise Creek—an inlet along the Rappahannock River, and sown fields that recall the time when what has become Belle Isle State Park was a working farm. Hike a mix of fields and woods, heading northwest, to reach Brewers Point and the small beach bordered by a grassy area. This is where boats using the campsite land. A short path leads into a pine- and oak-shaded camp. The sites are a tad close to one another but are well put together. So whether you paddle your way in or hike your way in, spend the night on the banks of the Rappahannock at Brewers Point.

chance to take a break should you desire to paddle back (be sure to get your boat off of the ramp). Another option is a foot/bike shuttle. It is but a 1.4-mile walk to the canoe/kayak launch from the Deep Creek boat ramp.

18 Mattaponi River

Follow this blackwater stream as it changes from slender stream to tidal waterway in a short span. A short, easy shuttle can be done on foot or bike.

Counties: King William; King and Queen
Start: Zoar State Forest Access, N37 48.542' / W77 7.280'
End: Aylett Ramp, N37 47.145' / W77 6.180'
Length: 5.0 miles
Float time: 2.6 hours
Difficulty rating: Easy
Rapids: None
River/lake type: Small river
Current: Slow
River gradient: 1.7 feet per mile
Water gauge: Mattaponi River near Beulahville, VA, no minimum runnable level

Season: Year-round; spring for blooming wild azaleas
Land status: State forest; private
Fees and permits: None
Nearest city/town: Aylett
Map: USGS: Aylett
Boats used: Kayaks, canoes; motorboats on lower stretches of paddle
Organization: Zoar State Forest, 4445 Upshaw Rd., Aylett, VA 23009; (804) 769-2962; www .dof.virginia.gov
Contact/outfitter: Mattaponi Canoe & Kayak; (800) 769-3545; www.mattaponi.com/index .html

Put-in/Takeout Information

To the takeout: From the intersection of US 360 and VA 600 / River Road in Aylett, take VA 600 / River Road south for less than 0.1 mile to turn left on the slender asphalt driveway-looking road just before St. David Episcopal Church. Follow this narrow road between the church and a house to your left to descend a hill and reach a Virginia Department of Game and Inland Fisheries parking area, dock, and boat ramp.

To the put-in from the takeout: Leave the ramp, turn right on VA 600 / River Road, and head north, crossing US 360. Stay with VA 600 / River Road for 1.6 miles, then turn right into signed Zoar State Forest, joining a gravel road. Quickly reach the nature trail parking lot and veer left, staying with the gravel road to soon dead-end at the canoe/kayak launch. From here it is a 30-yard carry to the canoe/kayak slide into Herring Creek.

Paddle Summary

This paddle starts at a woodsy launch in the Zoar State Forest. Briefly float Herring Creek before entering the Mattaponi River, its brooding dark waters inexorably moving toward the sea. The waterway is but a slender creek with alternating wetlands and bluffs on its shores. The twisting river makes a large arc, curving back to flow through Aylett, where the VDGIF ramp awaits. Its lower couple of miles are tidally

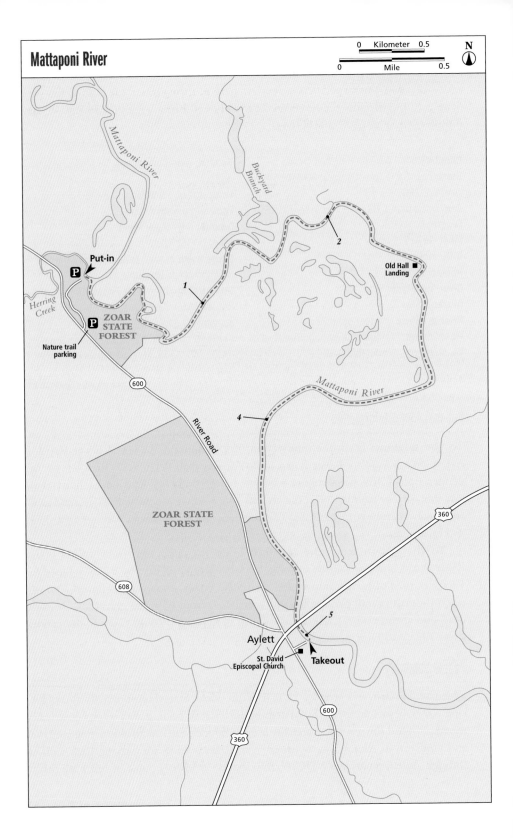

Mattaponi River

0 Kilometer 0.5
0 Mile 0.5

N

Mattaponi River

Buckyard Branch

Put-in

P

2

Old Hall
Landing

1

Herring Creek

P

ZOAR
STATE
FOREST

Nature trail
parking

600

Mattaponi River

River Road

4

ZOAR STATE
FOREST

360

608

5

Aylett

St. David
Episcopal Church

Takeout

600

360

affected, although the entire float is freshwater. Much of the banks are state forest, and the streamside scenery is pleasing and includes sandbars suitable for stopping and swimming. Lucky paddlers will come here in spring to see the wild-azalea gardens coloring the shoreline. Prepared paddlers will bring their bicycles for an easy shuttle—I have done it myself.

River/Lake Overview

The Mattaponi River has its headwaters in upper Spotsylvania County, below which the Mat, Ta, Po, and Ni Rivers merge (no joke). The Mattaponi River comes together near Bowling Green, where it flows through the Mattaponi Wildlife Management Area, keeping its southeasterly course and flowing through Caroline County. The Mattaponi then becomes the boundary between King William County and King and Queen County. It is in these reaches near Aylett where this paddle takes place. Below Aylett the Mattaponi becomes more and more tidal, quite wide, and broken with islands. Finally, it flows into the York River near the town of West Point.

The Paddling

It is a short carry from the parking area to the wooden boat slide on Herring Creek. This path is part of the greater hiking-trail system (worth your time) at Zoar State Forest. You will see some of these trails as they travel along the river during the first part of your paddle. Launch into Herring Creek, a shallow, small blackwater tributary of the Mattaponi River. Briefly wander down this sandy streamlet and immediately hit the Mattaponi River, passing a point that doubles as a bank-fishing spot. The waterway stretches 70 feet wide here, slipping reddish over sandy shallows, divided by deeper holes where the water seems black as night. Tan sandbars provide color contrast to the river. Spindly green willows overhang the waterway, along with other typical riverine species such as sycamore.

State forest land and private land are intermingled along the shore, and it is not always obvious whose land is whose. However, in places you will sometimes see camp chairs and such along the rivers that are obvious private property places. Nevertheless, the frequent sandbars allow for safe stopping spots. Fallen trees are common and some are embedded into the river bottom.

At 0.5 mile the Mattaponi splits around an island. Stay right here, along the state forest shore, where you can see trail bridges spanning little creeklets entering the Mattaponi. At 0.8 mile the river makes its first brush against the Mattaponi Bluffs, a series of hills by which the river flows. Here, scads of pink wild azaleas thrive among other vegetation. Rock runs along the river at the base of the bluffs. The stone is hollowed out in places. Ferns thrive in cool dripping areas. Beech trees rise on the hills.

The waterway continues bumping into bluffs time and again, as the stream meanders through a plain. At 1.4 miles Buckyard Branch comes in on your left after being dammed as a series of millponds, now wetlands. At 1.6 miles the Mattaponi River

A typical scene on the Mattaponi River

curves right as it bumps into more bluffs, on its left bank this time. At 2.5 miles the river curves right as a creek comes in on river left. This is the site of the old Oak Hall Landing. From here you can begin to see the effects of tides, as parts of the shoreline are exposed. The current may be slowed or sped up by the oceanic influence, despite salt water being a long way away.

Bump into more bluffs on river right at 3.9 miles. Lily pads grow in slow spots while azaleas and thick tree cover spread on the hills. Pass a few private accesses in this area. Come alongside another section of the state forest at 4.4 miles. From here it is a simple cruise on a widening waterway before you pass under the double bridges of US 360. Just beyond here on the right, reach the Virginia Department of Game and Inland Fisheries ramp. You will see it offers a fishing dock and large parking area as well as a dedicated boat ramp. As mentioned, despite being a 5-mile paddle, it is but a 2-mile shuttle. You could have someone watch the boat while you walk or bicycle back to the put in. River Road is not busy, and once you enter the state forest, traffic on the gravel road is minimal. While you are here, consider hiking the 0.4-mile Herring Creek Trail as well as the 1-mile Mattaponi Bluffs Trail.

Zoar State Forest is one of Virginia's smaller state forests. Covering 378 acres, it was donated to the state and is now home not only to the Mattaponi River but also agricultural and timber lands and dedicated habitats to enhance wildlife. Once the property of the man for whom Aylett was named back in the 1700s, the property passed into the hands of a man named Robert Pollard. After building his house Mr. Pollard named the dwelling Mount Zoar, unwittingly naming the state forest that was to come later. The house, although partially destroyed by fire, was rebuilt and is now the forest headquarters. Since the forest is virtually enveloped by civilization, hunting is not allowed. Paddling and hiking are the most popular activities here. See for yourself.

19 Swift Creek Lake

Make a paddling circuit around the shores of this popular impoundment at Pocahontas State Park, conveniently located near Richmond.

County: Chesterfield
Start: Swift Creek Lake ramp, N37 23.3665' / W77 34.5729'
End: Swift Creek Lake ramp, N37 23.3665' / W77 34.5729'
Length: 5.0 miles
Float time: 3.5 hours
Difficulty rating: Easy
Rapids: None
River/lake type: State park lake
Current: None
River gradient: None
Water gauge: None

Season: Year-round
Land status: Virginia state park
Fees and permits: Park entrance fee
Nearest city/town: Richmond
Maps: Pocahontas State Park trails; USGS: Chesterfield
Boats used: Kayaks, canoes, paddleboats
Organization: Pocahontas State Park, 10301 State Park Rd., Chesterfield, VA 23832; (804) 796-4255; www.dcr.virginia.gov/state-parks
Contact/outfitter: Friends of Pocahontas State Park, www.fopsp.org

Put-in/Takeout Information

To put-in/takeout: From exit 62 on I-95 south of downtown Richmond, take VA 288 / Chippenham Parkway north for 4.5 miles to Iron Bridge Road, VA 10 east / Chesterfield. Travel for 1.5 miles to Beach Road, Route 655. Turn right on Beach Road and follow it for 4.2 miles to turn right into the state park. Continue past the entrance station for 1.5 miles to turn right at the sign for the boat ramp. Follow the road past a large parking area, then descend past Picnic Shelter #2 to reach the boat ramp and a footbridge over Swift Creek Lake.

Paddle Summary

This paddle explores the natural wooded shores of Swift Creek Lake, situated in the heart of Pocahontas State Park. You will start on the west side of the slender impoundment at the boat ramp near the hiker bridge crossing the "no gas motors allowed" lake. From there, stick along the north shore, winding in and out of quiet coves, looking for wildlife on land and water. Make your way to the eastern end of the lake and find a fine stopping spot near the dam holding back Swift Creek. Your return route follows the southern shoreline and makes an additional turn into Third Branch embayment, a tributary of Swift Creek. The state park setting makes for a fine destination any time of year—they rent kayaks, canoes, rowboats, stand-up paddleboards, and paddleboats, too!

Swift Creek Lake

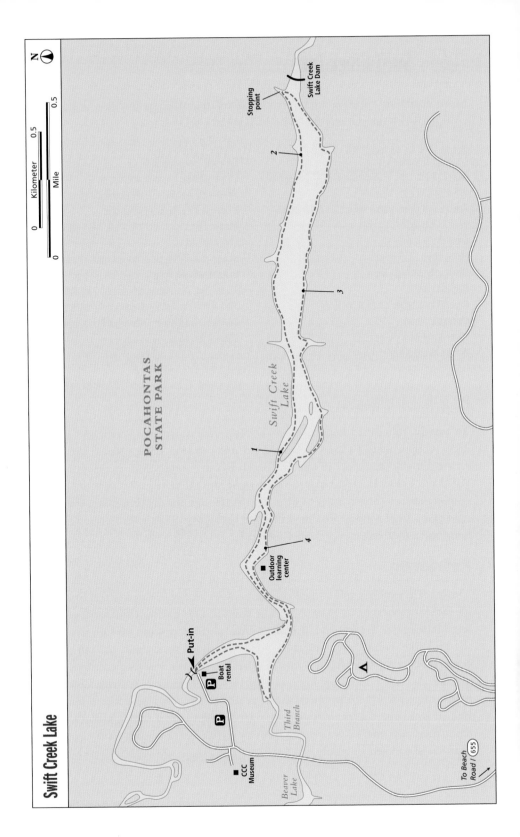

POCAHONTAS
STATE PARK

Swift Creek Lake

Swift Creek Lake Dam

Stopping point

2

3

1

4

Outdoor learning center

Put-in

Boat rental

P

P

CCC Museum

Beaver Lake

Third Branch

To Beach Road / 655

N

Kilometer
0   0.5

Mile
0   0.5

River/Lake Overview

Swift Creek Lake covers 225 acres, where Swift Creek was dammed to enhance the recreational opportunities at Pocahontas State Park. Swift Creek drains the southern part of Powhatan County and western Chesterfield County and is first dammed at 1,700-acre Swift Creek Reservoir, a much larger and wider impoundment—dammed to supply water for Chesterfield County—than narrow Swift Creek Lake. Beyond the park Swift Creek flows through the expanding suburbs connecting Richmond to Petersburg before eventually feeding the Appomattox River just before the Appomattox enters the mighty James River.

The Paddling

Swift Creek Lake and Pocahontas State Park are managed for both recreation and wildlife. This state park in what is now the south side of metro Richmond is easily the largest natural locale in the capital area. Having this place to paddle is important, but

Spring is a good time to kayak Swift Creek Lake.

TAKE THE FOREST EXPLORATION TRAIL

You will notice the trail bridge located at the put-in for this paddle. This is the beginning of the Forest Exploration Trail. This 2.2-mile trail loops its way on the north side of Swift Creek Lake. After bridging the lake the hike travels through multiple forest ecosystems. It also explores the cultural history of the park, visiting a pioneer homesite and cemetery. Consider adding this hike to your paddle while here at Pocahontas State Park. Attractive woodland of beech, hickory, oak, and pine with ample mountain laurel greets you on the loop. Interpretive information and resting benches are placed throughout the trek. Sweetgum, holly, and red bud fill the understory.

Park personnel use forest roads to manage the forest. Parts of the Forest Exploration Trail either follow or cross these forest roads. However, the loop is well marked and maintained, allowing you to focus on the natural beauty of the park. The beginning of the hike travels forest roads and nears Swift Creek Lake in bottomland where ash, sycamore, and pawpaw grow, more examples of forest types. Back on a ridgeline you will pass the pioneer homesite and cemetery of a nineteenth-century couple and their child. This is but one of the eighteen cemeteries identified within the boundaries of the nearly 8,000-acre state park. Look for privet and other homesteader-planted exotic species.

Find other past forest practices as you hike through a loblolly-pine grove planted in 1985. Count the years from now and gauge the tree's age. Maple, sweetgum, and vines grow amid the row-cropped evergreens. The evergreen world falls soon behind as you enter a hollow full of hardwoods. Note not only the change of forest type but also the smells of the woodland. In the hardwoods look for a rocky wet-weather cascade to your right. Another surprise lies downstream—some massive boulders coming seemingly out of nowhere.

The final part of the hike aims for Swift Creek Lake. Here it passes through a beech forest that has evolved precisely from the lack of fire. It should be primarily oak woodland, but fire suppression has allowed the beeches to grow. You begin to see an embayment of Swift Creek Lake before coming alongside some mountain laurel that will be showing off its pinkish-white blossoms in mid-May. And then you return to the trailhead, with a paddle and a hike under your belt here at Pocahontas State Park.

so is preserving the natural landscape. Managing the park to enhance wildlife is done through timber thinning, prescribed burns, and restoring natural plant species. At one time all fires were suppressed at the state park and resulted in a change of growth from its natural state, but now the park realizes that fires are a natural component of the forest and the prescribed burns are having a positive effect.

You will be observing the waterside forests throughout the paddle, as the lake is so slender that the rising hilly woods are always close. You will also see wildlife, especially deer, raptors, and waterfowl. Bring binoculars to enhance the experience. Leave the small boat ramp near the hiker bridge and boat-rental area and head southeast—although paddling west under the hiker bridge will take you up to the point where Swift Creek flows into the lake. You will soon be coming on to the widest part of the impoundment, where Third Branch creates an embayment. However, much of the effective paddling area can be covered over in lily pads and other waterweeds.

The lake narrows after 0.3 mile, and this is where you may even detect current. Open into the main part of the tarn, saddling along the left (north) shoreline. Occasional fallen trees stretch into the water while rock outcrops meld with soil banks. Alternating coves and points add natural lines to the shore and exploration possibilities. Long looks stretch easterly.

You begin to hear lake waters falling over the dam, as Swift Creek continues its run for the Appomattox River. Here, at 2.3 miles, you can swing left into a cove near the dam—but not too close—and stop for a bit. Here, a trail runs to the dam, allowing you to explore the weir. From there, join the south shoreline and begin the journey back. These north-facing hills are favorable for wildflowers in spring. Look for beaver dams banked against the shore, as well as herons fishing for a meal. A couple of larger coves are on this side of Swift Creek Lake. At 4.1 miles pass the outdoor learning center, marked with benches and a large fire ring. Here, groups engage in ecological education and demonstration. Beyond there, squeeze through the lake narrows and then tool up the less-visited cove of Third Branch. Interestingly, just upstream Third Branch is dammed, forming Beaver Lake, another state park impoundment. Boating is not allowed on Beaver Lake, however, fishing is allowed. Return to the boat ramp at 5 miles, completing the paddle. While here I recommend exploring other recreational possibilities at this park, including camping, mountain biking, and hiking the Forest Exploration Trail, with its trailhead at the boat ramp.

20 Rivanna River

Make a fun and historic float with Class I rapids and eye pleasing scenery east of Charlottesville.

County: Fluvanna
Start: Crofton Access, N37 55.121' / W78 17.875'
End: Palmyra Access, N37 51.468' / W78 16.022'
Length: 6.8 miles
Float time: 3.5 hours
Difficulty rating: Easy
Rapids: Class I rapids
River/lake type: Small river
Current: Moderate
River gradient: 4.2 feet per mile
Water gauge: Rivanna River at Palmyra, VA, minimum runnable level 180 cfs

Season: Apr–Oct
Land status: Mostly private; some parkland
Fees and permits: None
Nearest city/town: Palmyra
Maps: Rivanna River Crofton to Palmyra; USGS: Halifax, Scottsburg, Omega
Boats used: Kayaks, canoes
Organization: Rivanna Conservation Alliance, PO Box 1503, Charlottesville, VA 22902; (434) 977-4837; www.rivannariver.org
Contact/outfitter: Pleasant Grove Park, 271 Pleasant Grove Dr., Palmyra, VA 22963; (434) 589-2016; www.fluvannacounty.org

Put-in/Takeout Information

To the takeout: From exit 135 on I-64 east of Charlottesville, take US 15 south for 9 miles to cross the Rivanna River at Palmyra. Immediately turn right onto VA 53 and look right for the gravel parking area and a narrow ramp leading from the parking area down to the Rivanna River.

To the put-in from the takeout: Return to VA 53 and head west, driving for 4 miles to a roundabout. Stay right here, joining VA 600 north, and follow it for 3.3 miles, crossing the river and turning left into the river-access parking area. A concrete ramp leads down to the river.

Paddle Summary

This paddling trip follows a historic and scenic segment of the Rivanna River that works its way from the Blue Ridge toward the Piedmont. The clear stream rolls over a rocky bed and is bordered by trees nearly its entire length. Easy Class I rapids liven up the action as you roll past occasional bluffs and islands. At the end of the paddle, you reach Palmyra, site of a mill, a historic bridge, and other evidence of the Rivanna's past. Excellent accesses on both ends make the paddle user-friendly. The shuttle distance is short as well. However, there may be a little too much traffic for a bike shuttle. Although most of the land bordering the Rivanna River is private, the lower part of the paddle passes Fluvanna County's Pleasant Grove Park. This preserve features over

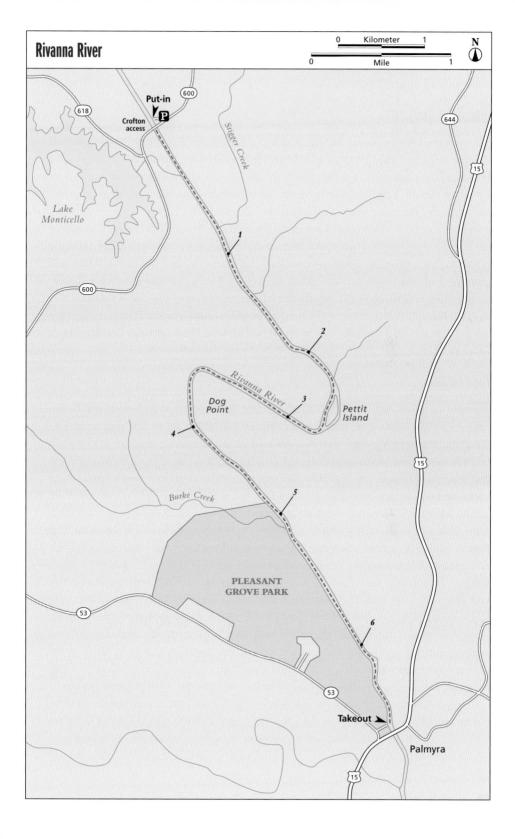

Rivanna River

0 Kilometer 1

0 Mile 1

N

618

600

Put-in
P
Crofton
access

Stigger Creek

Lake
Monticello

1

600

2

Rivanna River

3

Dog
Point

Pettit
Island

4

Burke Creek

5

PLEASANT
GROVE PARK

53

6

53

Takeout

15

Palmyra

644

15

15

20 miles of trails, some of which come alongside the river. Hikers, mountain bikers, and equestrians enjoy the paths. Parklands or not, this segment of the Rivanna is virtually devoid of development.

River/Lake Overview

The Rivanna River is now recognized as an important recreation destination and wildlife habitat flowing through Albemarle, Greene, and Fluvanna Counties. The Rivanna was named for Queen Anne (River Anne) and became shortened to its current moniker. The headwaters of the Rivanna River originate in Virginia's contribution to America's great national parks: Shenandoah National Park. Legendary waterways such as Moormans River and Doyles River flow out of the park to gather around Charlottesville. Sometimes known as Thomas Jefferson's river, the Rivanna River makes a 50-mile journey between Charlottesville and the James River and comprises a total watershed of 766 square miles. Along the way it leaves Charlottesville then cuts through the Southwest Mountains. From there, the Rivanna River keeps its southeasterly direction. Our paddle joins the Rivanna River at Crofton, where it winds through hills before reaching Palmyra. The waterway becomes even more rural between Palmyra and its mother stream the James.

The Paddling

The put-in is beneath the VA 600 bridge and you immediately launch into a fun little rapid. The river soon settles down, with banks about 80 to 100 feet wide. The Rivanna, like many Virginia waterways, was once used for transportation. A lock built in 1833 stood here at the site of the VA 600 bridge. You can still see remnants when the water is down in late summer. The translucent waters flow above underwater rocks. Still other stones stand above the water. Just ahead on the right is the site of the Union Mill Locks. When rivers were dammed by mills to harness waterpower, locks were built to allow traveling boats to raise or lower themselves around the dams. The Union Mill lock system is on the National Register of Historic Places. Sycamores, ash, and brush line the river. After a quarter mile you will have encountered your first sandbar. Depending on where they are some of them may be partly vegetated. You will also see gravel bars. The Rivanna settles down and the floating is fun and easy. Occasional fields come near the banks of 20 or so feet high. Sporadic riffles separate from slow pools. Oftentimes, the water will simply speed in the gravelly shallows without creating rapids, though you may have to pay attention to not get stuck in the shallows at summer water levels. Also, when the water is low and extra clear, you will see game fish such as smallmouth bass as well as suckers and other bottom feeders.

Stigger Creek comes in on the left at 0.9 mile. A gravel bar is usually formed here. An unnamed creek comes in on the left at 1.6 miles. The mix of woods and fields are favorable habitat for deer. Most paddlers going down this section will see at least one. At 2.3 miles make a serious bend to the right, passing straightforward shoals and small

Looking upriver at a shoal on the Rivanna River

rapids. Paddle around the wider right-hand channel of Pettit Island at 2.5 miles and bend northwest. A bluff rises above with scenic outcrops.

At 2.9 miles you paddle over timber and stones of the Broken Island canal and lock remains, originally built in the 1850s. Mostly made of wood, little is left of the lock. The Rivanna continues its winding ways, curving to its original southeasterly direction as it works around Dog Point. Pass another light rapid at 4.5 miles. By 4.7 miles you have come along the boundaries of Pleasant Grove Park. Here, see the first of several foot accesses in the park on the right-hand bank. More rock outcrops can be seen while floating down the bucolic Virginia stream. At 5.2 miles come to a straightforward rapid and Burke Creek coming in on your right. A shoal at 5.9 miles keeps you moving along. At 6.2 miles the river narrows and you wander through small islands and shoals, complemented with a gravel bar. The end is near, so stop here if you want to relax riverside.

The US 15 bridge comes into view just before paddle's end. Just upstream you will see old pilings of a former bridge built in the early 1800s linking the town of Palmyra to points south. This was once a covered bridge, first built in 1828, then damaged by flood. It was rebuilt the last time in 1884.

Because you end in the middle of a shoal and the takeout is just below the old bridge pilings, it pays off to stay right after seeing the US 15 bridge. The concrete ramp with squared-off steps at the base of the ramp is your takeout. From the takeout parking area, look downriver and you can find the basement of the old five-story Palmyra Mill, built in 1813, along with the remains of a dam just downstream of the takeout. Just across the river in Palmyra, you can also check out the old 1828 jail and county courthouse, still in its original configuration.

21 James River: Howardsville to Scottsville

Enjoy a scenic section of the middle James as it rolls through the Piedmont.

Counties: Albemarle; Buckingham
Start: Howardsville boat ramp, N37 43.978' / W78 38.721'
End: Scottsville boat ramp, N37 47.840' / W78 29.420'
Length: 12.0 miles
Float time: 6.0 hours
Difficulty rating: Easy–moderate
Rapids: Class I, one Class I+ rapid
River/lake type: Big Piedmont waterway
Current: Moderate
River gradient: 2.4 feet per mile
Water gauge: James River at Scottsville, no minimum runnable level, beware of river when well above average flows

Season: Mar–Nov
Land status: Private
Fees and permits: None
Nearest city/town: Scottsville
Maps: James River Water Trail; USGS: Howardsville, Glenmore, Esmont, Scottsville
Boats used: Kayaks, canoes, johnboats, and tubes in sections
Organization: James River Association, 4833 Old Main St., Richmond, VA 23231; (804) 788-8811; www.jamesriverassociation.org
Contact/outfitter: James River Reeling and Rafting, 265 Ferry St., Scottsville, VA 24590; (434) 286-4386; www.reelingandrafting.com

Put-in/Takeout Information

To the takeout: From exit 121A on I-81 near Charlottesville, take VA 20 south for 18 miles to downtown Scottsville. Here, turn left on Main Street / VA 6 east and follow it for 0.2 mile to turn right on Ferry Street. Follow Ferry Street south over the railroad tracks to reach the Scottsville boat ramp.

To the put-in from the takeout: Backtrack north on Ferry Street, then turn left on Main Street / VA 6 west and follow it 0.2 mile to turn right on VA 20. Follow VA 20 north for 0.6 mile, then turn left onto VA 6 west / Irish Road and follow it for 2.3 miles. Turn left on Langhorne Road and follow it for 2.9 miles, then turn right on James River Road and follow it for 6.1 miles to Baber Road and the signed left turn to the Howardsville boat ramp. *Note:* Most parking for the Howardsville boat ramp is well away from river. Do not park illegally here.

Paddle Summary

This is a big paddle on a big river. Do not let the distance of the adventure scare you. The James in this section has a steady current and some rapids to push you along. However, the width of the waterway does make it subject to winds. Just give yourself plenty of time, and enjoy the islands scattered along the route, as well as the overall quality Piedmont scenery. From Howardsville you will keep primarily east, rolling on the big river to reach a cluster of islands and a big rapid near Goosby Island. Take the intimate sneak route, snaking among smaller isles. Next, pass notable Rock Island. Downriver you will encounter Hatten Ferry, the last remaining ferry on the James. A fun rapid is here as well. Next, curve north beneath some hills, then float a wide section through light shoals to end your paddle at Scottsville, an intriguing small town with a lot of river history. An outfitter operates in Scottsville should you need to rent a boat or get a shuttle.

River/Lake Overview

The James River is Virginia's contribution to great rivers of the world, and it is Virginia's largest watercourse, flowing across the entire state from the mountains in the west to the Atlantic Ocean in the east. The James is born in the upper reaches of the Appalachians, fast against the West Virginia border in appropriately named Highland County, where the Cowpasture River and the Jackson River converge to form the James at a water pass between ridges known as the Iron Gate. Here in Botetourt County, the James officially begins its journey to Chesapeake Bay. It leaves the

A relaxing moment on the middle James River Keri Anne Molloy

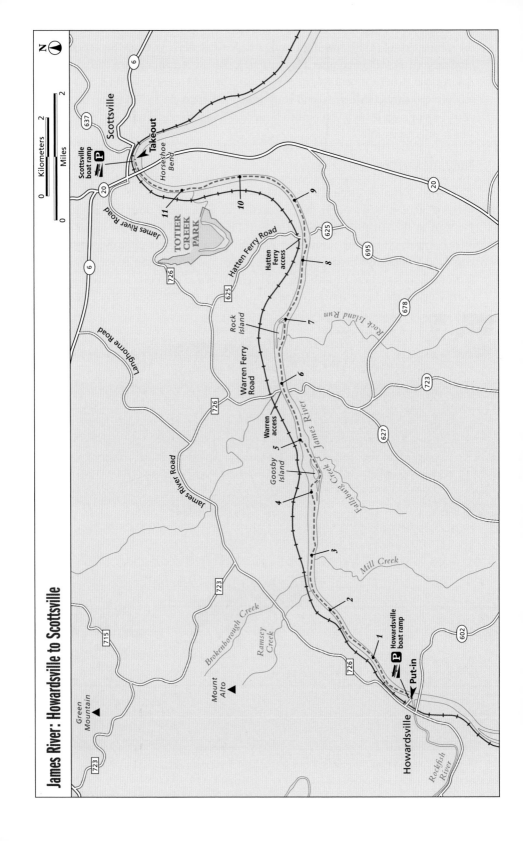

James River: Howardsville to Scottsville

mountains near Holcomb Rock, then passes Lynchburg. The river persists its endless quest for the ocean, churning through the Piedmont where this paddle takes place. The James drops off the fall line at Richmond (the reason for Richmond's location) in a crash of whitewater before pushing to the ocean. At 340 miles the James is one of the longest rivers in the United States that begins and ends in the same state. The James's watershed encompasses 25 percent of Virginia, around 10,000 square miles, draining the heart of the Old Dominion.

The Paddling

The Howardsville boat ramp is located at the confluence of the Rockfish River and the much bigger James River. Immediately launch into the huge James, normally flowing clear green. Small hills rise in the distance and occasional fields stretch behind a riverside screen of trees. The large size of the James allows for distant sweeps both upriver and downriver. At 0.6 mile flow through the first shoal, just a light riffle. Like most rapids in the middle James, standing rocks will be present in the moving waters. Float over another light shoal at 1.4 miles. The width of the river calls for picking a route as best as possible well ahead of rapids, since it is often impractical to ferry to one side or another of the river in midshoal. Additionally, being a big river, most sections of the James have a deceptively steady and strong current. At lower water levels, these light shoals will be bordered with gravel bars in places.

At 2.5 miles Ramsey Creek, then Brokenborough Creek, enters on river left. The James is now heading due east in shallows above various-size rocks. Mill Creek enters on river right at 2.9 miles. The mouths of these creeks help keep you apprised of your position as well as serve as potentially interesting exploration areas. Test the waters of these tributary creeks—they are generally cooler and clearer than the main stream and are potential wildlife-viewing areas.

Now you will see islands ahead while passing through a shallow rocky section. This is the grouping of isles centered by big Goosby Island. Start moving over to river

VISIT CANAL BASIN SQUARE

Scottsville is small but historic, and in their historic district on Main Street, near the Ferry Street boat launch used on this paddle, you can visit Canal Basin Square, an outdoor museum of sorts. In panels and displays the locale tells the transportation history of the James River and Kanawha Canal, starting before there was a Virginia to when the railroads rendered canals obsolete. You can also check out a replica bateaux, the boat used in river trade two centuries back. Also, view the scale-model demonstration canal lock and learn about Scottsville and the James River's place in the Civil War. Add a stop at Canal Basin Square to your paddle. It will enhance your historical appreciation for the James River.

Tubers and anglers also like this stretch of the James River.

right. The narrow channel around the right side of Goosby Island is much easier to navigate than the rocky rapids running on the much wider left side of Goosby Island. I recommend the right channel of Goosby Island. The islands begin at 3.7 miles. They are narrow teardrop-shaped lands with piled logs on the upstream ends and a tail of sand/soil on their lower ends. Here, begin working right, then get right of Goosby Island. Fallsburg Creek enters on river right as you pass Goosby Island, but you probably will not even notice it. Pass the downstream tip of Goosby Island at 4.3 miles. The shoals are milder here, with a final drop at the downstream tip of Goosby Island.

Float by the Warren access on river left at 6 miles. This was the site of a ferry in days gone by. Shallow waters keep you moving. Reach the light shoals of Rock Island at 6.4 miles. It is easy to see how the island got its name, with a tall stone precipice on its upstream end. Go to the right of Rock Island. Here big Rock Island Run adds its flow. Paddle beyond the east tip of Rock Island at 7.1 miles. The James is still leading you east. At 8.2 miles head left-center to run the rocky Class I+ Hatten Ferry rapids. Ahead, look for the old car ferry on either bank, linked by a cable. Established in 1870, the Hatton Ferry is purportedly the last pole-operated ferry in America. The old-time ferry operates on weekends from mid-April to mid-October and at other times by special arrangement. Hatten Ferry is also the last operating ferry on the entire James River. Early in Virginia's history literally hundreds of ferries crossed on this waterway. This locale is also used as a boating access, especially by tubers floating down to Scottsville.

By 9 miles a ridge rises on river right, forcing the James to bend left (northbound). The river widens more and becomes shallower but keeps moving, aiming for Scottsville. Totier Creek enters on your left at 10.9 miles. The final bend is to the right, the beginning of greater Horseshoe Bend. The VA 20 bridge and Scottsville come into view. Pass under the VA 20 bridge and the Scottsville boat ramp is on your left at 12 miles.

22 Farmville Blueway

Paddle three bodies of water and make an easy foot shuttle using a rail trail right in the heart of hip, happening Farmville. Start on Wilcks Lake and paddle that pretty little impoundment. Make a short portage and join serpentine Buffalo Creek, flowing through deep bottomland woods to meet the Appomattox River. Float down this historic stream to end in downtown Farmville.

Counties: Prince Edward; Cumberland
Start: Wilcks Lake boat ramp, N37 18.185' / W78 24.516'
End: Riverside Park ramp, N37 18.420' / W78 23.433'
Length: 3.9 miles
Float time: 2.0 hours
Difficulty rating: Easy–moderate
Rapids: Class I riffles
River/lake type: Small lake, small creek, medium-size river
Current: Can be fast on Buffalo Creek when water is up
River gradient: 2.1 feet per mile

Water gauge: Buffalo Creek near Hampden Sydney, VA, 50 cfs minimum runnable level, 180 cfs maximum runnable level
Season: Feb–June and after heavy rains
Land status: Some parkland; private
Fees and permits: None
Nearest city/town: Farmville
Maps: Farmville Blueway; USGS: Farmville
Boats used: Kayaks, canoes
Organization: Friends of the Appomattox River, PO Box 784, Farmville, VA 23901; http://far-va.org
Contact/outfitter: Town of Farmville, Virginia, 116 N. Main St., Farmville, VA 23901; (434) 392-5686; https://farmvilleva.com

Put-in/Takeout Information

To takeout: The takeout is located on the southwest bank of the Appomattox River at Riverside Park in downtown Farmville. Parking is off Elm Street. Before embarking on the paddle, walk down to the Appomattox River and find the small concrete ramp that must be accessed by walking through the grass to the Appomattox River. The ramp is about 50 yards upstream of the VA 15 / Main Street Bridge over the Appomattox River.

To put-in from the takeout: From the takeout, head south on VA 15 / Main Street for 0.4 mile, then turn right onto West Third Street. Follow West Third Street for 1 mile to the left turn into the park (just past the Farmville fire station) and ramp at Wilcks Lake.

Paddle Summary

This is one unique paddling trip. It is not often that you can paddle a lake, then a creek, then a river, all in the distance of 4 miles, but you can right here in the heart of Farmville. And to top it off, you can self-shuttle by foot or by bicycle using the High

Farmville Blueway

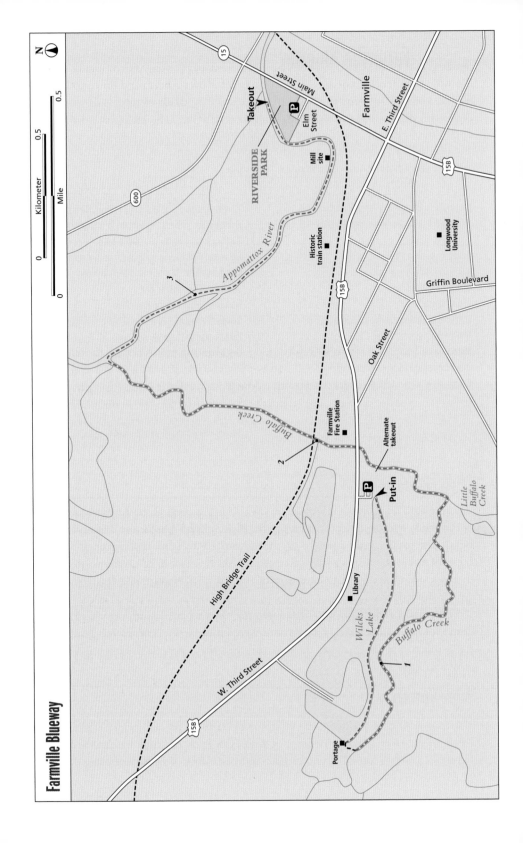

Bridge Trail, a Virginia state park rail trail. The first part of the paddle starts on linear Wilcks Lake. Here you tool along the shoreline (ringed with its own hiking trail by the way) then reach a portage. A short carry leads over a berm and down to Buffalo Creek, a slender stream coursing through extremely thick woods. Make your way down this tight passage to reach the Appomattox River. The bigger waterway takes you to the heart of downtown Farmville and paddle's end.

River/Lake Overview

Wilcks Lake, your starting point, is a 55-acre impoundment, a dammed tributary of Buffalo Creek. The lake is bordered by 100 acres of parkland. You can circle the lake by foot using the 2-mile Sarah Terry Trail. The next body of water is Buffalo Creek, a tributary of the Appomattox River. The slender stream drains the hills of western Prince Edward County, often breaking up into channels in its lower reaches before feeding its mother stream, the Appomattox River. The Appomattox River is born in hills just east of the town of Appomattox in Appomattox County. It gathers branches including Holliday Creek, part of Holliday Creek State Park. The river heads east, forming the boundary between several counties. It flows through Farmville, continuing to gain size, and is dammed as Lake Chesdin just west of Petersburg. At Petersburg the Appomattox drops off the fall line with several big rapids—Great Falls—before flattening out and giving its waters up to the James River. It is the falling water that led to Petersburg being established on the Appomattox for two reasons: The Great Falls water could be harnessed for power to operate machinery, and the rapids marked the limit of river navigability from the ocean.

The Paddling

Developed by the Friends of the Appomattox River, the Farmville Blueway ingeniously incorporates three different waterways into one fun little paddle with an easy shuttle that I have done by foot. And you can do only parts of the blueway if you please. Picnic tables and the Sarah Terry Trail ringing Wilcks Lake are both near the concrete boat ramp. Head west up Wilcks Lake. You will notice an elevated berm separates the impoundment from Buffalo Creek to the south. However, the north side of the lake is lower and is where most of the facilities of the park are located, including grassy play areas and picnic shelters. The lake is but 50 yards wide on its east end but continues to widen. After a quarter mile you will see the community library on the north bank of the lake. Paddle on over and check out a book. Much of the south shore is wooded with maples and river birch. At 0.4 mile pass by a wooded peninsula where park activities take place. Stay to the left of the peninsula.

Reach the portage trail to Buffalo Creek at 0.7 mile. You can continue to paddle the lake, but the portage is in the southwest corner of Wilcks Lake. Steps lead up to the berm upon which the Sarah Terry Trail runs. Once on the Sarah Terry Trail,

Wilcks Lake is but one of three bodies of water you experience on this paddle.

briefly head left then drop right to the banks of Buffalo Creek. This is but a short portage of hundred feet or so. The portage trail is signed.

You are now in a completely different world, as slim Buffalo Creek flows under a bottomland hardwood forest of ash, sycamore, and birch, exhibiting a primeval aura. Wildlife favors the area as well—expect to see beaver and deer as well as bird life. Although you cannot shut out the sounds of Farmville, the sights before you exude deep nature. The stream is around 30 feet wide, but the effective paddling area is much narrower, since fallen logs are a constant feature. You will be dodging around them and hopefully the route has been cleared recently. Expect to duck under a limb or two. At 1.1 miles the creek splits but a sign leads you right. The twists will keep you hopping at higher water levels. At 1.6 miles Little Buffalo Creek comes in on your right. Here, Buffalo Creek curves north. At 1.8 miles approach the West Third Street Bridge and, just before, find the grassy bank on river left that offers a takeout if you want to shorten your trip.

After passing under the West Third Street Bridge, you are in for a surprise: A pipeline crosses Buffalo Creek adjacent to the city waterworks. If the water is up, you may have to pull over this pipeline. At lower water you can float your boat under it. Exercise caution here either way. After making your way past the pipeline, pass under the High Bridge Trail, the popular converted rail trail that bisects the heart of Farmville.

A view of the Appomattox River as it flows through Farmville

Buffalo Creek is less junglelike down here. A canal comes in on your left at 2.5 miles. Meet and join the Appomattox River at 2.7 miles. Despite being less than 100 feet wide, the Appomattox seems very open compared to Buffalo Creek. At 3 miles an old canal goes left, but I do not recommend it for paddling. This canal was used in the early 1800s to allow bateaux—slender boats used for trade and transportation and moved by poling—to get around the Prince Edward Mill, where a dam was erected to harness waterpower. The Appomattox River was once used heavily for trade from Petersburg up to Plantersville—120 miles of riverway were improved to enhance moving the bateaux up and down the river.

Bluffs rise on river right, adding a scenic touch. Pass under a low bridge. Here, a sign indicates the old milldam 500 feet ahead. Come to the milldam site, just before coming into downtown Farmville. The left side is best for passage, but scout it before you run it. Make a final cruise past old tobacco-warehouses-turned-restaurants and such. Patrons may wave down to you—make us paddlers look good. When you see the VA 15 / Main Street Bridge, head over to river right. A sign marks the concrete ramp at Riverside Park. After floods the ramp can be muddy.

If executing a foot shuttle, you can lock your boat to a tree beside the takeout, then simply walk up Main Street to reach the High Bridge Trail and head right. Follow this trail for 0.3 mile west and leave it at the historic railroad station. From there simply walk along West Third Street over a hill to Wilcks Lake. Too bad there is not a direct link from the park to the High Bridge Trail. Should you want to explore the High Bridge Trail further, bicycles can be rented in downtown Farmville. The 31-mile High Bridge Trail travels roughly east–west between Pamplin City and Burkeville, with the trail's namesake High Bridge stretching over a half mile over the Appomattox River and 125 feet above the waterway, delivering a thrilling ride. It is one of the longest recreational trail bridges in the United States. Multiple trailhead accesses and picnic areas enhance the High Bridge experience.

23 Staunton River

This mellow, big-water, big-river Piedmont float cruises by historic Staunton River Battlefield State Park.

Counties: Halifax; Charlotte
Start: Watkins Bridge, N36 54.92' / W78 44.49'
End: Clover Landing at US 360 Bridge, N36 49.599' / W78 41.257'
Length: 8.8 miles
Float time: 4.0 hours
Difficulty rating: Easy
Rapids: None
River/lake type: Large river
Current: Moderate-swift
River gradient: 2.9 feet per mile
Water gauge: Roanoke (Staunton) River at Randolph, VA, no minimum runnable level

Season: Year-round, best in late summer
Land status: Private; state park; US Army Corps of Engineers
Fees and permits: None
Nearest city/town: Clover
Maps: Staunton River Watkins Bridge to Clover Landing; USGS: Saxe, Clover
Boats used: Kayaks, canoes, johnboats
Organization: Staunton River Battlefield State Park, 1035 Fort Hill Trail, Randolph, VA 23962; (434) 454-4312; www.dcr.virginia.gov
Contact/outfitter: Upper Reach, 274 Botetourt Ct., Boydton, VA 23917; (252) 213-9501; www.upperreach.org

Put-in/Takeout Information

To the takeout: From South Boston, take US 360 east for 15 miles to the Clover Landing access road on your right just before US 360 crosses the Staunton River.

To the put-in from the takeout: From the Clover Landing access, continue east on US 360, crossing the Staunton River, for 3 miles to turn left on VA 608. Follow VA 608 for 1.5 miles to turn left on VA 607. Follow VA 607 for 7.7 miles to reach a T intersection. Turn left here on VA 746 / Scuffletown Road and follow it for 0.5 mile to cross the Staunton River. Turn right to the Watkins Bridge ramp on your right.

Paddle Summary

This big-river paddle explores the Staunton River as it streams through Southside Virginia. Flowing amid a wide agricultural valley, the Staunton cruises southeasterly at a steady pace with easy floating—few obstructions or rapids. Reach Staunton River Battlefield State Park, site of a Civil War skirmish that can add hiking and historical exploration possibilities either during or after your paddle (you pass a portion of the park on the shuttle from the takeout to the put-in). The relaxing float continues downstream, passing under the VA 92 bridge and entering lands managed by the Army Corps of Engineers as part of the greater Buggs Island Lake project. Here you will pass remains of an old milldam before completing your paddle. Overall, the trip

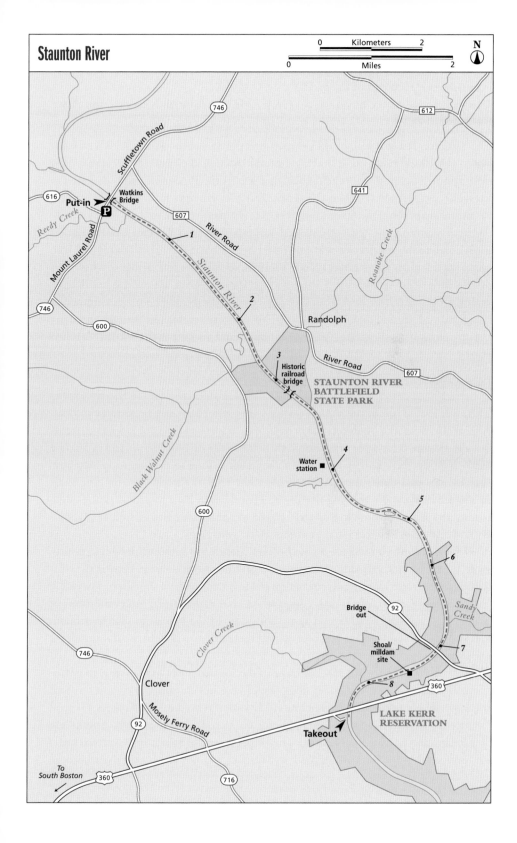

Staunton River

Kilometers 0 — 2
Miles 0 — 2

N

746

Scuffletown Road

612

616
Put-in
P
Watkins
Bridge

641

607

River Road

1

Reedy Creek

Mount Laurel Road

Staunton River

746

600

2

Randolph

Roanoke Creek

3
Historic
railroad
bridge

River Road

607

STAUNTON RIVER
BATTLEFIELD
STATE PARK

Black Walnut Creek

Water
station

4

600

5

6

92

Bridge
out

Sandy Creek

Clover Creek

Shoal/
milldam
site

7

746

Clover

8

360

LAKE KERR
RESERVATION

92

Mosely Ferry Road

Takeout

360

To
South Boston

716

amounts to a tranquil float on a big river without worrying about big rapids or not enough water. The Virginia Department of Game and Inland Fisheries offers quality boat ramps on each end of the paddle.

River/Lake Overview

The Staunton River is really a different-named portion of the Roanoke River, starting in the Blue Ridge, then flowing easterly through the town of Roanoke. It is next dammed as Smith Mountain Lake, then enters the Piedmont and is dammed as Leesville Lake. However, when the Roanoke River emerges from Leesville Dam, it has magically become the Staunton River, as it was named back in the 1700s for Lady Rebecca Staunton, the wife of Colonial Virginia Governor William Gooch. For 80 miles down to the confluence with the Dan River, the name remains Staunton River. Here, the 51 miles from Long Island, Virginia, to the US 360 Bridge—where this paddle ends—the Staunton is a Virginia State Scenic River. Below the confluence with the Dan, the river once again becomes the Roanoke and here it is dammed as Buggs Island Lake and then Lake Gaston. The river name remains Roanoke throughout its remaining mileage to Albemarle Sound and its end at the North Carolina coast.

The Paddling

This river can be run in late summer when other waterways may be too low to float. Also at this time, the Staunton River will have ample sandbars for stopping. Additionally, this can be a viable bike shuttle since the roads are mostly level and quiet. The Watkins Bridge boat ramp is a long concrete track leading to the big, wide Staunton. Immediately pass under the VA 746 bridge. The river is already stretching upwards of 200 feet wide and is moving steadily. You hardly even have to paddle much while passing the wooded shoreline of river birch, sycamore, and ash, as well as plentiful willows. At 0.3 mile Reedy Creek comes in on your right.

Where shallow, you will see a sand bottom. The steady current can be deceptively swift. It pays to pick one side of the river or another, since the waterway is so wide. Although the riverside flats are covered in fields, the immediate shoreline is wooded. At 2.4 miles Black Walnut Creek comes in on your right. By 2.7 miles the lands of Staunton River State Park extend along both sides of the waterway. The river bends and you see the railroad bridge, over which the battle was fought, floating under it at 3.2 miles.

Back in the summer of 1864, the cause of the Confederates was looking desperate. General Robert E. Lee was under siege east of here in Petersburg, trying to stave off the inevitable Union assault on Richmond. In order to hold off the Yankees, General Lee needed a reliable pipeline of supplies for his men. They came via the South Side and Richmond & Danville Railroad. The bridge over the Staunton River was critical to protecting the railroad supply line. This fact was not lost on the Northerners,

A Civil War battle was fought at this bridge crossing.

and General Grant set out to destroy the railroad bridge site under which you float. Over 5,000 Union soldiers headed for the Staunton River bridge, destroying railroad track along the way, while being harried by Confederate skirmishers. Back then the railroad bridge over the Staunton River was covered. Around that bridge 296 Confederate reserves stood waiting, knowing that thousands of Yankees were heading their way. Additionally, boys too young to fight and men too old for war gathered together a little under 500 strong to assist the Confederate reserves. Other citizenry came from nearby Halifax, Charlotte, and Mecklenburg Counties, raising the total to over 900 defenders at the bridge.

Union scouts were watching this gathering of defenders, and the Confederate leader, a man named Captain Benjamin Farinholt, kept sending empty trains back and forth to the west as if bringing in additional troops, to trick the scouts, making them believe the Southern contingent was much larger than it really was. The Union came after them anyway, and on a hot day in late June, the Yankees assaulted the bridge from the east and north, but the Southerners repulsed no less than four major charges on the bridge. By nightfall the Yankees had given up, making a night march back to Petersburg. This battle of the Staunton River Bridge became legend in Southside Virginia, the day when reserves, citizens, and local stragglers defeated 5,000 Union regulars. Today the area is the site of a 300-acre state park. Visitors can access the battlefield via hiking trails, the former railroad bridge, and enjoy interpretive information on both sides of the river. I strongly urge you to add this historic endeavor to your paddling trip, especially when you will be going directly by the park on your shuttle.

The paddle continues below the battlefield site, and at 3.6 miles Little Roanoke Creek, a big stream, enters on river left. At 4.3 miles pass a waterworks building. Exercise caution here, as the waterworks will sporadically cause turbulence when shooting water into the river. The Staunton curves to the southeast and you come to an unnamed island standing in midriver at 5.3 miles. The main channel goes left. The willowy isle surrounded by sand invites a stop. At 6.1 miles enter lands bordered by the Buggs Island Lake (Lake Kerr) Reservoir land, though you will not know the difference, as the river corridor has been nearly without development.

At 7.0 miles Sandy Creek enters on your left. Ahead, the indefinitely closed VA 92 bridge rises in front of you. Float under the silent span, now heading southwest. Drift into a small island and rock shoals. This is the remnants of an old milldam that once ground corn and wheat into meal. At 8.2 miles Clover Creek enters on river right. Sandbars form in this area with regularity. The US 360 / Clover bridge appears ahead. Get over on river right, and just beyond the bridge reach the boat ramp and large parking area of the takeout, finishing the paddle.

24 Banister River

Float an established blueway on the historic Banister River through virtually undeveloped banks, tracing a trade boat route from two centuries back, where you can still see evidence of wing dams and other construction that kept the Banister navigable.

County: Halifax
Start: Kings Bridge Canoe/Kayak Access, N36 46.640' / W78 55.034'
End: Terrys Bridge Canoe/Kayak Access, N36 44.697' / W78 50.486'
Length: 6.2 miles
Float time: 3.0 hours
Difficulty rating: Easy
Rapids: Class I riffles
River/lake type: Small river
Current: Moderate
River gradient: 2.7 feet per mile
Water gauge: Banister River at Halifax, VA, minimum runnable level 100 cfs
Season: Late Mar through mid-Nov

Land status: Some private; public wildlife management area
Fees and permits: None
Nearest city/town: Halifax
Maps: Banister River Blueway, Southern Virginia Wild Blueway; USGS: Halifax, Scottsburg, Omega
Boats used: Kayaks, canoes
Organization: Upper Reach, 274 Botetourt Ct., Boydton, VA 23917; (252) 213-9501; www.upperreach.org
Contacts/outfitters: Tri Rivers Canoe Rental; (434) 222-6182; http://tririverscanoerental .wixsite.com/canoes

Put-in/Takeout Information

To the takeout: From the intersection of US 501 and VA 360 in Halifax, take VA 360 east for 3.7 miles (passing the Kings Bridge access on the way) to turn right on VA 613 / Terrys Bridge Road. Turn right on VA 613 and follow it for 3.2 miles to turn right onto US 360 west. Immediately bridge the Banister River, then turn left and reach the Terrys Bridge / US 360 parking area. The access is under the bridge.

To the put-in from the takeout: Backtrack on US 360 east, then turn left on Terrys Bridge Road and follow it for 3.2 miles. Turn left onto VA 360 west and follow it for 3.1 miles to turn right into the Kings Bridge access on your right.

Paddle Summary

This float travels a part of the Banister that is a designated Virginia State Scenic River. Start at the elaborate Kings Bridge paddler access near downtown Halifax, enjoying the Banister River as it heads southeasterly under high vegetated banks. Along the way you will float over some simple Class I rapids that push your boat along. Look for historical weirs channeling the waters in sandy shallows. Later you enter the Wolf Trap Wildlife Management Area, keeping the banks wild. The takeout at Terry Bridge is a little more primitive than the Kings Bridge access.

A paddler's-eye view of the Banister River

River/Lake Overview

The Banister River is a tributary of the Dan River. Born in foothills east of the Blue Ridge in Pittsylvania County near Chatham, the smallish Banister flows first northeast beneath the slopes of White Oak Mountain before turning southeasterly into Halifax County, whereupon it is dammed as Banister Lake near Halifax, just upstream of this paddle's beginning. The Banister then flows free to meet the Dan River just east of South Boston, where both streams are slowed by the waters of Lake Kerr. A total of 63 miles of the Banister River, nearly the whole waterway, are distinguished as a Virginia State Scenic River.

The Paddling

As a paddler's river, the Banister has been through its incarnations. Aboriginal Virginians paddled the waterway, building camps and fish dams, weirs for trapping finned creatures for food. Later, colonial settlers and early Americans moving west from the Atlantic coast up the fingering rivers and creeks of the Staunton (Roanoke) River, made their way to the Banister River. Travel and trade in those days was largely done by water, as the forests were nearly impenetrable. Even the best roads were muddy ruts when wet and dust-blown, pothole-filled avenues when dry. Therefore, water was the way to go. Traders and travelers on the Banister and other rivers used what are known as bateaux—a shallow draft boat resembling a canoe except larger, with a rudder in the back and moved by paddle or pole—going upriver and downriver. Despite the shallow draft, these bateaux needed help in getting through shallows, and some of the old Indian fish dams were modified and other weirs were constructed to create a continuous moving—and deep enough—channel even when the Banister was low, typically late summer through autumn.

Banister River

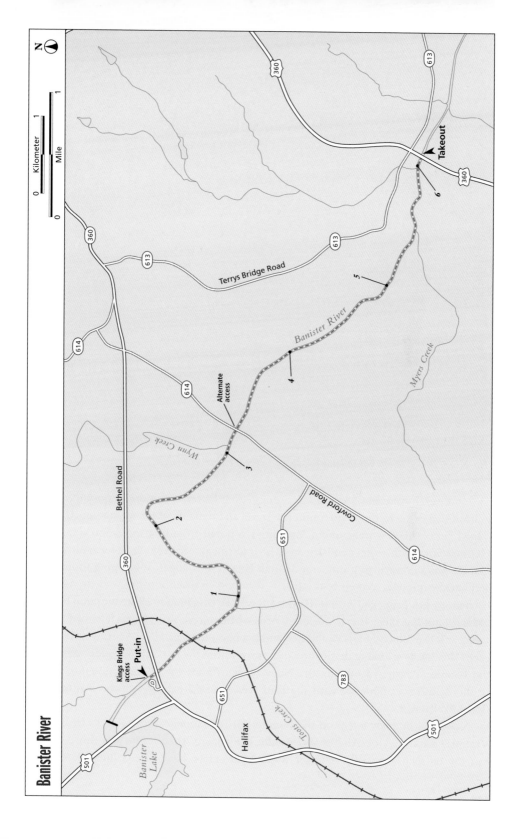

The Kings Bridge canoe/kayak launch is located near the town of Halifax.

However, by the late 1830s, roads were getting better, and more important, the railroad had come to the Old Dominion. Travel and trade by water was all but abandoned. Enter the new millennium. Paddling is a popular outdoor recreation activity. Communities with rivers and lakes in their midst begin developing water trails and blueways and constructing canoe and kayak launches in hopes of bringing tourism and healthy lifestyles to their backyards.

Thus it has happened on the Banister River. A cooperative effort by numerous agencies, among them the US Army Corps of Engineers and Halifax County, the Banister River Blueway was established and is a boon to us paddlers. Starting at Banister Lake (a lake-paddling destination just upriver from the start of this paddle, where the Banister River is dammed), the blueway then heads for 11 miles downstream to the Banister's confluence with the Dan River, itself a tributary of the Staunton (Roanoke) River.

Now we can enjoy a trip on the Banister for recreation, exercise, and to bask in Virginia's natural glory. And as you paddle, evidence of these weirs and fish dams can still be seen, especially at lower water levels. Here, hand-placed lines of rock channelizing the stream are exposed. At higher water levels you will flow right through them as riffles and low-grade rapids.

This particular segment of the Banister River Blueway runs from Kings Bridge Landing to Terrys Bridge. Access is excellent for beginner paddlers and those who want a relaxing float through nothing but nature. The adventure leaves the elaborately developed Kings Bridge access, with its large parking area, walkway to the river, and tiered concrete steps, then passes under the Bethel Road Bridge. Before embarking look just upstream at the old stone piling of Kings Bridge, for which the put-in is named. By the way, if the Banister is running slow, consider paddling upriver the short distance to the Banister Lake Dam outflow before making your downriver trek.

Once headed downstream you are in a wooded corridor, floating from Halifax. Steep, densely forested banks of soil mixed with some rock rise from the normally tannish water. Small auburn-colored gravel bars border swift shallows. All shoals are mere Class I, speeding over gravelly shallows that also provide easy stopping points, but most of the paddle is slower, deeper waters. Birdsong echoes under the tree canopy, which shades most of the 80-foot-wide river. On a hot summer day, you will be able to stay in the shade by paddling along one bank or another.

Stroke under the Norfolk Southern Railroad at 0.5 mile. At 0.9 mile Toots Creek comes in on your right, adding flow. At 1.3 miles the Banister River pushes over light shoals. At 2.1 miles you will pass the only riverside development, a private concrete boat ramp. Just beyond there the river curves right and goes over a series of light shoals. Look here for evidence of rock fish weirs and the hand-placed rock channelizing—wing dams—done by bateaux paddlers of two centuries back. It is amazing these are still in place to a degree. They will be most visible at lower flows. The shoals continue on and off for a little under a half mile.

Pass a rising rock hillside covered in mountain laurel and beech at 3.1 miles. At this point downstream you enter lands originally purchased by the Army Corp of Engineers as part of the greater Lake Kerr reservation, though it is miles before the waters of the Banister River (after flowing into the Dan River) are slowed in the impoundment. This keeps the banks undeveloped, although shores are in their natural state nearly the entire route. Birch, sycamore, and ironwood rise above you.

Reach Cowford Bridge at 3.2 miles. This ingress/egress, part of the Banister River Blueway, is on the northeast side of the small two-lane bridge. Make a long straightaway in gentle waters beyond Cowford Bridge. Trees fallen into the river are kept cut back by local paddlers. By 3.7 miles the river starts a long southeasterly direction. Tributaries cut steep gullies in the banks. Around 5.5 miles the river speeds again in shoals. Here, Myers Creek enters on river right. At 6 miles an unnamed but decent-size creek enters on the left. By this point the rumbles from US 360 drift upriver. Come to the pair of spans crossing the Banister at 6.2 miles. Your exit is on river right, at the second of the two parallel auto conduits. It is but a short carry to the parking area, but the area under the bridge may be a bit muddy and steep rising from the water.

25 Meherrin River

Follow this swift, sandy, and shallow State Scenic River from historic Whittles Mill past numerous tributaries to end at quiet Dix Bridge.

Counties: Mecklenburg; Lunenburg
Start: Whittles Mill at Max B. Crowder Memorial Park, N36 48.08' / W78 10.11'
End: Dix Bridge, N36 47.00' / W78 2.58'
Length: 9.3 miles
Float time: 4.5 hours
Difficulty rating: Easy-moderate
Rapids: Class I shoals
River/lake type: Small river
Current: Moderate
River gradient: 3.8 feet per mile
Water gauge: Meherrin River at VA 637 near South Hill, VA, minimum runnable level 120 cfs
Season: Mar-Nov

Land status: Private
Fees and permits: None
Nearest city/town: South Hill
Maps: Meherrin River Canoe Trail; USGS: North View, Forksville
Boats used: Kayaks, canoes
Organization: Virginia Department of Game and Inland Fisheries, 7870 Villa Park Dr., Ste. 400 (Villa Park 3), Henrico, VA 23228; (804) 367-1000; www.dgif.virginia.gov
Contact/outfitter: Town of South Hill, 211 S. Mecklenburg Ave., South Hill, VA 23970; (434) 447-3191; www.southhillva.org

Put-in/Takeout Information

To the takeout: From exit 15 on I-85 near South Hill, take US 1 north for 2.4 miles to angle left on VA 621 / Dix Bridge Road. Follow VA 621 for 1.7 miles, passing over I-85, then reaching Dix Bridge. Parking is on the left after crossing the Meherrin River.

To the put-in from the takeout: From Dix Bridge, backtrack on VA 621 and US 1, returning to exit 15 on I-85. Now, continue on US 1 south for 2.7 miles into South Hill, then turn right on VA 47 north / East Atlantic Street. Stay with VA 47 for 4 miles, then turn right on VA 654 / Whittles Mill Road. Stay with Whittles Mill Road for 1 mile, then curve left, joining VA 636 (Whittles Mill Road dead-ends ahead). Stay with VA 636 for 1.7 miles, then turn left into Max B. Crowder Memorial Park on your left just before crossing the Meherrin River. The launch is on the gravel sandbar below the park's milldam.

Paddle Summary

This paddle starts at historic Whittles Mill, where a still-standing dam backs up the water of the Meherrin River. Join the outflow and begin scooting down the scenic, shallow, sandy stream in a corridor of tall trees. Since the river is so sandy and scattered with fallen trees, the Meherrin keeps a steady speed, with neither significantly long pools nor extended rapids. Several notable tributaries come in as you pass under a pair of tall bridges that provide difficult or poor access. The float continues easterly, skimming past sandbars on bends to reach Dix Bridge, a much lower span with easier access. Little in the way of development will distract you from the Meherrin's scenery, deserving of its status as a State Scenic River.

River/Lake Overview

The Meherrin River begins on the east side of Charlotte County in the Piedmont. Here, the North Fork, Middle Fork, and South Fork merge to form the Meherrin. Additional smaller streams add their flow as it works easterly, forming the county line dividing Lunenburg County from Mecklenburg County. The river skirts around the north side of South Hill and is where this paddle takes place. The waterway keeps easterly, gaining in size before passing through the town of Emporia, where it drops off the fall line. The river morphs into a serpentine, twisting swamp river before entering North Carolina. From there it keeps a southeasterly course before giving its waters to the Chowan River in the Tarheel State. Fifty-four miles of the Meherrin

The historic dam on the Meherrin River

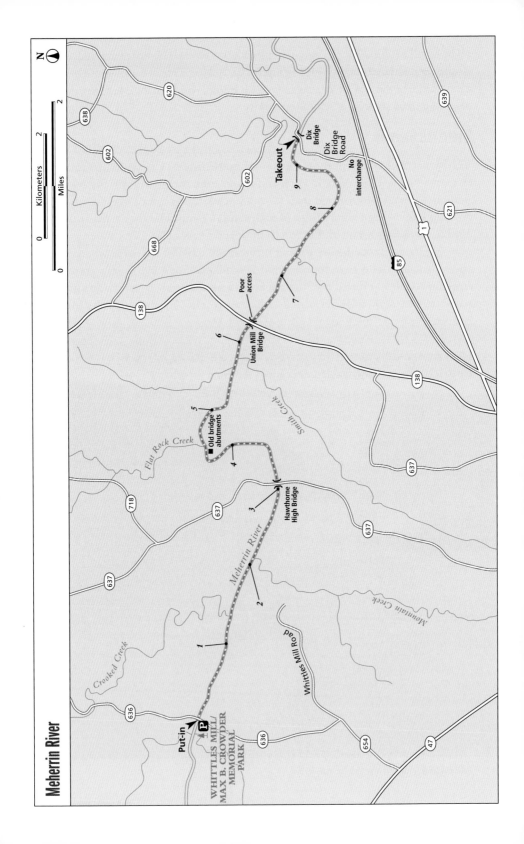

Meherrin River

River are a designated Virginia State Scenic River. This special segment stretches from the confluence with the North Meherrin River down to the Brunswick-Greensville County line, a little west of Emporia. Our paddle is within the State Scenic River portion of the Meherrin.

The Paddling

The gravel bars below Whittles Mill are popular fishing and water play areas. This is also the launch for this paddle. The dam was erected on the Meherrin River to provide hydropower to run a mill. Including the river itself and its tributaries, over 35 mills were once scattered in the Meherrin River valley. The first mill on this site, Whittles Mill, was erected in the mid-1700s by a fellow named John Brooks. The site then went through a succession of owners. In the early 1800s a Revolutionary War veteran named Thomas Bedford raised the height of the milldam and improved the structure. The Whittle clan got hold of the mill in the later 1800s and lent their name, which lasts to today. Even after the mill was bought by A. W. Hankey, throughout the community it was still known as Whittles Mill. Hankey raised the milldam yet again, increasing its power and capacity to turn grain to meal or to saw logs. Interestingly, Hankey eventually turned the waterpower into electricity and operated his mill using electrical power, a newfangled concept at the time.

In 1962 the dam at Whittles Mill failed, sending a rush of water and sand accumulated over time downstream. This adversely affected the water supply for the town of South Hill and other neighboring communities, fouling the pipes, as they were receiving water from the Meherrin River. However, the dam was repaired, ensuring a stable water supply for South Hill, plus a park locals can enjoy and a place we paddlers can use as a point of embarkation.

Whittles Mill lives on. The park around the mill is named for a local historian and Meherrin River enthusiast by the name of Max B. Crowder, who was instrumental in helping to establish the paddling trail on the Meherrin River. You will put in on the gravel bar below the dam. The float quickly leads you under the VA 636 bridge, a newer high span. The tan-colored waterway stretches around 60 feet wide and is bordered by high banks rising in thick forests. Fallen trees and sandy shallows are a regular feature of the river, narrowing the effective paddling area. However, even if you pick the wrong channel, there is no harm, as you will just slow into shallow gravel.

The Meherrin flows easy, sliding over sand. At 1.4 miles Crooked Creek enters on river left. Sandbars are common on bends and make for laidback stopping spots. Mountain Creek comes in on river right at 2.1 miles. The upper stretches of Mountain Creek drain the town of South Hill. High hills rise on the right downstream of Mountain Creek. At 2.6 miles the Meherrin River narrows as it is squeezed by a massive rock outcrop on river right. Come to the Hawthorne High Bridge / VA 637 at 3 miles. This is a difficult access simply because the distance from the river to the road is significant—therefore I do not recommend it as a put-in or takeout.

The banks of the Meherrin River grow thick with trees.

The Meherrin River curves north beyond Hawthorne High Bridge. Gravel bars are more frequent among these bends, as the Meherrin continues its shallow ways. At 4.5 miles pass the abutments of a forgotten bridge. Flat Rock Creek comes in at this point on your left. Wooded hills and rock outcrops adorn the scenery. Big Smith Creek enters on your right at 5.8 miles. Meet the VA 138 / Union Mill Bridge at 6.2 miles. This newer, high span has made river access at this point very difficult. Also, watch out for logs accumulating on the central bridge abutment here, potentially impeding the river. Watch for the remains of an old bridge and an old stone dam, all that remains of Union Mill, just below the VA 138 bridge. The dam remnants create a little shoal here.

Continue southeasterly downstream, above the sands and around fallen trees (in places fallen trees are half-embedded in the sand). At 8.2 miles the river bends left. Look for the noteworthy outcrop on river right. At 9.3 miles Dix Bridge appears before you. Although a newer span, it is not high. The takeout is on the left, up a steep but short bank directly at the span.

26 Nottoway River

Trace the attractive and remote Nottoway on this all-day paddle that takes you through fun rapids as it drops off the fall line.

Counties: Brunswick; Dinwiddie; Greensville; Sussex
Start: Cutbank Bridge Access, N36 54.08' / W77 40.40'
End: Double Bridge Access, N36 50.800' / W77 33.614'
Length: 11.5 miles
Float time: 6.5 hours
Difficulty rating: Moderate-difficult due to distance
Rapids: Class I-II rocky rapids
River/lake type: Small-medium river
Current: Moderate
River gradient: 5.1 feet per mile
Water gauge: Nottoway River at Route 609 near McKenney, VA, minimum runnable level 150 cfs

Season: Late Mar through mid-Nov
Land status: Private
Fees and permits: None
Nearest city/town: Jarratt
Maps: USGS: McKenney, Smokey Ordinary, Cherry Hill, Purdy
Boats used: Kayaks, canoes
Organization: Virginia Department of Game and Inland Fisheries, 7870 Villa Park Dr., Ste. 400 (Villa Park 3), Henrico, VA 23228; (804) 367-1000; www.dgif.virginia.gov
Contact/outfitter: Virginia Department of Conservation and Recreation, 600 E. Main St., Richmond, VA 23219; (804) 786-6124; www.dcr.virginia.gov

Put-in/Takeout Information

To the takeout: From exit 20 on I-95 near Jarrett, take VA 139 west and stay with it for 1.2 miles, then turn left onto Allen Road, staying with VA 139. After 1 mile turn right onto VA 608 / Wyatts Mill Road and follow it 4.1 miles to turn right onto VA 651 / Nottoway Road. Follow it for 1.1 miles to the VDGIF Double Bridge access on your right.

To the put-in from the takeout: Continue on VA 651 for 0.2 mile, then turn right onto VA 619. Follow VA 619 5.3 miles to turn left onto VA 617 and keep straight at 1.5 miles as it becomes VA 616 / Ridge Road. Reach a T intersection after 1.8 miles and turn left on VA 609 / Cherry Hill Road. Follow VA 609 for 4.2 miles, reaching the access just after bridging the Nottoway River. The access is on the southwest side of the bridge.

Paddle Summary

This paddle wanders down a secluded segment of the Nottoway River where it tumbles off the fall line. Although you do experience rapids on this float, most of them are simple Class I and Class I+ maneuverings around rocks, making for a fun

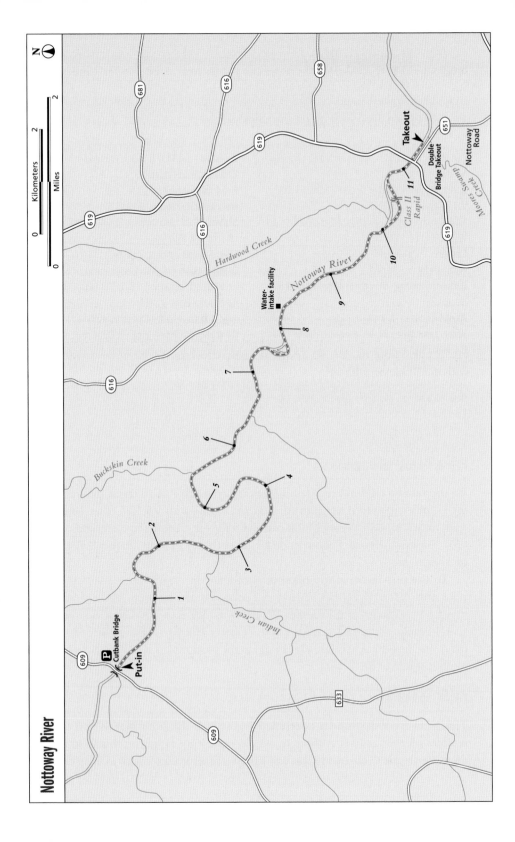

Nottoway River

venture. The adventure leaves Cutbank Bridge and begins down a steady current broken by speedy shallows. The first rapid comes in at a little under 2 miles in the adventure. There is very little development here, so the banks are mostly wild. The waterway continues winding and most of the rapids occur in the last few miles of the float, where the Nottoway divides around islands. Although the current is decent, allow plenty of time to make the full 11.5-mile float.

River/Lake Overview

The Nottoway is a Virginia-only watercourse. The uppermost reaches of the Nottoway River are found in the Piedmont southwest of Burkeville. Here, the Nottoway flows southeasterly, picking up numerous tributaries before being dammed at Fort Pickett, as Fort Pickett Reservoir. From there, the waterway continues its winding southeasterly course, passing the area of our float east of I-85 and west of I-95, where it drops off the fall line. The Nottoway turns north in Sussex County before curving back south, reincarnated as a swamp-bordered river of the coastal plain. Just before entering North Carolina, it meets the Blackwater River, where the two streams form the Chowan River. The Nottoway River is a designated Virginia State Scenic River for 72 miles, from the VA 40 bridge at Stony Creek to the Nottoway's confluence with the Blackwater River.

The Paddling

Interestingly, the river gauge for this paddle is at Cutbank Bridge, where we start. The Cutbank Bridge is small and the area remote, exuding an aura of getting out to the back of beyond. You are unlikely to see another kayaker or canoeist. Carry your craft down to the water's edge. Here, the Nottoway is about 70 feet wide and shallow, with a rock-and-sand bottom. Immediately pass a fish camp on your right. Development is infrequent on this stretch of waterway, though you do see a house or two and other fish camps. The banks are mostly natural, with sycamore, river birch, and musclewood. Small creeks cut deeper clefts while bigger tributaries come in wide. Since this area is near the fall line, rocks are common in and along the river and are concentrated in the rapids.

The river waxes up to 110 feet wide but is canopied on both sides. Occasional hills rise from the stream and are dotted with mountain laurel. At 1.3 miles the river bends to the left, passing a rocky shoreline and hill. An unnamed tributary comes in on your left at 1.5 miles. The Nottoway continues its bending ways, then reaches the first rapid at 1.9 miles. You will see gatherings of rocks at these rapids and it is up to you to pick the best channel getting through, which is usually a simple matter. In addition, if you are stopped among the rocks, just keep the boat pointed downstream and do not let your craft get sideways to the current. Sandy shallows and sandbars form at the base of these Class I rapids.

Indian Creek, a major tributary, comes in on the right at 2.8 miles. The Nottoway presents long shallow stretches, deep enough for self-propelled craft but not much else. The river is rarely deeper than your paddle. After making some major bends,

The Nottoway River features several rock rapids.

the Nottoway resumes its primary course—southeasterly—at 5.1 miles. Buckskin Creek, another significant tributary, comes in on your left at 5.4 miles. Rocky riffles occasionally liven up the paddling. Pass another Class I rapid at 6.4 miles, a short, river-wide rocky drop.

At 6.8 miles the Nottoway splits around an island among rocky light shoals, then comes a slower segment. At 7.5 miles, as the waterway is heading south, the river splits around a pair of islands. Stay right here, and work your way through a long set of shoals, ending at 8.1 miles. This is a fun stretch of river. Just ahead, at 8.3 miles, you make another short drop. Look for a water-intake facility hereabouts. Downriver, the Nottoway continues pushing among shallows and rocks. The rapids begin to pick up. Pass around a small island at 9.5 miles, then paddle under power lines at 10 miles.

Ahead, be on your toes as the Nottoway again divides among some relatively big islands. If you stay right, you will come to the biggest rapid of the paddle. It will be easy to spot since there is a conspicuous house on the hill above the rapids. You will see this house before reaching the shoal. If necessary, scout the rapid before doing it, although it is a straightforward drop. No matter which side of the islands or channels you take, the river is narrow and it becomes a little more challenging to figure out the best route. Hardwood Creek comes in on the left side of these islands, though you may not even see it unless you are in that left channel. These island areas of the Nottoway are quite scenic.

The Nottoway comes back together, then divides again before passing under the VA 619 bridge, known as Double Bridge, at 11.2 miles. Once beyond the bridge get over to the right bank and dance through a final onset of shoals, reaching the Virginia Department of Game and Inland Fisheries ramp at 11.5 miles, the end of this paddling adventure.

27 Jamestown Island Circumnavigation

Undertake a scenic and historic paddle by circling around Jamestown Island, site of the first successful English colony in Virginia, located along the lower, tidal James River.

County: James City
Start: James City County Marina, N37 13.599' / W76 46.744'
End: James City County Marina, N37 13.599' / W76 46.744'
Length: 9.4 miles
Float time: 4.5 hours
Difficulty rating: Difficult due to flatwater paddling distance
Rapids: None
River/lake type: Massive tidal river, plus smaller bodies of water
Current: Tidal
River gradient: None
Water gauge: None

Season: Mar–Oct
Land status: National park
Fees and permits: Marina launch fee
Nearest city/town: Williamsburg
Maps: Colonial National Historical Park, Historic Jamestowne; USGS: Surry, Hog Island
Boats used: Kayaks, canoes
Organization: Colonial National Historical Park, PO Box 210, Yorktown, VA 23690; (757) 856-1200; www.nps.gov/colo
Contact/outfitter: James City County Marina, 2054 Jamestown Rd., Williamsburg, VA 23185; (757) 565-3699; www.jamescitycountyva.gov. This marina is the paddle's launch point. They rent canoes and kayaks.

Put-in/Takeout Information

To put-in/takeout: From downtown Williamsburg, take Jamestown Road southwest for 4.2 miles, then keep straight, joining VA 31, still on Jamestown Road. Drive for 1.4 more miles, then turn left onto Colonial Parkway and follow it for 0.1 mile to turn left into James City County Marina. The canoe/kayak launch is near the main building of the marina.

Paddle Summary

This aquatic adventure combines colonial history with scenic paddling in several bodies of water. First, you start at James City County Marina then break out into Powhatan Creek, a gentle tidal waterway that meets Sandy Bay. Cut under Colonial Parkway and open onto the massive tidal James River. Begin circling around Jamestown Island, site of the first successful English colony in Virginia. Pass the actual location of the colony and observe the statue of John Smith, leader of the group. Continue around the island, passing small beaches and grassy shores as well as wooded banks. Reach Black Point beyond Passmore Creek, with distant views down the James. Turn into The Thorofare, a bay closing to the Back River. Trace the tidal waters of Back River to successfully circumnavigate Jamestown Island, returning to James City County Marina.

River/Lake Overview

Powhatan Creek is a tributary of the lower tidal James River draining south from Williamsburg. It opens onto the James River. The James River is Virginia's contribution to great rivers of the world and is Virginia's largest watercourse, flowing across the entire state from the mountains in the west to the Atlantic Ocean in the east. The James is born in the upper reaches of the Appalachians, fast against the West Virginia border in appropriately named Highland County, where the Cowpasture River and the Jackson River converge to form the James. Here, the James officially begins its 340-mile journey to Chesapeake Bay, making it one of the longest rivers in the United States that begins and ends in the same state, passing through the Piedmont and Tidewater. The James's watershed encompasses 25 percent of Virginia, around 10,000 square miles, draining the heart of the Old Dominion.

The Paddling

James City County Marina not only offers canoes and kayaks for rent, they also have an excellent launch for self-propelled craft as well as a covered picnic area and slips for boats. Leave the marina and soon join Powhatan Creek. Turn right on this tidal tributary of the James, heading downstream to float under Colonial Parkway at 0.2 mile. Powhatan Creek is bordered in cypress, pine, and hardwoods. It exhibits moderate tidal influence. Open onto shallow Sandy Bay at 0.7 mile. Begin your counterclockwise circumnavigation of Jamestown Island by aiming for the narrow channel opening onto the James River, paddling under Colonial Parkway at 1.1 miles. It is better to go this route because if the winds are not blowing at the beginning of your paddle, you might as well get out on the James River first, since it is over a mile wide in most places near Jamestown Island.

Notice the riprap bordering Jamestown Island. The rock bank protects the island from wave action, not only from wind and watercraft but also from the large ferryboats crossing from Jamestown to Scotland, Virginia, across the river. Keep these ferries on

EXPLORING JAMESTOWN ISLAND

Add to your paddle by visiting the island you just circled. Preserved as Colonial National Historical Park, this island was the site of the first successful English colony in Virginia, begun in 1607, and is an important part of the Old Dominion's history. Not only can you tour the visitor center, viewing the informative exhibits, you can also walk through the re-created colony on your own or with a guided park tour specializing in history or archaeology. Bicycle the roads on the island. There is a 3-mile loop road and a 5-mile loop road on the island. The nearby Colonial Parkway heads 23 miles one-way to Williamsburg. For more information, visit www.nps.gov/colo.

Jamestown Island Circumnavigation

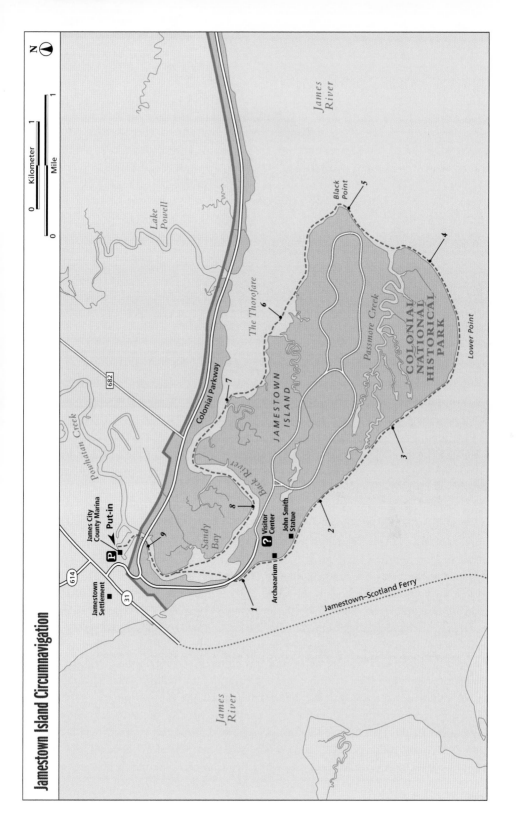

Taking a break at this sandy beach on Jamestown Island

your radar as they will kick up some big waves that dash against the island and will rock your boat. Forest rises above the riprap. Be apprised that this riprap makes landing on the island very difficult. I suggest executing your paddle then making the short drive to the colony site from the marina and touring the historic site on foot.

Despite being tidally influenced, the James River at this point is entirely freshwater. At 1.4 miles pass the archaearium located near the original colony site. Come to the statue of John Smith at 1.6 miles. It is easily visible from the water and is an outstanding marker. You can see other structures in the distance, enticing you to make a tour. Watch for pilings of old piers in the water. By 1.9 miles you have paddled past the primary interpretive area. Ahead, breaks in the riprap appear and you can access small beaches near channels of Passmore Creek. The beaches make ideal stopping spots. An experienced paddler with GPS-loaded maps could make his or her way through the heart of the island on Passmore Creek, but I recommend staying on the outside of the island for simplicity's sake. Passmore Creek breaks up into multiple channels. Do not enter without a map, or at least use the satellite map feature on your phone.

The beaches continue sporadically as you curve around the southwest side of Jamestown Island. Here, tan sands form a narrow strip rising to mixed woods and grasses. By now paddlers have passed several stationary waterfowl blinds. These are primitive structures on stilts camouflaged by brush to allow hunters a place to seek out waterfowl. Circle past Lower Point at 3.6 miles. This is the most southerly tip of Jamestown Island. The river at this point is miles across, and you can enjoy even more distant views to the east. Hope a southerly wind does not kick up. Begin the curve around the east side of the island, opening onto the mouth of Passmore Creek at 4.5 miles. Much of the shoreline is grassy at this point. Pine-covered Black Point stands out ahead of you. Reach this spot at 5.1 miles. Bank fishermen and river observers are often found here, having reached it via the end of the interior roads of the national park that is Jamestown Island.

Turn into The Thorofare, relatively smaller than the James River but still large. Channel markers keep motor boaters in the deeper waters. However, paddlers can cruise along the scenic winding shore of Jamestown Island in the shallows. The Thorofare gradually narrows until it is riverine by 6.8 miles. The road off to your right is Colonial Parkway. Enter the Back River, the channel curving past the north side of Jamestown Island. Its banks are both grass and woods.

Keep Jamestown Island to your left, and you can see the park visitor at 8 miles. Again, it is easier to stick with the paddle then drive to the park rather than visit in mid paddle. Ahead, turn into Sandy Bay, reaching the mouth of Powhatan Creek at 8.7 miles. From here it is a simple backtrack to James City County Marina, completing the paddling adventure at 9.4 miles.

This statue of John Smith can be seen from the water. Note the riprap bank.

28 Lake Drummond

Paddle a historical canal leading to one of Virginia's two natural lakes, located in the heart of the Great Dismal Swamp.

County: Chesapeake City
Start: Arbuckle Landing, N36 35.43' / W76 23.13'
End: Arbuckle Landing, N36 35.43' / W76 23.13'
Length: 7.2–10.6 miles
Float time: 4.0–6.0 hours
Difficulty rating: Moderate–difficult
Rapids: None
River/lake type: Canals, natural lake
Current: None
River gradient: None
Water gauge: Portsmouth Ditch near Deep Creek, VA, no minimum level
Season: Year-round

Land status: US Army Corps of Engineers; national wildlife refuge
Fees and permits: None
Nearest city/town: Chesapeake
Maps: Great Dismal Swamp; USGS: Lake Drummond
Boats used: Kayaks, canoes, motorboats with 25 or less horsepower
Organization: Great Dismal Swamp National Wildlife Refuge, 3100 Desert Rd., Suffolk, VA 23434; (757) 986-3705; www.fws.gov
Contact/outfitter: US Army Corps of Engineers, Norfolk Office, 803 Front St., Norfolk, VA 23510; (757) 201-7500; www.nao.usace.army.mil

Put-in/Takeout Information

To put-in/takeout: From exit 294 on I-64 just west of Chesapeake, take US 17 north / US 17 Business south, then turn right onto US 17 Business south and follow it for 1.1 miles. Take a quick left and right, still on US 17 Business south. Stay with the road for 4.1 miles, then turn right onto US 17 south. Stay with US 17 south for 6.7 miles to turn right on Ballahack Road. Follow Ballahack Road for 0.1 mile, then turn left onto Dismal Swamp Canal Trail and follow it for 0.6 mile to a dead end and gate. Here, wooden steps lead right under pines to the dock at Arbuckle Landing.

Paddle Summary

This paddle briefly joins the Dismal Swamp Canal, the oldest continuously operating man-made body of water in the United States, before turning onto Feeder Ditch. Trace this linear waterway to a dike and camping area. Here, a short self-operating tram helps you make a short crossing to the balance of Feeder Ditch that soon opens onto majestic Lake Drummond, the aquatic heart of the Great Dismal Swamp, a wild, untamed, cypress-ringed body of water that is a fine example of Virginia's wondrous watery variety. From here, a suggested 3-mile circuit around part of the lake will reveal this beauty.

River/Lake Overview

Natural Lake Drummond stands in the center of the Great Dismal Swamp, which at one time was much bigger than its size today. Lake Drummond at 3,142 acres is a sizable lake, yet is only 6 feet deep at its maximum. Tannin-stained blackwater gives it an additionally brooding aspect, befitting a swamp lake. The first ditches draining the Great Dismal Swamp were cut in the 1700s. Our access route uses two canals to reach Lake Drummond. Once visited only by aboriginals, colonials altered the swamp makeup with canals and roads. The swamp was later logged, but today Lake Drummond and surrounding wetlands are protected as the Great Dismal Swamp National Wildlife Refuge.

The Paddling

Lake Drummond is only one of two natural freshwater lakes in Virginia (The other is Mountain Lake in western Virginia's Giles County, near Pembroke). Lake Drummond lies deep in the Great Dismal Swamp, much of which is protected as the Great

Paddlers explore the waters of Lake Drummond. DANIELLE EMERSON

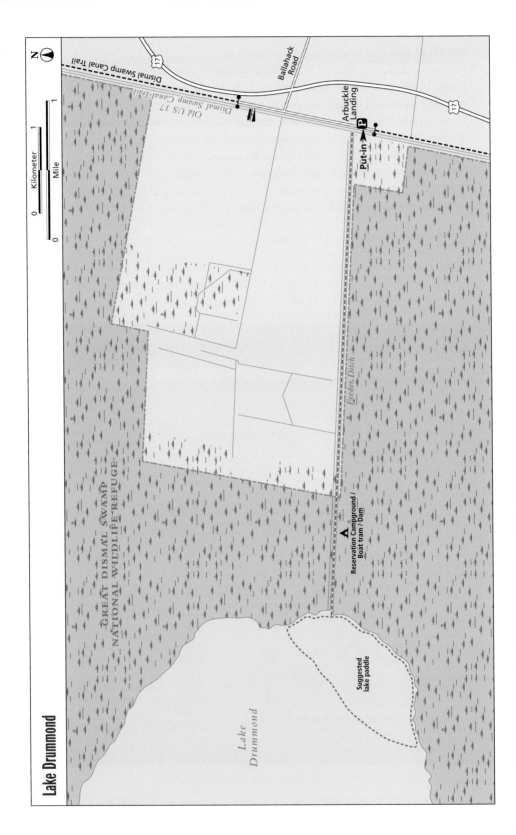

Lake Drummond

N

Kilometer

0   1

Mile

0   1

Dismal Swamp Canal Trail

17

Ballahack Road

Old US 17

Dismal Swamp Canal Trail

17

Arbuckle Landing

P

Put-in

GREAT DISMAL SWAMP
NATIONAL WILDLIFE REFUGE

Feeder Ditch

Reservation Campground /
Boat tram / Dam

Suggested
lake paddle

Lake
Drummond

Dismal Swamp National Wildlife Refuge. The preserve harbors not only Lake Drummond but also encompasses deep forests, wetlands, and plenty of bears. The wildlife refuge bleeds over into North Carolina. Lake Drummond, in fact, is but a few miles north of the border with the Tarheel State.

For early Virginians the Great Dismal Swamp was seen as potentially fertile ground—if it could be drained. Already, coastal farming land was becoming scarce and valuable. None other than George Washington himself got behind the effort to "drain the swamp." Canals and ditches were dug, but it seemed the swamp could not be drained. The massive wetland was too big and the efforts were too feeble. The plan was abandoned, for George Washington had bigger challenges, such as leading the United States to independence from England. Yet during our Revolutionary War, the Great Dismal Swamp came to Washington's attention. For America in defending herself was attentive to creating an alternate passage to the Atlantic Ocean from Chesapeake Bay to Albemarle Sound in North Carolina, whereby nations threatening America (read: England) couldn't successfully blockade Chesapeake Bay.

A north–south canal was dug, and passage through the Great Dismal Swamp was made. Other canals were dug to drain the land for timbering and farmland. At one time the swamp was thought to be near 1 million acres. Today's Great Dismal Swamp NWR harbors 112,000 acres. Interestingly, the swamp itself is higher than the land around it. Therefore, rainwater flows out of the swamp rather than into it.

ABOUT THE DISMAL SWAMP CANAL TRAIL

Starting near the put-in for this paddle is the trailhead for Dismal Swamp Canal Trail. Once a section of US 17, the highway-turned-pathway travels south for 8.3 miles to the North Carolina state line. The Dismal Swamp Canal Trail is popular with walkers and especially bicyclers, who tool up and down the paved route. Visitors to the trail often get their picture taken with Chessie, the big carved bear statue at the trailhead. An additional portion of the Dismal Swamp Canal Trail runs north for 3 miles to Deep Creek Park. The Great Dismal Swamp National Wildlife Refuge stands to the west of the trail, as does the actual Dismal Swamp Canal.

Paddlers ply the Dismal Swamp Canal, using accesses at Deep Creek Park, as well as the primary hiking trailhead, the boat ramp just north of Ballahack Road, and at Arbuckle Landing. Interestingly, the Dismal Swamp Canal is a route of the Intracoastal Waterway here in southeastern Virginia. Annually, canoers and kayakers undertake the "Paddle for the Border" whereupon paddlers head down the canal to reach the North Carolina state line. Speaking of North Carolina, that state offers a welcome center off current US 17 just south of the Virginia–North Carolina state line. The welcome center includes scads of interpretive information about the Great Dismal Swamp and is worth a visit.

Lake Drummond, our paddling destination, lies at once was the heart of the swamp. Our paddle begins at Arbuckle Landing to join the Dismal Swamp Canal—the oldest operating man-made waterway in the United States, and briefly travels that historic track before turning west along industrially named Feeder Ditch, a blackwater canal bordered with tall trees and plentiful wildlife, from birds to deer. The steep but short walled channel is narrow enough to offer shade much of the day.

After 3 miles you reach what is known as Lake Drummond Reservation. Here stands a narrow dam—a dike if you will—artificially raising the level of Lake Drummond. A side channel leads to a boat tram that crosses a slender spit of land. A small campground / picnic area with restrooms and screened shelters stands here. Camping here is a good idea for paddlers who want to fully explore Lake Drummond. To paddle to Lake Drummond and then completely circumnavigate the scenic lake (a 9-mile paddle around the tarn) and return to the put-in requires a 17-mile day! However, camping at Lake Drummond Reservation will make it easy to completely explore the lake. A suggested shorter lake exploration adds 3 miles to the 7.2 miles there and back on the canals, making a doable day paddle.

Lake Drummond is a half mile distant from the boat tram and campground. And there you will open onto this incredible cypress-lined body of water. The distant shore is but a low line. However, closer shores rise to your left and right. Scattered lone cypresses stand as picturesque sentinels in the open water. The suggested paddle heads left (south), working along the ragged line of trees meeting the water. It can be fun to wind among these trees. Cruise along the shore to a point, then angle across Lake Drummond back toward Feeder Ditch. If undertaking the lake paddle, be sure to save enough energy to paddle back. Consider the winds and other weather. Lake Drummond is wide-open and a fairway for winds if big blows are pushing across the water. Again, the best way to do a full exploration of Lake Drummond is to camp at the Lake Drummond Reservation. However, if you do camp overnight, you are required to leave your automobile at the parking area at the boat ramp just north of Ballahack Road (shown on the map) and not at Arbuckle Landing. This adds about 0.7 mile each way to your paddle.

29 West Neck Creek

This paddle in suburban Virginia Beach starts on West Neck Creek, then travels through West Neck Creek Natural Area, passing a massive old-growth cypress tree, to trace the ever-widening wildlife-rich stream to meet the North Landing River. Follow this wide State Scenic River to your endpoint, just a few miles from where you began.

County: Virginia Beach City
Start: Dozier Bridge Canoe/Kayak Access, N36 45.349' / W76 2.423'
End: North Landing River Canoe/Kayak Access, N36 43.060' / W76 5.949'
Length: 10.0 miles, can be shortened
Float time: 5.5 hours
Difficulty rating: Moderate to difficult
Rapids: None
River/lake type: Small tidal creek, larger tidal river, intracoastal waterway
Current: Tidal
River gradient: None
Water gauge: West Neck Creek at Dam Neck Road at Mapleton, VA, no minimum runnable level

Season: Year-round
Land status: Some public; mostly private
Fees and permits: None
Nearest city/town: Virginia Beach
Maps: USGS: Princess Anne, Pleasant Ridge
Boats used: Kayaks, canoes, motorboats on lower stretches of West Neck Creek and on North Landing River
Organization: City of Virginia Beach Parks & Recreation, 2408 Courthouse Dr., Virginia Beach, VA 23456; (757) 385-1100; www.vbgov.com
Contact/outfitter: Wild River Outfitters Inc., 3636 Virginia Beach Blvd. #108, Virginia Beach, VA 23452; www.wildriveroutfitters.com

Put-in/Takeout Information

To the takeout: From exit 286 on I-64 in Virginia Beach, take Indian River Road southeast for 7.6 miles, then turn right onto North Landing Road. Follow North Landing Road for 1.2 miles to reach the North Landing River and a left turn onto a canoe/kayak launch and fishing area just before crossing the swivel bridge over the Intracoastal Waterway.

To the put-in from the takeout: From the takeout, backtrack on North Landing Road and stay with it for 4.2 miles, then meet Princess Anne Road coming in from your left. Keep straight at this intersection as North Landing Road becomes Princess Anne Road and continue for 0.8 mile, then veer left to join the Dozier Bridge Canoe/Kayak access road and quickly dead-end at the canoe/kayak access.

Paddle Summary

This paddle covers a lot of territory while offering a variety of scenery and paddling possibilities. West Neck Creek is but a slender stream at first as it passes through

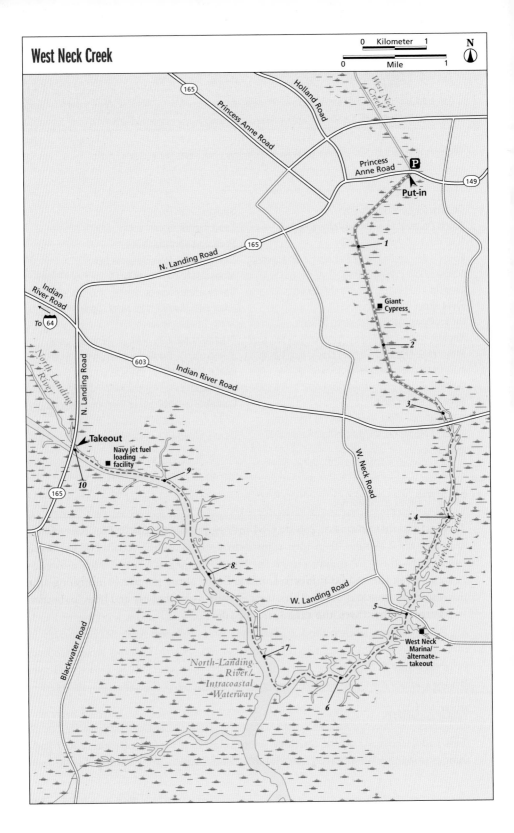

West Neck Creek

0 Kilometer 1
0 Mile 1

N

165

Holland Road

West Neck Creek

Princess Anne Road

Princess Anne Road

P

Put-in

149

165

N. Landing Road

1

Giant Cypress

2

Indian River Road

To 64

603

Indian River Road

North Landing River

W. Neck Road

3

Takeout

Navy jet fuel loading facility

9

10

165

8

West Neck Creek

4

W. Landing Road

5

West Neck Marina/ alternate takeout

7

6

North Landing River/ Intracoastal Waterway

Blackwater Road

Wild irises brighten the banks of West Neck Creek.

West Neck Creek Natural Area. Below the Indian River Road Bridge, West Neck Creek becomes more winding and bordered with scenic sloughs begging exploration. You will then paddle under the West Neck Road Bridge, passing a potential stopping point and marina after 5 miles. Ambitious paddlers will continue down the widening waterway to meet North Landing River, a sizable river that doubles as the Intracoastal Waterway. The paddle turns north, where you will be observing sailboats, motor yachts, and other users of the North Landing River / Intracoastal Waterway before ending the paddle at North Landing Road, also a popular bank-fishing area. Although the shuttle is only 6 miles, the two-lane roads are busy and bicycle shuttlers will be taking their lives into their hands pedaling.

River/Lake Overview

Upper West Neck Creek has been channelized and links northward to London Bridge Creek, which in turn connects to the Lynnhaven River, providing a route north to Chesapeake Bay. Southbound, West Neck Creek is channelized until Indian River Road. Below there, the waterway is all natural, bordered by swampy terrain with many arms jutting into swamps. North Landing River, a Virginia State Scenic River, is a large tidal waterway entering Virginia from North Carolina and Currituck

Sound. The river becomes narrower in the Old Dominion and continues winding through swamplands, becoming channelized near the end of this paddle. The watercourse continues north to meet the Eastern Branch Elizabeth River, also reaching Chesapeake Bay.

The Paddling

The Dozier Bridge launch has limited parking, so try to get there early on a nice Saturday. A short carry leads to a wooden dock and landing. Quickly float under brick Dozier Bridge on West Neck Creek. The stream ranges about 50 feet wide and is shaded by sweetgum, maple, and other hardwoods, as well as cypress and gum trees, both swamp dwellers. Although West Neck Creek is canalized here, the natural growth along the waterway makes it seem less so. Furthermore, you are paddling within the West Neck Creek Natural Area. Lesser old canals cut away from West Neck Creek. Look for low piles of spoil bordering the waterway. Potential stopping spots are frequent and evident. This upper part of West Neck Creek is only marginally tidal. Interestingly, the hiking trails of West Neck Creek Natural Area run to your right (westerly), originating off North Landing Road near the Virginia Beach Municipal Center. The natural area functions as a wildlife corridor within ever-expanding Virginia Beach. Expect to see abundant bird life as well as some land creatures such as deer.

Parts of West Neck Creek are arrow straight.

At 0.9 mile the stream bends from a southwesterly direction to a south-southeasterly direction. Most side canals morph into mini-swamps. Fallen trees narrow the effective paddling area, but you should be able to get through under normal conditions. Paddling advocates help keep this waterway open. This upper stretch is narrow enough to be partly shady in summer and protected from the wind in winter, making it a favorable year-round paddling destination. At 1.6 miles, on your left, look for a massive cypress tree rising amid the swamp woods. This old-growth giant has been here since before the United States was a country. It stands proud despite being struck by lightning at its top. The wide diameter remains well up the tree. Other tall cypresses populate the creek-side forest, but none of them compete with this one.

At 2.3 miles the creek again bends left. The swamps widen around the creek, making the stream the centerpiece of a seeping wetland. Pass around an island at 2.7 miles. Channels break off West Neck Creek. Pass under the Indian River Road Bridge at 3.1 miles. You may have to duck under the span if the water is high. There is no public access here, so plan on going at least to West Neck Road, although you could do a 6.2-mile out-and-back paddle to this point, returning to the Dozier Bridge access.

The banks of the river are natural from here on out and have widened in excess of 100 feet. The banks undulate with wide sloughs, but the main channel is clear. Cypress and gum are more prevalent along the shores, as the banks often morph into swamp. Expect to see osprey nests in lone standing trees. The waterway expands more.

Pass under the West Neck Road Bridge at 5 miles. You will not have to duck under this newer high span. Here a channel leads left to West Neck Marina and a potential stopping spot, making for a 5-mile one-way paddle. The river is over 200 feet wide now, with next to no development. Pick one side or another of the waterway to best enjoy the melding of land and water. Channel markers help keep motor boaters in the deeper waters. Paddlers have no such concerns. Grasses and brush have become common along the shores, continually punctuated with bays.

Open onto the North Landing River at 6.6 miles. This waterway stretches up to 300 feet across yet has a mostly natural shoreline. It is also part of the Intracoastal Waterway and is a designated Virginia State Scenic River. Additionally, over 3,400 acres along the waterway are a Virginia state nature preserve. Mostly natural banks cover the shores. Prepare to see motor yachts, sailboats, and other craft using the Intracoastal Waterway. Expect a few waves from these boats, but the creek is wide enough for you to easily handle them. Paddle by a few houses on river right at 7.6 miles. This area is known as West Landing. Continue paddling northwest. The waterway is upwards of 400 feet wide. Side channels finger into deep swamps. Paddle past a facility used for naval jet fuel loading on your right at 9.6 miles. You are almost at the takeout. Here, the swiveling North Landing Road Bridge stands just before the takeout, which is on river right. This locale is a popular bank-fishing spot and paddler ingress/egress. There is no boat ramp for larger craft. Complete the paddle at 10 miles.

30 Ashville Bridge Creek Circuit

Make a loop among creeks flowing through portions of Back Bay National Wildlife Refuge.

County: Virginia Beach City
Start: Horn Point Launch, N36 42.493' / W75 58.222'
End: Horn Point Launch, N36 42.493' / W75 58.222'
Length: 6.0 miles
Float time: 3.0–3.5 hours
Difficulty rating: Moderate
Rapids: None
River/lake type: Bay, canals, winding creek
Current: Lightly tidal
River gradient: None
Water gauge: None
Season: Mar–Nov

Land status: Mostly national wildlife refuge; some private
Fees and permits: None
Nearest city/town: Sandbridge
Maps: Back Bay National Wildlife Refuge; USGS: North Bay
Boats used: Kayaks, canoes, a few motorboats on parts of the loop
Organization: Back Bay National Wildlife Refuge, 1324 Sandbridge Rd., Virginia Beach, VA 23456; (757) 301-7329; www.fws.gov
Contact/outfitter: City of Virginia Beach Parks & Recreation, 2408 Courthouse Dr., Virginia Beach, VA 23456; (757) 385-1100; www.vbgov.com

Put-in/Takeout Information

To put-in/takeout: From exit 286 on I-64 in Virginia Beach, take Indian River Road east for 4.6 miles, then turn right to stay on Indian River Road. Continue for 9.3 miles to turn left onto North Muddy Creek Road. Follow North Muddy Creek Road for 1.4 miles to turn left onto Horn Point Road. Follow Horn Point Road for 0.8 mile to dead-end at the refuge parking area and canoe/kayak launch.

Paddle Summary

This loop paddle winds through a portion of Back Bay National Wildlife Refuge. Starting at view-filled Horn Point, the paddle heads north through open North Bay then into Hells Point Creek Canal, taking you north to paddle under Sandbridge Road. Leave the ever-narrowing waterway to join Ashville Bridge Creek, a gorgeous waterway. Cross back over Sandbridge Road at the renowned Lotus Garden, where Ashville Bridge Creek can be full of blooms. Crossing Sandbridge Road requires a short portage over the sometimes busy road. Finally, make your way down an avenue of cypresses as Ashville Bridge Creek returns to North Bay and Horn Point.

River/Lake Overview

Back Bay National Wildlife Refuge and the tributaries feeding it are located just west of the sand spit separating southeastern Virginia Beach City County from the Atlantic Ocean. North Bay is one of several bays that constitute the open-water portions of Back Bay National Wildlife Refuge. Hells Point Creek Canal is one of several man-made channels and natural waterways running through this marshy portion of greater Virginia Beach. Ashville Bridge Creek links north to Lake Tecumseh and also wanders south. Its most famous stretch is at the Lotus Garden, where a small park alongside Sandbridge Road allows visitors to view these fragrant flowers bloom in season. Below the Lotus Garden, Ashville Bridge Creek is a winding stream leading to North Bay.

The Paddling

Horn Point is located in the northwest portion of North Bay and thus paddlers do not have to face too much open water on this paddle, in case the winds are howling. Launch your craft from a simple, small beach landing, then set out on North Bay, aiming north-northeast for Hells Point Creek Canal. It is a long way east to the houses of Sandbridge overlooking the Atlantic Ocean. Avoid the nest of pilings cut to the water level near the put-in. Ahead, Ashville Bridge Creek comes in from your left and is your return route. By 0.5 mile you have left North Bay and have entered the Hells Point Creek Canal, running about 100 to 120 feet wide and lined with trees and brush. You are still inside the bounds of the wildlife refuge, although portions of this paddle do leave and enter the refuge. Nevertheless, the vast majority of the paddle is within refuge confines.

The canal crosses Hells Point Creek at 0.8 mile. Keep straight (north), still on the canal, flanked by both trees and grasses. Red-winged blackbirds twitter from the banks. Ahead, a small canal heads left, westerly. At 1.3 miles pass the Indian Cove Resort, an RV enclave perched on the edge of the refuge. Observe the big-rig campers lined up against the canal. Leave the resort at 1.7 miles. The low bridge of Sandbridge Road stands dead ahead. If the water is high, you will have to duck to get under the small span, passing under it at 1.8 miles. The waterway is now narrower and angles northwesterly flanked by wooded banks of wax myrtle, sweetgum, maple, and ever-present pine. Pass a small canal on your left at 2.1 miles. However, at 2.3 miles, come to Ashville Bridge Creek. The way you can be sure this is the correct route is the canal you have been on now curves right (northeasterly) and becomes Ashville Bridge Creek, then comes to a golf-cart bridge ahead. If you come to the golf-cart bridge, you have gone a little too far.

Turn left onto Ashville Bridge Creek. The correct route heads southwesterly, now on a canalized portion of Ashville Bridge Creek. The stream here is but 30 feet wide and overhung with trees, an intimate waterway. Fallen trees will be on the edges of

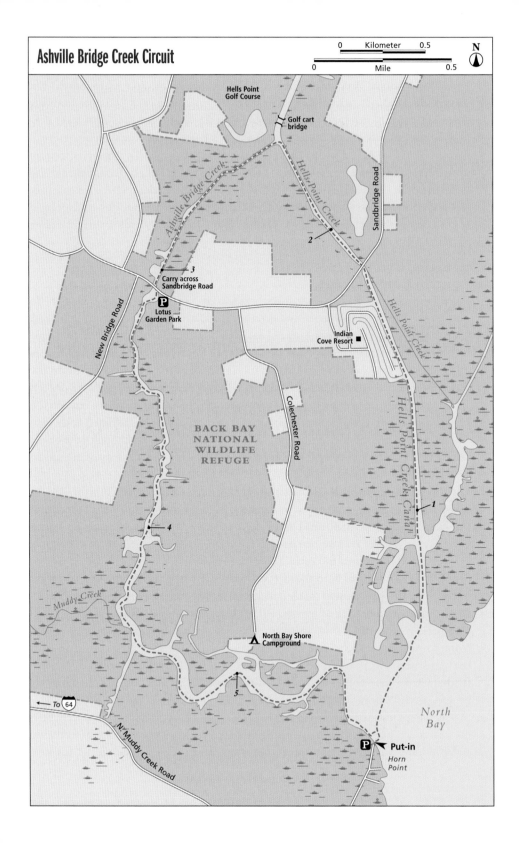

Ashville Bridge Creek Circuit

0   Kilometer   0.5

0   Mile   0.5

N

Hells Point
Golf Course

Golf cart
bridge

Hells Point Creek

Ashville Bridge Creek

Sandbridge Road

2

3
Carry across
Sandbridge Road

P
Lotus
Garden Park

New Bridge Road

Hells Point Creek

Indian
Cove Resort

Colechester Road

BACK BAY
NATIONAL
WILDLIFE
REFUGE

Hells Point Creek Canal

1

4

Muddy Creek

North Bay Shore
Campground

To 64

5

North
Bay

N. Muddy Creek Road

P   Put-in

Horn
Point

the waterway, but the stream should be cut clear of brush and easy to get through. Cypress trees find their place. What a difference from the open water you were paddling through earlier! The creek widens a bit as it wanders southwesterly.

Come to Sandbridge Road at 3.1 miles. Unfortunately, you have to carry your boat across the road with you. Small user-created landings are to the left and to the right. Neither is ideal, though the landing to the right avails a shorter carry, but you are also closer to the road while unloading and loading your boat. Exercise caution

CAMP AT FALSE CAPE STATE PARK

A trip to nearby False Cape State Park, located just across Back Bay from this paddle, can be a rewarding experience. Here, you can hike trails, paddle Back Bay, and camp in maritime woods with either the Atlantic Ocean or Back Bay within a short distance. In fact, the four campsite areas are accessed by paddlers as well as backpackers. However, whether you are backpacking or paddling to the campsites, preparation and planning are necessary.

The first order of business is to reserve your campsites for the dates you specify through reserveamerica.com. Then you arrange your overnight parking at Little Island City Park through either False Cape State Park or the city of Virginia Beach parks department, depending on the season. During holidays or the off-season, a False Cape State Park ranger may meet you at Little Island City Park to assist with your permit. If hiking, you will need to pay a fee to pass through Back Bay National Wildlife Refuge, which can be done in person. Parking is never available at Back Bay National Wildlife Refuge for overnight guests.

Sound like a hassle? It is, but you will find camping at False Cape State Park worth the effort. From Little Island City Park, you must first decide whether to paddle to the camps, to walk the beach to False Cape, or take the doubletrack trails through Back Bay refuge (Little Island City Park has a canoe/kayak launch). If hiking, I recommend taking the trails if possible on the way out and returning by the beach if you desire (From November 1 through March 31, the trails through Back Bay National Wildlife Refuge are closed, necessitating backpackers to access False Cape State Park by walking the beach only. The refuge trails are open the rest of the year. False Cape State Park trails are open year-round).

The campsites have a tent pad, picnic table, and lantern post. There's no fire ring—campfires are not allowed at False Cape State Park. Outhouses and drinking water are nearby. If you are going through the motions of camping here, make it at least two nights in order to allow exploration time and to soak in this special part of Virginia. Consider staying at a couple of different campsites. Relax on the beach or find a favorite overlook of Back Bay. It may be an experience you will always remember.

Looking down Ashville Bridge Creek as trees form a green canopy

here. You are now at Lotus Garden Park. A small parking area on the south side of the road is used as both a paddler put-in as well as an observation post to see the aquatic flowers.

Ashville Bridge Creek is pond-like in this area, and its course is all natural from here out. Grasses and pine border the serpentine, tidal waterway. Cypresses stand as sentinels guarding the route. At 4.5 miles unpleasantly named Muddy Creek comes in on your right. At 4.6 miles another canal leads south to a landing on Muddy Creek Road. Ashville Bridge Creek continues to widen and curves easterly. By 5 miles paddle past a small portion of the North Bay Shore Campground on your left. At 5.6 miles open onto North Bay. Here, you can stick with the shoreline, avoiding open water if the winds are blowing. Paddle alongside a grassy shore, then come to the cut pilings near Horn Point. Reach the landing after skirting around the pilings, completing the circuit paddle at 6 miles.

West Virginia Paddles

Paddlers enjoy river and mountain scenery on the Cheat River.

Southern West Virginia Paddles

31 Coal River Water Trail

Paddle the Coal River, from below Upper Falls at Meadowood Park to just above Lower Falls. This section is wide, relaxing, and has year-round paddling possibilities.

County: Kanawha
Start: Meadowood Park Canoe/Kayak Access, N38 20.622' / W81 50.455'
End: Lower Falls Canoe/Kayak Access, N38 22.781' / W81 51.415'
Length: 6.2 miles
Float time: 3.0 hours
Difficulty rating: Easy
Rapids: Class I
River/lake type: Medium river
Current: Slow–moderate
River gradient: 3.0 feet per mile
Water gauge: Big Coal River at Ashford, minimum runnable level 1.9 feet, maximum 5.0 feet

Season: Year-round
Land status: Private, but does start at county park
Fees and permits: None
Nearest city/town: Tornado
Maps: Coal River Water Trail; USGS: Alum Creek, Saint Albans
Boats used: Kayaks, canoes, a few johnboats
Organization: Coal River Water Trail; (304) 722-3055; www.coalriverwatertrail.org
Contact/outfitter: Meadowood Park– Kanawha County Parks & Recreation, 375 Henry C. Hoppy Shores Dr., Charleston, WV 25302; (304) 341-8000; www.kcprc.com

Put-in/Takeout Information

To the takeout: From exit 44 on I-64 west of Charleston, take WV 817 south and stay with it for 4.5 miles to turn right onto Coal River Road. Follow Coal River Road for 1 mile, then turn left onto Strawberry Road. Follow it for 0.2 mile to the Lower Falls public access on your right.

To the put-in from the takeout: From the Lower Falls access, drive 0.2 mile back on Strawberry Road, then turn left on Coal River Road and follow it for 4.4 miles to Tornado. Then turn left on Smith Creek Road. Immediately bridge the Coal River, then turn left into Meadowood Park just after crossing the bridge. Upon entering the park you will see a canoe/kayak access to your left. Do not use that access unless you want to tackle Upper Falls. Instead, continue into the park, passing the Coal River Group Center and boat rental. Continue just a short distance more, then look left for a parking area and Picnic Shelter #1. This is the put-in. Here, follow a trail along the line of trees before dropping to the river below Upper Falls.

Paddle Summary

This paddling trip is sandwiched between two major rapids on the Coal River, Upper Falls and Lower Falls, both once locations of locks that helped coal barges go up and down the river. Today, they are free-flowing and you can run them if you please. However, most paddlers start below Class II+ Upper Falls, paddle up to it for a view, then turn downriver, enjoying a winding lazy float in sun or shade, depending on the weather. Wooded shores and houses populate the banks. Toward the end you will come upon a long line of man-made islands, once part of the navigation system used on the river. Take out just above Class II Little Falls. Note the river bends significantly during the paddle, making the river shuttle shorter than the actual river trip.

River/Lake Overview

The north-flowing Coal River is a major tributary of the Kanawha River, draining much of southern Virginia south and east of Charleston with an 840-square-mile watershed. Its two primary feeders are the Little Coal River and the Big Coal River, meeting at Forks of Coal, a little south of the community of Alum Creek. From here, the Coal River flows approximately 25 paddleable miles to meet its mother stream, the Kanawha. Of the three major paddling rivers that comprise the collective Coal River Water Trail—Little Coal, Big Coal, and Coal—the Coal River has the longest paddling season, while the other two can run too low from late summer to fall.

The Paddling

Back two decades ago, residents of the greater Charleston area recognized that they had a jewel in the rough in the greater Coal River watershed. At that time the New River and Greenbrier River were the go-to waterways for Charleston-area paddlers. Sure, the Coal River watershed had been neglected over the years, but the natural beauty of the Little Coal, Big Coal, and Coal Rivers was undeniable. Plans were enacted, the Coal River Group formed in 2004, and hard work began. Seemingly endless meetings, river restoration, trash removal, and establishments of paddling accesses have resulted in a clean watershed with three major water trails. This was accomplished by hundreds of volunteers removing tires, the building of the Coal River Group Center at Meadowood Park, where this paddle begins, and river restoration, working with the West Virginia Department of Environmental Protection and West Virginia Department of Natural Resources. We can now paddle over 88 miles of designated water trail using seventeen accesses. This allows us to make multiple adventures among the three waterways.

While executing this particular paddle, make sure you visit the Coal River Group Center. It is full of interpretive information inside and out, with science and educational treats related to the Coal River, and is the heartbeat of the Coal River Water Trail system. The view from the back porch looking over Upper Falls is pretty good, too! You can also rent canoes and kayaks here and even reserve a shuttle for this very

The Coal River flows clear while flanked by green trees.

paddle. Then you can literally buy the T-shirt after your adventure. Also, walk the trails of Meadowood Park if you please. At least go check out Upper Falls up close and remnants of the 1855-era lock that boats used to bypass Upper Falls.

Now, time to paddle the Coal River. You will find the boat carry from the parking area to the river a little on the long side. Consider consolidating your gear to make fewer runs. At least it is downhill from the parking area at park shelter #1. First, walk along the woods line, then drop left downhill through forest to reach a rocky landing looking upstream at Upper Falls. Make sure to paddle up to the falls for a closer look. Under normal conditions a big sandbar collects at the fall's base, making a fun spot to walk around as the roar of the river wafts into your ears.

After getting your fill of Upper Falls, turn downstream and begin your relaxing float trip down the Coal River. At this point the waterway stretches over 140 feet across, flowing steadily over a sand bottom. The clear-green waters allow looks at aquatic life below, from turtles to fish. Trees grow thick along the banks. At 0.3 mile the Coal River bends right, and a gravel bar forms on river right, allowing for a stop if you need to get organized. Just ahead, sizable Smith Creek enters on river right. The waterway then makes the first of several major bends. Sandbars will be found inside these bends. A big bluff rises on river right. The pools here are the deepest in the entire Coal River Water Trail system. Big boulders find their way to the river's

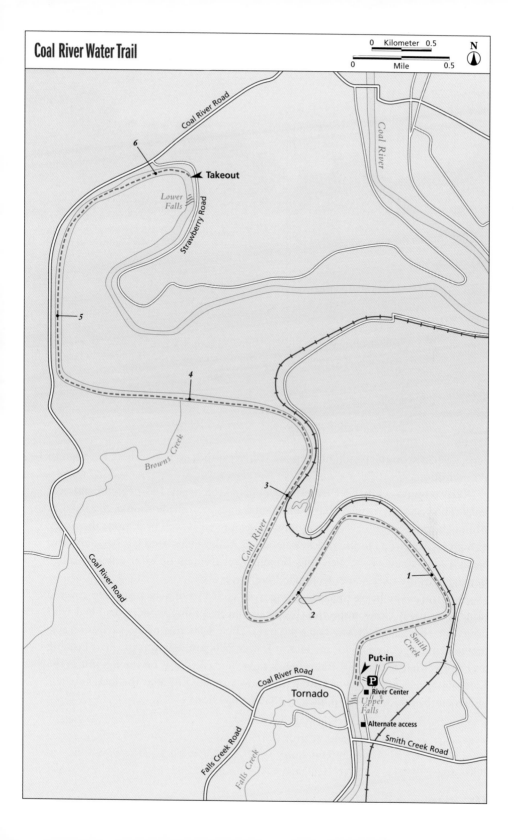

Coal River Water Trail

0 Kilometer 0.5

0 Mile 0.5

N

Coal River Road

Coal River

6

Takeout

Lower Falls

Strawberry Road

5

4

Browns Creek

Coal River

Coal River Road

3

1

2

Smith Creek

Put-in

P

River Center

Coal River Road

Tornado

Upper Falls

Alternate access

Falls Creek Road

Falls Creek

Smith Creek Road

Looking upstream at Upper Falls

edge, especially on the bends, making me wonder if they were put there long ago to aid navigation.

Keep cruising with the Coal as you undertake a major 180-degree bend at 2 miles. The waterway is wide, but overhanging trees avail shade should you need it. Although some banks have houses, most development is well back from the water, or high up banks, due to intermittent flooding. At 3.3 miles bend left (westerly) and begin a long straightaway. Very big Browns Creek enters on river left at 4 miles. Beyond here, the river comes alongside Coal River Road.

At 5.5 miles you begin to paddle along an extended set of man-made tree-covered islands that upon closer inspection have been erected using wood cribs filled with stone. They have since grown over with trees. These were part of the navigation system to help barges line up for the lock at Lower Falls, just downstream. Start heading over to river left as the Coal River bends right. The takeout is on the left just as the waterway speeds over rocks at Lower Falls, now running free after the lock here was blown out by floods two years after its 1859 completion.

32 Little Coal River Water Trail

This historic river makes for a fun paddle on clear waters with easy, straightforward rapids.

County: Boone
Start: Madison boat ramp, N38 3.563' / W81 49.486'
End: Donald Kuhn Juvenile Center Canoe/ Kayak Access, N38 8.183' / W81 50.182'
Length: 8.2 miles
Float time: 4.0 hours
Difficulty rating: Moderate
Rapids: Class I shoals
River/lake type: Small river
Current: Moderate
River gradient: 3.2 feet per mile
Water gauge: Little Coal River at Danville (National Weather Service gauge), minimum runnable level 1.0 foot

Season: Mar-Sept
Land status: Private
Fees and permits: None
Nearest city/town: Madison
Maps: Coal River Water Trail; USGS: Madison, Julian
Boats used: Kayaks, canoes
Organization: Coal River Water Trail; www.coal riverwatertrail.org; (304) 722-3055
Contact/outfitter: Meadowood Park– Kanawha County Parks & Recreation, 375 Henry C. Hoppy Shores Dr., Charleston, WV 25302; (304) 341-8000; www.kcprc.com

Put-in/Takeout Information

To the takeout: From exit 89 on I-64 / I-77 east of Charleston, take WV 94 / WV 61, then join WV 94 south for 9.8 miles to Racine and a stop light. Turn right on WV 3 west and follow it for 14 miles to turn right onto US 119 north, and follow US 119 north for 5.1 miles then turn left into the Daniel R. Kuhn Juvenile Center. Immediately look left for a signed gravel road leading down to the Little Coal River. The lower part of this gravel access road is very steep so check it before you drive down to the bottom. Before heading to the put-in, walk down to the river and view the access so you can remember it.

To the put-in from the takeout: From the Daniel R. Kuhn Juvenile Center access, leave right (southbound) on US 119 and follow it for 4.8 miles to a traffic light and turn left onto Riverside Drive. Stay with Riverside Drive for 2.4 miles, then turn left onto Spruce Fork Road, immediately bridging the Little Coal River, then take a quick left into Madison City Park. The boat ramp is on the left down by the river.

Paddle Summary

This paddle begins in the uppermost reaches of the historic and scenic Little Coal River. From the Madison boat ramp, you will join a swift, clear stream winding north and shadowed by steep hills. The speedy waterway passes through the towns of

Cruising a clear, rocky-strewn section of the Little Coal River

Madison and Danville, continuing its northbound ways. Fun shoals and larger pools keep the action going. At some point you will notice the river improvements, when large stone blocks were placed in and alongside the river to keep it moving, ridding the waterway of silt gathered in its industrial past. Today, these stone improvements keep you moving along. Sandbars are frequent along the way, allowing for stops, and you soon find yourself at the takeout, with another West Virginia water trail under your belt.

River/Lake Overview

The Little Coal River is a significant tributary of the Coal River. The Little Coal River begins where this paddle starts, at the town of Madison where Pond Fork and Spruce Fork merge. Upstream, these two tributaries drain extremely folded hill country, rising to over 3,000 feet west of Beckley. From Madison the Little Coal River begins its winding northbound journey to meet the Big Coal River, forming the Coal River. The Coal River merges into the Kanawha below Charleston. Finally, the Kanawha empties into its mother stream, the Ohio River. The Little Coal River is paddleable for over 30 miles from the put-in for this paddle at Madison to its confluence with the Big Coal River. *Note:* The Little Coal River is usually the first of the Coal River waterways to become too shallow to paddle.

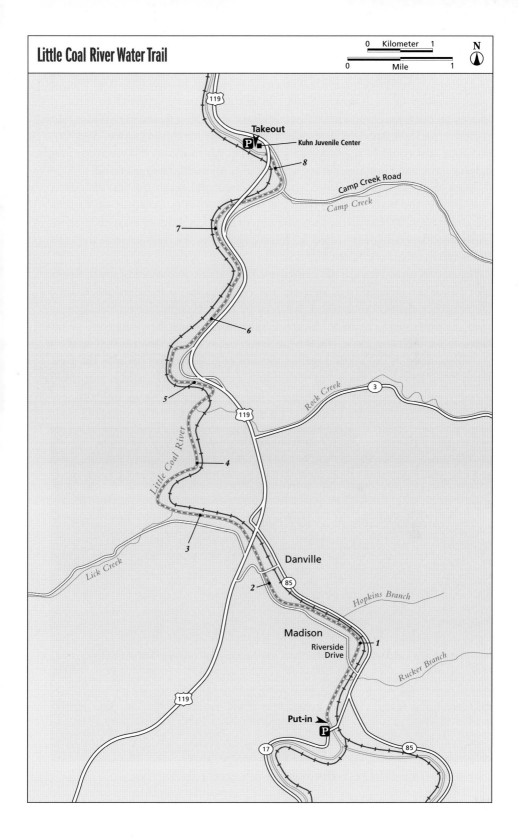

Little Coal River Water Trail

0   Kilometer   1

0   Mile   1

N

119

Takeout
P   Kuhn Juvenile Center

8

Camp Creek Road

Camp Creek

7

6

5

Rock Creek

3

Little Coal River

119

4

3

Lick Creek

Danville

2   85

Hopkins Branch

Madison
Riverside
Drive   1

Rucker Branch

119

Put-in
P

17   85

The greater Coal River basin has historically been rich in resources. And being a major tributary of the Kanawha River that in turn connects to the Ohio River, it allowed an early America to use water transportation to ship resources to where they were desired. It all started with the discovery of something called cannel coal. This particular coal could be used to produce coal oil, which in the 1800s was used for lighting homes and businesses. It replaced more costly and limited whale oil.

Back then extracting coal was a rough business, and moving it was difficult as well. To ship the black mineral, the Coal River Navigation Company of Virginia spent over $200,000 enhancing the waterways of the Coal River to make them more efficiently float coal down toward St. Albans, located at the confluence of the Coal River and the Kanawha River.

Later, eyes turned toward the tree-covered hills where massive old-growth forests lay ripe for the picking. Trees were cut and driven down to the river, where large log rafts were floated downstream, managed by men who did not mind hazardous work. Sawmills sprang up by St. Albans. Finished lumber was then shipped to points beyond.

The coming of the railroad spelled the end of river transportation in the Coal River basin. The river returned to what it had been since it was settled as part of old Virginia, a place where people gathered, fished, swam, floated canoes, and witnessed church baptisms on Sunday. Therefore, it is only natural that we have come full circle

Stonework channels placed by the West Virginia DNR speed up the waterway.

and once again see the river as a gathering place, a haven of recreation and enjoyment, a destination where we can float the clear waters, relax in the deep pools, enjoying the nature of wild, wonderful West Virginia.

Our paddle begins in the heart of Madison, where the shallow, fast-moving Little Coal River takes you through a corridor of greenery, although the sounds of town drift into your ears. River birch, sycamore, and alder line the 100-foot-wide waterway, rolling over rocks. Hills rise in the yon. This is what modern-day outdoor enthusiasts strive for, places where we can enjoy nature's bounty in the backyard of our homes.

Bigger boulders are scattered along the waterway while small grassy islands lie along shoals. Look for rough fish darting in the waters. On your right, at 0.6 mile, just before going under a bridge, look for the cupola of the Boone County Courthouse in Madison. The waterway is swift, shallow, and wide under a tree canopy. Paddle under another road bridge at 0.9 mile. Hopkins Branch comes in on your right via culvert at 1.1 miles. Float under another bridge at 2.1 miles. You are now in Danville, though it is hard to tell from the river, as houses are scattered here and there. The river narrows and goes down several shoals. At 2.2 miles Turtle Creek enters on the left. Just ahead on your right, pass a boat ramp access in Danville off Phipps Avenue. Next comes your crossing under the massive twin spans of US 119.

Float by the signed Danville alternate access on your left at the Danville Community Center at 2.6 miles. Start looking for the embedded stone blocks in the water that keep it moving and also along the banks, there to keep silt from overabundantly gathering.

The river now flows into a more remote section, having left the towns of Danville and Madison. The sheer amount of river restoration stonework is amazing, especially around 3.8 miles, where a series of stonework channels form a fun fast section. Rock Creek, which includes some little shoals, enters on river right at 4.6 miles. Pass under a railroad bridge just ahead.

The Little Coal River then bends left. Here you enter a veritable big-boulder field, around which the river divides and flows. There is no hazard here, however. It is a simply scenic section different from the rest of this particular paddle.

Float under a low road bridge at 6.1 miles. Easily missed Dry Branch enters on your right a little downstream of a low road bridge. At 6.9 miles watch for a long-broken-down concrete ford that poses little danger but does speed up the river. Steep hills rise. Camp Creek comes in on river right at 7.8 miles. At 8.2 miles, as you bend left, the Donald Kuhn Juvenile Center access is on river right. It is a small sand/rock bar leading up to the steep gravel road. It is less risky to carry your boat up the steep road than to drive down to your boat. Exercise common sense here, especially if it has rained recently.

33 Big Coal River Water Trail

Take a fun ride on this clear waterway running between steep hills, where straightforward shoals alternate with slower pools.

County: Boone
Start: JM Protan Community Center Canoe/Kayak Access at Orgas, N38 3.884' / W81 34.553'
End: John Slack Park Canoe/Kayak Access, N38 8.224' / W81 38.799'
Length: 11.1 miles
Float time: 4.5 hours
Difficulty rating: Moderate
Rapids: Class I shoals
River/lake type: Small river
Current: Moderate
River gradient: 4.0 feet per mile
Water gauge: Big Coal River at Ashford, minimum runnable level 1.9 feet, maximum 5.0 feet

Season: Apr–Sept
Land status: Private
Fees and permits: None
Nearest city/town: Racine
Maps: Coal River Water Trail; USGS: Sylvester, Belle, Racine
Boats used: Kayaks, canoes
Organization: Coal River Water Trail; www.coalriverwatertrail.org; (304) 722-3055
Contact/outfitter: Meadowood Park–Kanawha County Parks & Recreation, 375 Henry C. Hoppy Shores Dr., Charleston, WV 25302; (304) 341-8000; www.kcprc.com

Put-in/Takeout Information

To the takeout: From exit 89 on I-64 / I-77 east of Charleston, take WV 94 south for 9.8 miles to Racine and a stop light. Then turn left on WV 3 and follow it for 0.8 mile to turn right into John Slack Park. Follow the loop road a short distance to the boat ramp on your left.

   To the put-in from the takeout: From John Slack Park, resume east on WV 3 and follow it for 10 miles to the JM Protan Community Center at Orgas. Follow the road leading behind the community center to reach a boat ramp on your left.

Paddle Summary

This can be a fun float with the water running. Despite the name, the Big Coal River is fairly small in this upper segment and offers a delightful but not scary endeavor should you want to float some fun shoals without getting in over your head. Starting behind the Protan Orgas Community Center, the Big Coal River quickly moves you along bordered in deep hills lined with deep woods. The clear waters flow fast over a rock bottom. Time and again the river narrows along gravel bars or sycamore-covered islands to charge down shoals, then widen and slow, but not too much, before reaching another riffle. The river winds through a valley also shared with a companion road

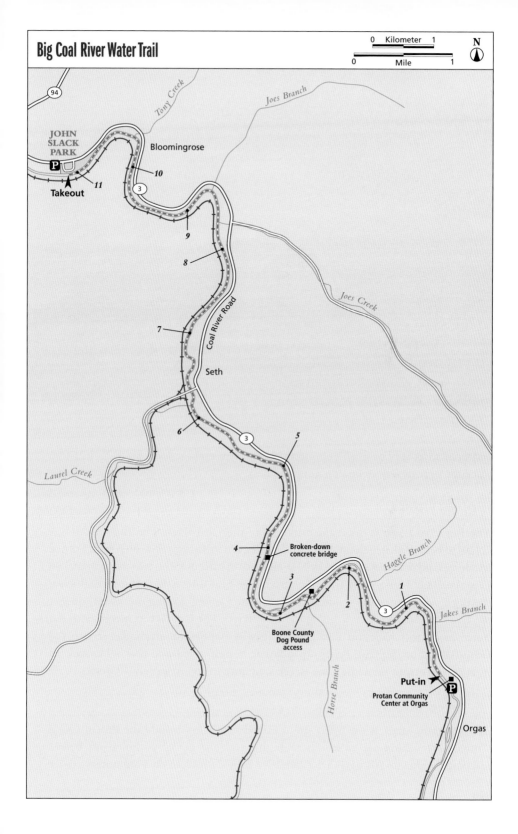

Big Coal River Water Trail

0 Kilometer 1

0 Mile 1

N

94

Tony Creek

Joes Branch

JOHN
SLACK
PARK

Bloomingrose

P

Takeout — 11

10

3

9

8

Joes Creek

7

Coal River Road

Seth

6

3

5

Laurel Creek

4 — **Broken-down
concrete bridge**

Haggle Branch

3

2

1

3

Jakes Branch

**Boone County
Dog Pound
access**

Horse Branch

Put-in

P

**Protan Community
Center at Orgas**

Orgas

This section of the Big Coal River narrows in fast, fun channels.

and railroad as well as small communities. The trip ends at John Slack Park, a fine place for a picnic before or after your paddle.

River/Lake Overview

The Big Coal River is the major tributary of the Coal River. The Big Coal River comes to be in Raleigh County, west of Beckley, where streams flow west from Spruce Mountain and other adjacent peaks. This network of streams forms two major branches, Clear Fork and Marsh Fork, which in turn merge near Whitesville. At this confluence the Big Coal River comes to life, entering Boone County, flowing northwest to meet the Little Coal River, then forming the Coal River. The Coal River merges into the Kanawha below Charleston. Finally, the Kanawha empties into its mother stream, the Ohio River. The Big Coal River is paddleable from its formation near Whitesville to its confluence with the Little Coal River, a distance of approximately 40 miles.

The Paddling

The adventure starts at the often sand-covered boat ramp behind the Protan Orgas Community Center. Be careful as there are a couple of big potholes just before reaching the put-in. Also, go ahead and drive your car back to the community center

Summertime finds the banks of the Big Coal River heavy with lush vegetation.

parking area directly beside the road—it will be safer there than leaving it screened behind the trees beside the Big Coal River. The waterway stretches about 70 feet across here. The rocky, pebble river bottom is easily visible in the translucent water, assuming normal flow rates. Sycamore and ash trees rise tall along the shallow waterway. Immediately pass under a bridge. After 0.1 mile you come to the first rapid typical of the Big Coal River. Here, the waterway narrows as it passes by a gravel bar partially vegetated with sycamores, then slows in a pool. If you can make it down this one fairly easy rapid, then you can make it the whole way down the Big Coal River. Generally speaking, the rapids have an even gradient and few irregular rocks, making them an easy mark for all but the most incompetent paddler.

However, you are not just going to be pushed down the river the entire way. It is an 11-mile paddle, and there are some slow sections, especially toward the end of the paddle when you may be a bit fatigued.

Remember that sections of the waterway go directly beside WV 3. Here, motorists driving by can look down on you, jealously wishing they were on the Big Coal River Water Trail. They will also be watching you run the shoals, so do a good job for your audience.

At 0.6 mile Jakes Branch comes in on your right, forming a gravel bar. Almost anywhere along this river, either shoals form or the water speeds where a side creek comes in. Densely wooded hillsides rise high in the distance while pawpaw grows in thick ranks on riverside flats. Occasional remnants of swinging footbridges still stretch across the river in places, adding a rustic touch. Haggle Branch enters on your right at 1.8 miles. Take note that civilization is always nearby—despite the junglelike growth of vegetation along the river you will see houses and hear cars, and the rail is nearby. The river continues to wind snakelike yet keep a northwesterly tack. Occasional modest bluffs add contrast to the shoreline.

At 2.5 miles paddle beside the Boone County Dog Pound access on your right. This large gravel bar certainly has appeal. Unfortunately, the road from West Virginia 3 to the gravel bar is often very rough at the end so exercise caution and avoid getting stuck if using this access. Horse Branch enters on river left at 2.7 miles, and ahead you make a long bend. At 3.8 miles come to the only potentially hazardous situation—a broken-down former low-water concrete bridge now damaged by floods. Note that when this bridge was cut off, the houses on the west side of the river were abandoned. Approach the bridge with caution as waters continue to alter it. It will likely require a pullover no matter which side you try to carry around. Absolutely do not try to paddle over it.

Beyond here, the paddling is easy as you wind your way downriver. Paddle under a bridge at 5.4 miles. Big Laurel Creek enters on river left at 6.1 miles. You will not miss this sizable stream. Shoals continue among grassy islands. You will see more houses in this vicinity and also pass under another bridge at 6.3 miles. The river is now meandering through Seth, one of the larger communities along Big Coal River. The pools between shoals are getting bigger, including a huge pool and swimming hole at 6.6 miles. Downriver, the Big Coal River flows over long stretches with sandy bottom. At 8.3 miles Joes Creek, another large tributary, enters on river right. You will not miss this stream either. More bends and shoals continue, then you float under yet another bridge at 8.9 miles.

You are closing in on John Slack Park. Paddle under another bridge at 10.4 miles, in the community of Bloomingrose. At 10.8 miles come alongside the park on river right. You can see the picnic shelters. Enjoy the last parts of the float before reaching the park boat ramp at 11.1 miles, ending this segment of the water trail.

34 Hawks Nest Lake

Do you want to paddle in the New River Gorge without the rough rapids? Then Hawks Nest Lake—an impoundment in the gorge—is the place for you.

County: Fayette
Start: Hawks Nest State Park boat ramp, N38 7.120' / W81 7.180'
End: Hawks Nest State Park boat ramp, N38 7.120' / W81 7.180'
Length: 6.3 miles, with additional mileage possibilities
Float time: 3.4 hours
Difficulty rating: Moderate
Rapids: On upper end of lake where it merges with New River
River/lake type: Flood reservoir
Current: Mostly on upper lake when water is up
River gradient: None
Water gauge: None
Season: Apr–Oct, later summer is best

Land status: West Virginia state park; national river
Fees and permits: None
Nearest city/town: Ansted
Maps: Hawks Nest State Park Map & Trail Guide; National Geographic Trails Illustrated map #242—New River Gorge; USGS: Fayetteville
Boats used: Kayaks, canoes, motorboats
Organization: Hawks Nest State Park, PO Box 857, 49 Hawks Nest Park Rd., Ansted, WV 25812; (304) 658-5212; www.hawksnestsp.com
Contacs/outfitter: New River Gorge National River, PO Box 246, 104 Main St., Glen Jean, WV 25846; (304) 465-0508; www.nps.gov/neri

Put-in/Takeout Information

To put-in/takeout: From the New River Gorge Visitor Center just north of the New River Bridge on US 19, drive north on US 19 for 4.8 miles to the US 60 exit, Hico/Rainelle. Take US 60 west for 6.3 miles to the town of Ansted. Here, near the Rite-Aid store on the right-hand side of US 60, split right on one-way Rich Creek Road, which is near Cemetery Road, then curve left onto Hawks Nest Road / County Road 60/2, and immediately pass under US 60. Continue on gravel WV 60/2 to reach the boat ramp and Hawks Nest Lake at 2 miles.

Paddle Summary

Set deep in the lower end of the New River Gorge, Hawks Nest Lake allows you to experience paddling in the gorge without having to tackle crazy whitewater. After reaching the bottom of the gorge on a bouncy gravel road, you will paddle up the impoundment, where towering headlands rise high above the slender lake. Depending on flow rates of the New River, you may experience the current. After 3 miles come to some rapids, and if you can make it up them, you can turn the corner to see the magnificent New River Bridge. On your return trip hug the other shore and

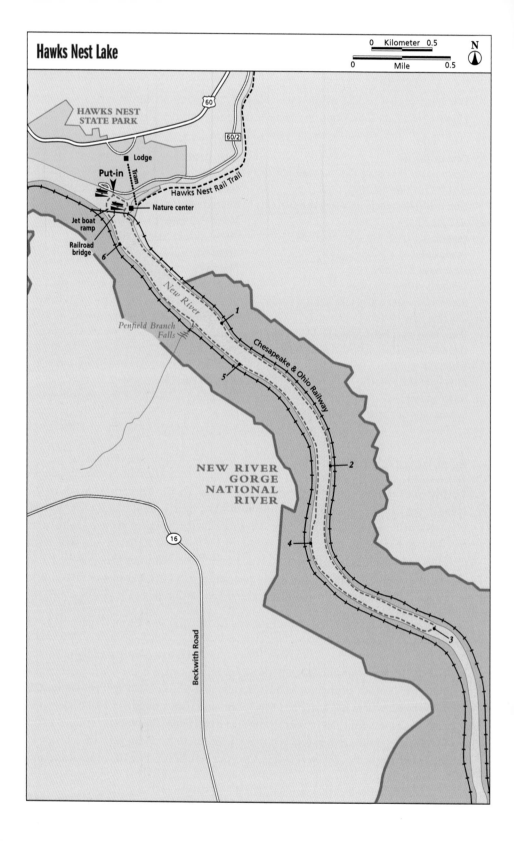

Hawks Nest Lake

HAWKS NEST
STATE PARK

60

60/2

Lodge

Tram

Put-in

Hawks Nest Rail Trail

Nature center

Jet boat
ramp

Railroad
bridge

6

New River

Penfield Branch
Falls

Chesapeake & Ohio Railway

1

5

2

NEW RIVER
GORGE
NATIONAL
RIVER

4

16

3

Beckwith Road

0   Kilometer   0.5

0   Mile   0.5

N

paddle to visit Penfield Branch Falls, a cataract accessible by going under a short tunnel on the adjacent railroad line. Just as elsewhere in the New River Gorge, railroad lines border the water. Additionally, you will see imaginatively built fish camps as well as decrepit shacks.

River/Lake Overview

Hawks Nest Lake is a 250-acre impoundment of the New River. Located at the lower end of the gorge for which the New River is famous, the lake dam was completed in the 1930s to provide flood control as well as hydroelectric power for the adjoining

HAWKS NEST STATE PARK OFFERS MORE

Seeing Penfield Branch Falls may whet your appetite for more cataracts and other highlights. Well, there are plenty of waterfalls here at Hawks Nest State Park. Consider taking the Hawks Nest Rail Trail up the valley of Mill Creek, making pools and cascades of its own. Here you will reach a trestle that provides a first-rate view of Fox Branch Falls as it tumbles upwards of 60 feet to flow under the trestle after a half mile, then walk a bit farther to enjoy 20-foot Mill Creek Falls, a wide, more powerful cataract.

To access the rail trail from the boat ramp, cross the road bridge over Mill Creek. Pass by the tram facility, nature center, and jet boat landing. Walk toward the railroad bridge, then pick up the Hawks Nest Rail Trail. Look for mining machinery and rail tracks embedded in the soil. Slightly ascend along Mill Creek after picking up the Hawks Nest Rail Trail, a former mining rail line. Along the way you will pass a cave with a spring emanating from it, and then come to the trestle and 60-foot Fox Branch Falls. The trestle makes for a fine viewing platform, but photographers and admirers can get closer with ease via paths just beyond the trestle. A picnic table near the falls adds a little civilization to the cataract. Note the bridge abutments and old hiker bridge below the current rail trail trestle.

Continue up the former track to meet Mill Creek Falls, also marked with a picnic table. A stone promontory allows a good look at the cataract from its top, but getting to the base of the falls is more challenging. However, the waterfall is worth a look and the Mill Creek valley exudes beauty throughout.

Still more hiking trails at Hawks Nest State Park avail still more cataracts and cliffs, as well as the famed Hawks Nest Overlook, where you can look up Hawks Nest Lake. Ride the tram up to the top of the gorge. Take the jet boat ride up the lake to review your paddling trip. With all there is to do here, consider booking a room at the lodge and give yourself an extra day to sample the outdoor menu.

area. Named for the abundance of osprey nests in the area, the lake and surrounding properties were purchased by the state of West Virginia and turned into a park. The facilities were enhanced in the 1960s with the building of the lodge overlooking lake. Today, the impoundment is popular with anglers and paddlers alike.

The Paddling

The boat ramp is located in the depths of the gorge. You already have a sense of being "down there." Start paddling toward the railroad bridge crossing the lake (although if you head the other way, toward the dam, you will see tan cliffs rising amid the for- ested gorge walls). Curve along the embayment of Mill Creek, passing near the nature center and tram, as well as the dock for the jet boat rides that head up the lake. The jet boat is named because it is moved by water jets rather than a propeller. You will see the jet boat cruise by while you are paddling. Paddle under the very low railroad bridge after a few hundred feet, then begin your trip in earnest. The rail line stands above the wooded shore. It is not long before you come to the first fish camp. Some

Penfield Branch Falls flow into Hawks Nest Lake.

Looking under a railroad tunnel out to Hawks Nest Lake

were built with the blessings of the railroad via leases while others were just put up quickly with a prayer that the rail line does not dismantle them. According to a fish camp owner I talked to, the railroad leaves them alone as long as they stay off the rail lines and right-of-way. It seems these homemade shacks are in a constant state of repair/disrepair, some being built while others are long abandoned. They are perched between the water and the railroad tracks on sloped terrain. Most of the terrain is wooded, and land emerges steeply from the shoreline.

   Big boulders line the shoreline in places. Trees and brush overhang the lakeshore. The lake itself stretches 400 to 500 feet wide and about 4 miles long. Make a bend to

Hawks Nest State Park Lodge looms above a low railroad bridge crossing Hawks Nest Lake.

the right at 1.6 miles. Tall wooded ramparts rise overhead, a "gorge-ous" sight indeed. At 2.2 miles you curve back to the left. By this point the current may be increasing as you are nearing the upper end of the lake.

At 3 miles the gorge bends to the right. Large boulders are strewn along the left shore. Rapids begin to form. At lower flows you can work your way past the shoals and turn the corner to the right. Ahead, the famed New River Bridge will come into view. However, if the New River is charging, getting past the lower rapids will be a pipe dream.

Your return trip takes you along the other shore. Enjoy more great views and look left for the tunnel leading under the rail line at 5.2 miles. Here, Penfield Branch makes a 20-foot angled stairstep drop, ending just before flowing under the tunnel (you may have to walk partway to reach the falls). Ahead, enjoy vistas of the state park lodge before passing under the railroad bridge a second time and ending your paddle at the boat ramp at 6.3 miles. If you want to extend the trip, you can paddle down toward the dam, but be careful.

35 New River: New River Gorge

This super-scenic stretch of the New River Gorge is the most paddleable section of the entire gorge.

Counties: Raleigh; Fayette; Summers
Start: Sandstone Public Access, N37 46.370' / W80 53.537'
End: Glade Creek Campground & Day-Use Area, N37 49.757' / W81 0.898'
Length: 9.0 miles
Float time: 4.0 hours
Difficulty rating: More difficult due to rapids
Rapids: Class II+
River/lake type: Huge mountain river
Current: Swift in rapids, otherwise steady
River gradient: 5.5 feet per mile
Water gauge: New River at Thurmond, no minimum runnable level, novices stay off above 6,000 cfs
Season: Apr–Oct

Land status: National river
Fees and permits: None
Nearest city/town: Sandstone
Maps: National Geographic Trails Illustrated map #242–New River Gorge; USGS: Meadow Creek, Prince
Boats used: Rafts, kayaks, funyaks, canoes
Organization: West Virginia Department of Natural Resources, 324 Fourth Ave., South Charleston, WV 25303; (304) 558-2771; www.wvdnr.gov
Contact/outfitter: New River Gorge National River, PO Box 246, 104 Main St., Glen Jean, WV 25846; (304) 465-0508; www.nps.gov/neri

Put-in/Takeout Information

To takeout: From exit 124 on I-64 east of Beckley, take the Beckley Bypass north for 1 mile, then stay straight at a traffic light, reaching Stanaford Road at 2.2 miles from the interstate. Turn right on Stanaford Road, WV 41 north. Follow Stanaford Road for 4.4 miles, then turn right at a stop sign and the intersection with WV 61. Here, stay right with WV 41 north for 3.8 miles, descending into the New River Gorge. Stay right with Glade Creek Road just before WV 41 crosses the New River via a bridge. Trace Glade Creek Road for 5.6 miles to a T intersection. Here, turn left and follow the road to the takeout and a large parking area next to the New River.

To the put-in from the takeout: Backtrack to exit 124 on I-64, then take I-64 east toward Lewisburg to exit 139, Sandstone/Hinton. Next, head left (southbound) on WV 20 towards Hinton. Follow it for 0.4 mile to turn right on River Road, WV 20/CR 7. Cross the railroad tracks, take an immediate left, then follow the public access signs a short distance to the put-in. Be apprised the final part of the gravel road to the gravel bar put-in is very steep. It may be wiser to carry your boat down this short but steep hill.

New River: New River Gorge

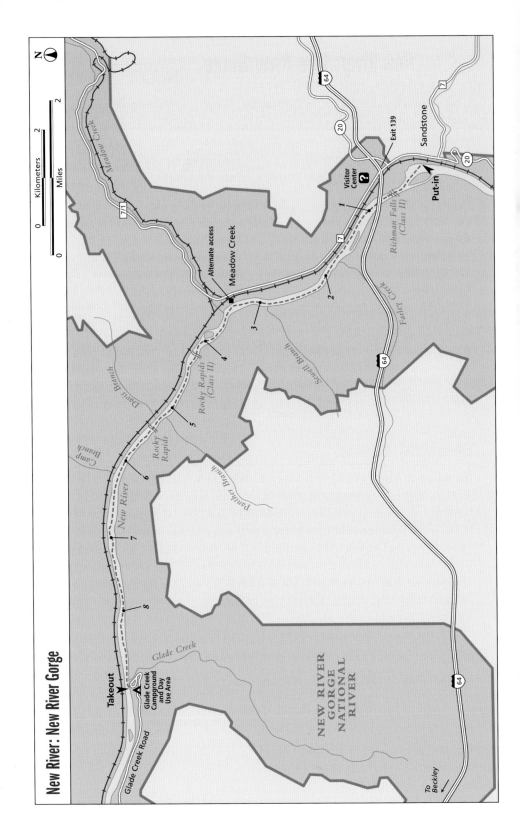

Gazing into the one and only New River Gorge

Paddle Summary

This trip leads 9 miles through the New River Gorge, from the community of Sandstone to Glade Creek. The scenery is spectacular and the rapids are the least difficult of any stretch within the gorge. Right off you tackle Class II Richman Falls, then later Class II Rocky Rapids is navigated. Other shoals will be encountered. Wildlife is plentiful in this stretch. The lack of commercial outfitters in this section of the gorge keeps the atmosphere serene. Be apprised the auto shuttle is above average in mileage (35 miles one-way).

River/Lake Overview

The New River is one of America's great waterways. Many aquatic enthusiasts believe the segment of the New River through the New River Gorge to be the best of the best. Born in the North Carolina highlands near the Blue Ridge town of Boone, the New River winds north and east through the Tarheel State, where it makes for a mostly casual paddling venture. The New enters Virginia at Independence. By then it has gained steam and has become a medium-size river. Dammed at Fries, the New pushes forth past Mount Rogers National Recreation area and beyond to

Foster Falls. Hereabouts the 57-mile New River Trail—a rail trail—parallels the river. Slowed again at Claytor Lake, the New pushes west, brawling through high ridges to enter West Virginia. A now truly massive mountain waterway, the New is dammed again at Bluestone Lake then enters the New River Gorge National River, with abundant recreation opportunities. Here, the entire New crashes over incomparable Sandstone Falls, just a mile above the start of this paddle, then cuts deeper into the Appalachian Plateau. The scenery and history of the New River Gorge is the setting until the New is dammed at Hawks Nest State Lake Park, another paddle included in this guide. From there, the New pushes a few more miles to meet the Gauley River and together form the Kanawha River. Overall, the New offers 250 plus or minus miles of paddling opportunity from mild Class I floats to raucous whitewater

SEE GLADE CREEK FALLS AND KATES BRANCH FALLS

The site of the takeout, Glade Creek, also offers hiking, camping, and historical study—plus two cool waterfalls by the names of Glade Creek Falls and Kates Branch Falls. Start the hike near the old village site of Hamlet, worth a side exploration. The Glade Creek Trail, a former railroad grade, takes you up an untamed valley on a foot-friendly path. After a mile reach a huge pool fed by 10-foot Glade Creek Falls. Glade Creek Falls spills over a ragged, creek-wide ledge into a pool that far outstrips the waterfall in size, creating a picturesque scene as viewed from the elevated trail. A somewhat steep user-created path leads to the base of the pools for a straight-on look at the falls. From the swimming hole you can see the trail ahead was built up with a creek-side floodwall. Continue up a deep mountain vale, savoring the everywhere-you-look loveliness. Look for old settler relics in flats and daunting rock bluffs. Come to the spur to Kates Falls after bridging Glade Creek. Make a final climb and discover the 25-foot cataract diving off a naked rock ledge. Kates Branch Falls, another 3.7 miles past Glade Creek Falls, is flanked by a rising bluff to the right of the falls and a sea of rhododendron to the left. Here, the stream dives 5 feet over a rock rampart then hits another ledge to pour 20 feet down a widening rock face then splatter onto rocks.

You can also camp at Glade Creek river access. I have spent many a night here. The camp stands underneath thick and towering woodland of locust, river birch, buckeye, sycamore, and tulip trees. Five campsites are strung along a gravel road. A picnic table, fire ring, and lantern post adorn each flat spot. A restroom building rises nearby. Five riverfront walk-in tent sites stand on a beach near the New River boat launch. Park your car and walk down the sandbar, shaded in river birch and sycamore, and pick one of the five marked campsites. All the campsites are free of charge.

for helmeted kayakers and rafters. It is truly a first-rate American paddling resource flowing through both Virginia and West Virginia.

The Paddling

Make no mistake, the shuttle for this paddle is a bear. However, the adventure presents the best opportunity for recreational paddlers to float the New River Gorge without having to tackle rough Class III and higher rapids. This way you can enjoy the magnificent scenery of the gorge yet not be excessively concerned with the challenges of whitewater. That being said, you will have a couple of exciting Class II rapids that can get pushy when the water is up. However, when the water is up, you can usually work around the biggest haystacks—waves gathering where the waters merge in a froth of white.

Start your paddle at the Sandstone public access. You are across from an island, and another island stands downstream. Begin downriver and move left to get your first taste of whitewater on the New River–Richman Falls. Not a fall in the true sense of the word, but it is a solid Class II rapid with big haystacks. Avoid the biggest haystacks if the water is up. If you make it through this, you can make the rest of the trip just fine. Float under the I-64 bridge at 0.7 mile. "Gorge-ous" scenery rises before you—a broad waterway with islands beyond which rise forested highlands. Rock, grass, and gravel banks stretch along the green river. Along these shores you will often spot deer. Islands will be cloaked in willow and sycamore. Pass some light rapids and islands near Farley Creek at 1.7 miles. The railroad is to your right.

You are heading northwest. The river is hundreds of feet across. Pass a shoal at 2.8 miles. At 3.3 miles look right for the Meadow Creek boater access. Meadow Creek flows in below there. At this point the New River is once again scattered with islands. Watch ahead as the river narrows and becomes rocky. Reach the Rocky Rapids at 4.1 miles. These are lesser shoals than Richman Falls, but standing boulders present different challenges than haystacks of frothing water. A beach lies on river left just after Rocky Rapids.

A series of fun ledges continue, keeping you downriver. At 5.4 miles, after passing Panther Branch, bounce through lower Rocky Rapids, a lesser Class II shoal. By 6.5 miles the New River has widened and is mostly slow from here out, with a few shoals. The scenery remains outstanding. Paddle by eight abutments of a former bridge crossing the New at 8.2 miles. Ahead, you can see where the river narrows and becomes rocky again. Your takeout is at 9 miles, after one last straightforward drop. Here, Glade Creek enters on river left, and just beyond it is a concrete ramp. Note that Class II–III Grassy Shoals rapid is downstream of the takeout.

36 Greenbrier River

Make a fun float on one of West Virginia's iconic waterways.

County: Greenbrier
Start: Caldwell boat launch, N37 46.909' / W80 23.911'
End: Island Park, N37 44.703' / W80 27.932'
Length: 5.1 miles
Float time: 3.0 hours
Difficulty rating: Easy
Rapids: Class I
River/lake type: Mountain river
Current: Moderate
River gradient: 6.9 feet per mile
Water gauge: Greenbrier River at Alderson, WV, 300 cfs minimum runnable level
Season: Mar–Oct

Land status: Private
Fees and permits: None
Nearest city/town: Ronceverte
Maps: USGS: Lewisburg, Ronceverte
Boats used: Kayaks, canoes
Organization: Friends of the Lower Greenbrier River, 549 WV 12, Alderson, WV 24910; (304) 445-2005; www.lowergreenbrierriver.org
Contact/outfitter: Greenbrier River Campground, 4316 Highland Trail, Alderson, WV 24910; (304) 445-2203; www.greenbrierriver.com. Runs shuttles for this trip and others on the Greenbrier, also rents boats and offers camping.

Put-in/Takeout Information

To the takeout: From exit 169 on I-64 near Lewisburg, take US 219 south through Lewisburg and onward for a total of 6.5 miles from the interstate to reach Ronceverte. Continue through Ronceverte to turn left on Island Park Road just before crossing the US 219 bridge over the Greenbrier River. The takeout is in Island Park near a covered shelter overlooking the Greenbrier River.

To the put-in from the takeout: Backtrack from Ronceverte on US 219 north to downtown Lewisburg, then turn right (eastbound) on US 60 / Washington Street. Follow US 60 / Washington Street for 3.1 miles, then turn right into the Caldwell boat ramp just before crossing the Greenbrier River.

Paddle Summary

This is but one leg of many paddling adventures on the famed Greenbrier River. This particular float takes you from Caldwell to Ronceverte on a picturesque stretch of the waterway, with visual highlights and some moving water. The float is perfect for novices and those who just want to relax and take in the mountain scenery. Light but fun shoals keep you moving with only one rapid of note, Whitcomb Rapid, a Class I+ shoal just downstream of the CSX Railroad bridge. Island Park makes for a fine ending point, with easy water access, shelters, and a restroom in little downtown Ronceverte.

River/Lake Overview

The Greenbrier River is born high in the mountains of the Monongahela National Forest, picking up tributaries just south of West Virginia's high point at Spruce Knob, rising 4,865 feet above sea level. The Greenbrier River picks up enough tributaries to form the West Fork Greenbrier River and East Fork Greenbrier River, divided by Middle Mountain. Flowing southwesterly, the two forks join at the town of Durbin, and the Greenbrier winds its way between Back Allegheny Mountain and Little Mountain, flowing below the nearby Snowshoe ski resort. The river courses through state and national forest land and is generally considered paddleable as it flows through the town of Marlinton. At this point the clear waters are some of the most renowned trout and smallmouth-bass fishing waters in the Mountain State. Equally famed Anthony Creek enters the Greenbrier as it leaves the national forest just before reaching Caldwell and the start of this particular paddle. The upper section of the Greenbrier is also known for having one of the premier rail trails in the

The Greenbrier River presents several fun rapids such as this. KERI ANNE MOLLOY

Greenbrier River

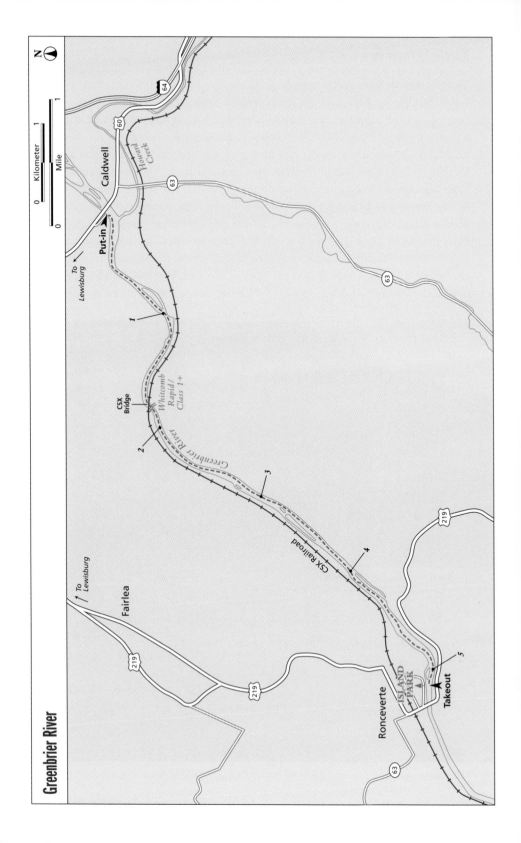

Southeast—the Greenbrier River Trail. This spectacular path winds for 78 plus miles, offering a riverside path for hikers, bicyclers, and equestrians. The lower Greenbrier River continues its southwesterly ways and gains size while becoming less used, save where it flows through small towns before meeting its mother stream, the New River, near the town of Hinton. It is said the 173-mile-long Greenbrier River delivers up to 30 percent of the entire flow of the massive New River. The Greenbrier is truly one of West Virginia's finest paddling resources. I have floated much of the river, pedaled the entire Greenbrier River Trail, and claim them both to be superlative West Virginia outdoor resources.

The Paddling

The put-in offers shaded parking and a wide ramp. Here, the Greenbrier is about 120 feet wide as it flows normally clear. Rocks and underwater life can be seen as the sun pierces the surface. As you float, Howard Creek enters the Greenbrier across from the ramp, partially screened by downstream-bent low sycamores rising from a gravel bar. The Greenbrier speeds down an easy shoal, indicative of the rapids found downstream. These are simple, straightforward riffles, flowing over evenly sized rocks, with little in the way of obstacles. At 0.7 mile pass a long linear island, the primary channel of which is on river right. River birch and sycamore are the main streamside trees. Rocks and grasses are also represented on the shoreline.

ABOUT THE GREENBRIER RIVER TRAIL

Just upstream of this paddle begins the Greenbrier River Trail, the most acclaimed rail trail in the Mountain State. Stretching from Caldwell to Cass, the 78-mile path follows the Greenbrier River its entire length. The pea-gravel track presents remote sections traversing deep forests, other segments running through small hamlets and weekend retreats, with still other sections including bridges spanning the Greenbrier, where fantastic vistas await. Historic logging communities can be found in the back of beyond. Evidence of the days as an active railroad can be seen, such as an old water tank, track signs, and even old tunnels! The trail elevation changes a mere 220 feet over 78 miles, making the grade not difficult even when going uphill. I have pedaled all the way up and all the way down and I admit going down is a tad easier. Nevertheless, what makes the trail even better are the designated campsites and shelters along the way. The trail also passes through civilization in Marlinton, where supplies and accommodations can be had. Outfitters can provide bicycles and shuttles. So, whether you are going for a day or a week, add a bike trip on this stellar path to enhance your Greenbrier River experience.

Beyond the island, the Greenbrier returns to its customary width, allowing for expansive views. Float over another Class I riffle that keeps you moving at 0.9 mile. The even gradients make for easy river running—just be careful about becoming stranded in the shallows. At 1 mile bend right. More riffles keep the paddling easy. Slow in a deeper hole after a quarter mile as a big rock bluff rises on your left, with a few riverside habitations on river right.

At 1.7 miles the Greenbrier narrows and bends left, then passes under the CSX Railroad bridge. Brace yourself for Whitcomb Rapid, a Class I+ shoal that narrows and drops. The waters gather in haystacks at higher flows. The wave train is easily avoidable by running just alongside the waves to the right. Do not go to the left of the wave train as the chute is very close to shore. Rhododendron-cloaked bluffs rise on river left. These bluffs are what forced the rail line across the Greenbrier.

The waterway slows, and you drift among waters of varying depths, with sporadic bigger boulders standing in the stream, which pose no hazard unless you are paddling backwards with your eyes closed. That is one of the joys of this float—it's fun, easy, and pleasing to the eye. By 2.4 miles the river speeds and you shoot another easy rapid at 2.8 miles. Easy views continue to be had floating the wide waters.

Scan the river bottom around 3 miles and you may note some rock structures that were once efforts at increasing the navigability of the Greenbrier. Like many rivers in the two Virginias, the Greenbrier was used for trade and transportation in the early days of America, when the forests were trackless thickets inhabited by often hostile aboriginals. Alas, today, we paddlers are the primary navigators of the Greenbrier, with nearly all of us going downstream, needing but a few inches of river clearance for our kayaks and canoes.

A straightaway leads to a long island at 3.6 miles. This isle has a man-made look to it and may have been built for navigation and deepening of the Greenbrier. Look for log frames and revetment used to channel the river. At 4.2 miles pass another long island. At 4.6 miles bounce down a few rapids as the US 219 bridge comes into view. Head over to river right and reach your takeout at Island Park, known also as Ronceverte Island Park. By the way, the unusual name of Ronceverte is French for "Greenbrier."

37 Lake Sherwood

Circle the shoreline of this mountain-rimmed, no-gas-motors-allowed impoundment, arguably West Virginia's most beautiful lake, nestled deep in the Monongahela National Forest.

County: Greenbrier
Start: Lake Sherwood boat launch, N38 0.484' / W80 0.575'
End: Lake Sherwood boat launch, N38 0.484' / W80 0.575'
Length: 3.5 miles
Float time: 2.0 hours
Difficulty rating: Easy
Rapids: None
River/lake type: National forest mountain lake
Current: None
River gradient: None
Water gauge: None
Season: Apr–Oct
Land status: National forest

Fees and permits: Entrance fee required
Nearest city/town: Neola
Maps: Monongahela National Forest, Lake Sherwood Area Hiking Trail & Map; USGS: Lake Sherwood
Boats used: Kayaks, canoes, pedal boats, stand-up paddleboards, a few johnboats
Organization: Monongahela National Forest, White Sulphur Springs District, 410 E. Main St., White Sulphur Springs, WV 24986; (304) 536-2144; www.fs.fed.us
Contact/outfitter: West Virginia Department of Natural Resources, 324 Fourth Ave., South Charleston, WV 25303; (304) 558-2771; www.wvdnr.gov

Put-in/Takeout Information

To put-in/takeout: From exit 181 on I-64 at White Sulphur Springs, drive 15 miles north on State Road 92 to Neola. From Neola, travel east on Lake Sherwood Road for 11 miles and come to the recreation area. Pass the entrance gatehouse, then follow signs for the boat ramp, a right turn, quickly reaching the ramp on your left.

Paddle Summary

Make a circuit paddle at quiet, relaxing, and super-scenic Lake Sherwood. Start your adventure at the recreation area boat ramp, then make a clockwise trip around the impoundment, turning into coves, passing the recreation area's campground, and reaching the lake's headwaters on Meadow Creek. From there, turn south down the lake, enjoying the scenery near and far. Come alongside Lake Sherwood's dam, exploring more coves and soaking in big-time mountain views. Finally work around a pair of islands, completing the circuit paddle. The no-gas-motors-allowed lake keeps the locale easy on the ears and eliminates worrying about motorboats blasting across the water.

Lake Sherwood is great for family paddling.

River/Lake Overview

Lake Sherwood lies within the Monongahela National Forest near the Virginia state line. Here, Meadow Creek flows bordered by Meadow Creek Mountain on one side and Allegheny Mountain—the mountain dividing West Virginia and Virginia—on the other, and is the setting for what may be the Mountain State's most beautiful lake. Back in 1958, Meadow Creek was dammed and Lake Sherwood came to be, opening for recreation in the year 1959. Ever since then the 164-acre lake has been the centerpiece of a popular getaway that presents activities for recreationalists of all stripes. In addition to paddling, the lake also draws in fishermen. Largemouth bass, bluegill, and catfish are the most sought-after species. However, tiger muskie are also stocked here and can run 15 pounds or more.

The Paddling

Paddlers can rent canoes, kayaks, johnboats, and stand-up paddleboards in season at the kiosk next to the small boat ramp with dock. Leave the boat ramp and begin a clockwise circuit of Lake Sherwood. The beauty of the lake is immediate and evident, from the clear water to the mass of woods beyond the shore to the mountains themselves rising above. The sounds of nature reign. You will soon be paddling alongside the campground, with some sites near the water and still other areas where campers can launch their canoes and kayaks without leaving the campground. The state-line ridge rises across the water. Waterweeds grow in parts of Lake Sherwood. Serenity usually stretches over all, save for the occasional thunderstorms that pass over during the summer paddling season.

Do not be surprised as you paddle along if the smell of campfire smoke, hot dogs, and hamburgers wafts from the wooded campsites to the open lake. Continue winding in and out of coves. At 0.8 mile turn into the marshy headwaters of Lake

DO MORE AT LAKE SHERWOOD

Lake Sherwood Recreation Area is a true highlight of the Monongahela National Forest. The well-kept, well-managed destination started with natural beauty, and the enhancements did nothing to spoil the natural allure—in fact they made a good thing better. The lake, swim beach, campground, picnic areas, and trails are the venues by which you can indulge in the area's resources.

As you drive up, Lake Sherwood will be on your right. The swim beaches and main boat landing are over that way too. The campground is a real winner. White pine, oak, and hickory, with scads of dogwood, dominate the rich forest. The sites are very spacious and this spaciousness adds to the campsite privacy. The loops have accesses leading to the water's edge, where paddlers like us can launch directly from the campground. Recreation-area managers and hosts give Lake Sherwood that well-cared-for look. Water spigots and hot showers are available, and campsites can be reserved.

Hikers can have a ball here. The Lake Sherwood Trail makes a 3.6-mile loop around the reservoir, roughly following the route of this paddle trip. The Virginia Trail spurs off the Lake Sherwood Trail and heads 0.6 mile up to the Allegheny Mountain Trail. From here, you walk the state-line ridge for 3.6 miles and gain views down on Lake Sherwood and over to Lake Moomaw in Virginia, a first-rate Virginia paddling destination, also detailed in this guide.

The Meadow Creek Trail starts at the head of Lake Sherwood and parallels Meadow Creek, crossing the stream several times amid thickets of rhododendron, intersecting the Connector Trail at 2.7 miles. Here, you can turn right and make a 10-mile loop back to Lake Sherwood using the Allegheny Mountain and Lake Sherwood trails. This is one of my favorite long day hikes in the two Virginias. So start your Lake Sherwood adventure with a paddle. It may lead to swimming, fishing, camping, hiking, and hopefully a little relaxing, too.

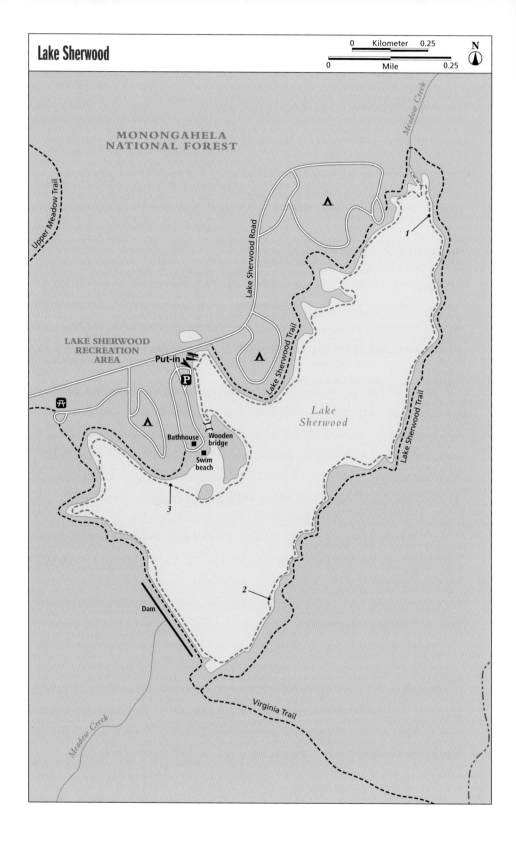

Lake Sherwood

0   Kilometer   0.25

0   Mile   0.25

N

MONONGAHELA
NATIONAL FOREST

Upper Meadow Trail

Meadow Creek

Lake Sherwood Road

Lake Sherwood Trail

1

LAKE SHERWOOD
RECREATION
AREA

Put-in

P

Bathhouse

Wooden
bridge

Swim
beach

3

Lake
Sherwood

Lake Sherwood Trail

2

Dam

Meadow Creek

Virginia Trail

Lake Sherwood at dawn

Sherwood. Here, Meadow Creek empties its clean, clear waters into the impoundment. See how far you can get up the creek, winding your way among the shallows and fallen logs before running out of lake. You should get close enough to see the Lake Sherwood Trail hiker bridge crossing Meadow Creek. This is part of the loop trail circling Lake Sherwood. Alder grows thick in these parts.

Turn south along the shore, leaving Meadow Creek. The reservoir dam is visible in the distance, and you will soon be paddling beside it. Look also for the Lake Sherwood Trail as it often runs close to the water. At 1.5 miles turn into a cove. Here, scan across the lake for the boat ramp and launch area. It is almost directly across the impoundment.

Continuing south, you enter the deeper part of the tarn. The maximum depth is 20 feet with an average depth of 10 feet, according to the West Virginia Department of Natural Resources. By 2.1 miles you are in the southeastern corner of Lake Sherwood. Turn west here, paddling along the dam. At this point Meadow Creek Mountain stands out in bold relief. Beyond the dam, your circuit paddle leads into a pair of coves filled with cattails. Paddle by a fishing pier, then come to the recreation area swim beach. This is another aquatic draw. One beach is on the main shore and the other is on an island accessible by a wooden bridge. The swim area is between the two beaches. The scenery near and far will enhance your swimming experience.

Be sure to stay outside the swim-beach-delineation buoys and to the outside of the only two islands in the lake. After coming around the two islands, the end is near, but most paddlers like to inspect the arched bridge linking one of the islands to the mainland. After that, it is but a short distance to the boat ramp and paddle's end at 3.5 miles.

Northern West Virginia Paddles

38   Ohio River: Middle Island Loop

Enjoy a big-river paddle, leaving the small town of St. Marys to execute a circuit around historic Middle Island, a wooded wild parcel on the Ohio River.

County: Pleasants
Start: St. Marys Marina boat ramp, N39 23.625' / W81 12.406'
End: St. Marys Marina boat ramp, N39 23.625' / W81 12.406'
Length: 4.6 miles, with additional mileage possible
Float time: 2.4 hours
Difficulty rating: Moderate
Rapids: None
River/lake type: Massive river
Current: Strong in main river
River gradient: 1.0 foot per mile
Water gauge: Ohio River at Parkersburg, no minimum runnable level

Season: Year-round
Land status: Middle Island is national wildlife refuge
Fees and permits: None
Nearest city/town: St. Marys
Maps: Middle Island Trail; USGS: Raven Rock
Boats used: Kayaks, canoes, johnboats, motorboats
Organization: Ohio River Islands National Wildlife Refuge, 3982 Waverly Rd., Williamstown, WV 26187; (304) 375-2923; www.fws.gov/refuge/Ohio_River_Islands
Contact/outfitter: City of St. Marys, 418 Second St., St. Marys, WV 26170; (304) 684-2401; https://local.wv.gov/stmarys

Put-in/Takeout Information

To put-in/takeout: From the intersection of WV 16 and WV 2 just north of downtown St. Marys, take WV 2 south for 0.5 mile to turn right onto Clay Street and follow it for 0.2 mile to turn right onto Riverside Drive. Follow Riverside Drive for 0.2 mile to turn left into St. Marys Marina. Follow the main marina road to the boat ramp on the Ohio River.

Paddle Summary

On this paddling adventure you will start at St. Marys Marina, a quieter place than its name implies. From there you will paddle up The Thoroughfare, a channel lying between the West Virginia mainland and Middle Island. This channel passes the inflow of Middle Island Creek, a paddleable stream that also lays claim to being the longest creek in West Virginia. Continue to the northern end of Middle Island, then open onto the main body of the Ohio River. You will then turn south, cruising along

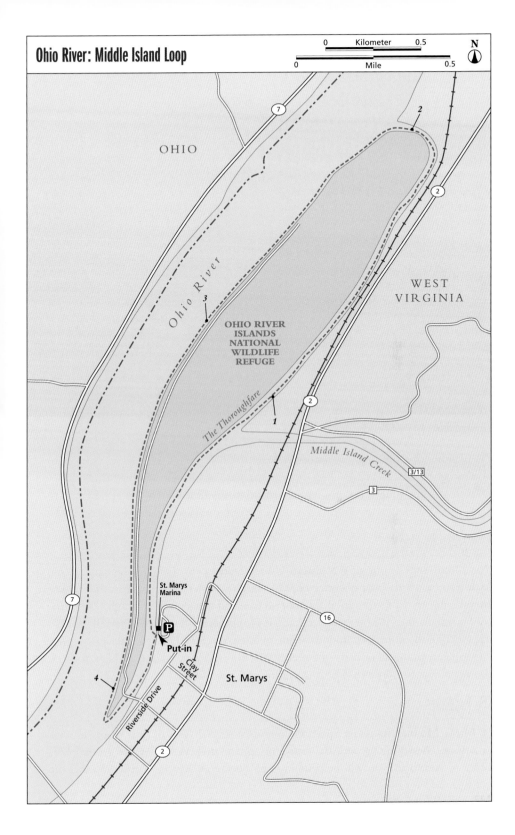

Ohio River: Middle Island Loop

0   Kilometer   0.5

0   Mile   0.5

N

OHIO

Ohio River

7

2

2

WEST
VIRGINIA

3

OHIO RIVER
ISLANDS
NATIONAL
WILDLIFE
REFUGE

The Thoroughfare

1

2

Middle Island Creek

3/13

3

7

St. Marys
Marina

P

Put-in

16

4

Riverside Drive

Clay
Street

St. Marys

2

A barge floats by Middle Island.

the island with wide-open views of the huge Ohio River, as well as the rising hills bordering the waterway, including those in the state of Ohio, across the water. Upon returning to the southern tip of Middle Island, you will paddle by quiet downtown St. Marys, completing the loop.

River/Lake Overview

The Ohio River is one of the eastern United States' primary waterways and is the river into which the vast majority of West Virginia waterways flow. It is the single-largest tributary of the mighty Mississippi River, and it starts at Pittsburgh where the Monongahela and Allegheny Rivers merge. From there it flows southwesterly, forming much of the northwest boundary line of West Virginia. The Ohio River runs for 981 miles, draining all or parts of fifteen states, from extreme southwest New York all the way down to northern Alabama, ending at Cairo, Illinois.

The Paddling

St. Marys Marina provides a fine launching spot, several lanes of boat ramps, as well as a dock. The adjoining park has restrooms, picnic shelters, and ample green space. Once in your boat, you will be paddling The Thoroughfare, the narrow channel on the east side of Middle Island. This is the preferred route for looping around Middle Island since The Thoroughfare has less current and is less subject to wind than is the balance of the Ohio River, extending hundreds of yards across on the west side of Middle Island. The Thoroughfare stretches about 150 feet across. Middle Island is a riot of vegetation while the mainland shore of The Thoroughfare is composed of, first, the marina park, a campground, then assorted fish camps and woods. In the distance bold wooded hills demark the flatlands along the river.

By 0.8 mile you have come alongside Middle Island Creek, named for the isle to where it flows. At 77 miles in length, Middle Island Creek is a worthy paddling destination in its own right, and since it lays claim to being the longest creek in West Virginia, the stream begs the question: When does a creek become a river? You can look upstream at the rail bridge and auto bridge spanning Middle Island Creek. Interestingly, Middle Island Creek, depending on upstream weather, can either push in clear or silty water into the Ohio River, itself subject to inflow from a thousand other tributaries.

Continue beyond Middle Island Creek. The Thoroughfare is now much narrower. Paddle past occasional broken-down fish camps as well better-kempt places. This

WHAT ARE THE OHIO RIVER ISLANDS?

The Ohio River has always been important for the people who lived around it, from pre-Columbian aboriginals to today's American citizens. As what became West Virginia was coming to be, the Ohio was a free-flowing waterway, laced with a series of islands formed from sand and gravel pushed downriver. These islands were used as campsites and homesites, but later, when segments of the Ohio River were dammed, much of these islands' acreage went underwater, making the still-standing parts of the islands all the more valuable.

Ohio River islands began to be purchased—most of them in West Virginia—and in 1990 the Ohio River Islands National Wildlife Refuge came to be. Now, the refuge preserves twenty-two islands along a 362-mile segment of the Ohio River, as well as four parcels of mainland. This amounts to 3,440 acres of protected land in West Virginia alone. Today, the refuge is working to restore ideal conditions for flora and fauna as well as underwater life such as mussels. Among other beneficiaries are migratory birds, found along the Ohio River Flyway. Refuge headquarters are in Williamstown, West Virginia.

Middle Island, at 235 acres, is one of the most famous of the Ohio River Islands, and it is also the only refuge isle accessible by auto bridge. Today you can drive 1.5 miles on the island as well as enjoy over 3 miles of hiking trails. The access road to the island is just a short distance from St. Marys Marina. You would be remiss not to explore Middle Island by auto and foot as well as by canoe or kayak.

The St. Marys Bridge links West Virginia to Ohio.

segment resembles a small river. Begin bending left. The balance of the Ohio River opens before you at 2.1 miles. If you are looking to extend your trip, you can turn right up the Ohio River and circle smaller Grape Island, adding a 3-mile round-trip to the 4.6-mile endeavor. Otherwise turn left, downstream, on the mighty Ohio, hugging the shore of Middle Island while hundreds of yards stretch out between you and the state of Ohio to the west. Notice the riprap along the shoreline of Middle Island. This is to cut down on erosion from not only windborne waves but also barge traffic going up and down the valley, as well as lesser boats.

At lower flows, tan sand beaches will be exposed in areas. Look for animal tracks on these beaches. However, should you want to actually get out of your boat and explore Middle Island, you are best served doing it after the paddle, accessing the island by auto, and walking some of the 3.5 miles of trails. The island is densely wooded and junglelike with brush. Looking at the island now, it is hard to imagine it being settled in the 1700s, cultivated, and generally civilized.

Continue curving down the teardrop-shaped isle. Downstream, you begin to see the white St. Marys Bridge linking West Virginia to Ohio. Reach the southern, slender tip of Middle Island at 4.2 miles. Here, join the southern entrance to The Thoroughfare. Downtown St. Marys stands on the mainland and includes a public library. Ahead, pass under the old span that once crossed the Ohio River but now provides a link only to Middle Island. The rest of that particular bridge was dismantled after the bridge over the Ohio River connecting Point Pleasant to Gallipolis, Ohio, collapsed in 1967. They were of the same design.

The last part of the paddle leads to the St. Marys Marina, ending at 4.6 miles. After your paddle, consider a picnic at the marina park, followed by a land tour of Middle Island.

39 North Bend Lake

Paddle among picturesque standing tree snags at this winding state park impoundment set among wildlife-rich forest, brush, and tree-covered hills.

County: Ritchie
Start: North Bend State Park canoe/kayak launch, N39 12.665' / W81 4.374'
End: North Bend State Park canoe/kayak launch, N39 12.665' / W81 4.374'
Length: 6.2 miles, with additional mileage possible
Float time: 3.4 hours
Difficulty rating: Moderate
Rapids: None
River/lake type: Small narrow lake
Current: None
River gradient: None
Water gauge: None

Season: Mar–Oct
Land status: State park
Fees and permits: None
Nearest city/town: Harrisville
Maps: North Bend State Park; USGS: Harrisville
Boats used: Kayaks, canoes, johnboats
Organization: North Bend State Park, 202 North Bend Park Rd., Cairo, WV 26337; (304) 643-2931; https://wvstateparks.com/
Contact/outfitter: West Virginia Department of Natural Resources, 324 Fourth Ave., South Charleston, WV 25303; (304) 558-2771; www.wvdnr.gov

Put-in/Takeout Information

To put-in/takeout: From the intersection of WV 16 and WV 31 in downtown Harrisville, take Main Street / County Road 5 west for 0.9 mile, then make a sharp right toward the canoe/kayak launch, quickly descending to reach the launch and parking area.

Paddle Summary

North Bend Lake offers a different and scenic paddling experience. The long and meandering reservoir is populated with scattered tree snags as well as open areas from which rise attractive hills. Start at the park canoe/kayak launch, then work your way along the shoreline toward the park dam. The standing tree snags lend a picturesque air to the water as you twist and turn among them. Reach open water near the main park boat launch, then continue working your way down the dammed North Fork Hughes River, scanning the hills for deer and other wildlife. Enjoy extensive bird life as well. After coming near the dam, work your way along the shoreline turning into Lost Run embayment. The final part of the trip takes you back to the canoe/kayak launch. Note that motors up to 10 horsepower are allowed on the impoundment, but the practical result of the standing and fallen tree snags makes motorboat travel difficult, effectively keeping their usage to a minimum.

North Bend Lake

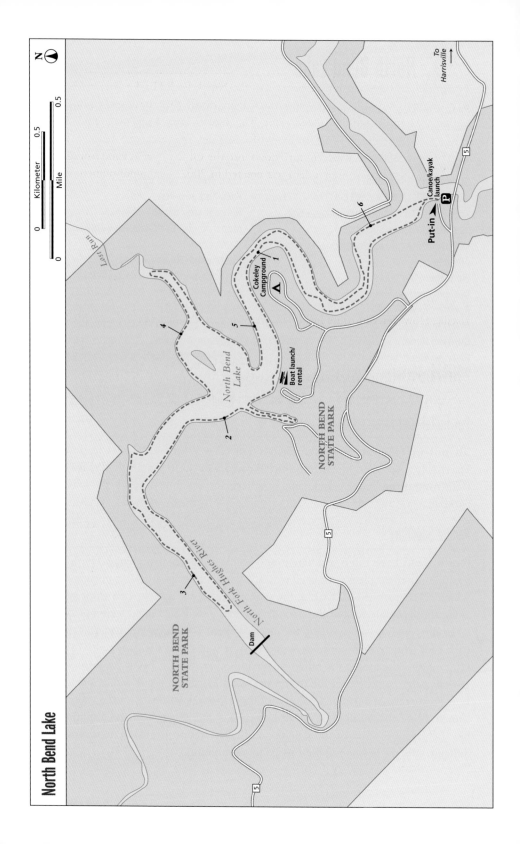

River/Lake Overview

North Bend Lake is a dammed portion of the North Fork Hughes River. The North Fork starts in the hills of western Doddridge County, then flows west into Ritchie County, where our paddle takes place. The North Fork and South Fork Hughes River meet near the small community of Cisco before their merged waters join the Little Kanawha River, which in turn flows into the Ohio River at Parkersburg. North Bend Lake came to be after a dam was erected in 2002. The impoundment stands at 305 acres, winding for 8 linear miles. Its average depth is 12 feet, with the deepest point at 36 feet.

The Paddling

Leave the quiet canoe/kayak launch, located in the Third Run embayment of the lake, nearly its center. Paddle north, opening onto the primary part of the impoundment. To your right, the watercourse makes a slender serpentine way toward Harrisville. However, our route heads left, westerly into the heart of the state park and its

STILL MORE TO NORTH BEND STATE PARK

North Bend State Park is the heart of the North Bend Rail Trail, one of West Virginia's most scenic and successful rail-to-trail conversions. The rail-to-trail conversion began in 1989 and currently covers over 70 miles, running from near Parkersburg 27 miles to North Bend State Park and then east for another 43 miles to Wolf Summit. North Bend State Park makes a fine base camp for paddling and pedaling the rail trail, but there's more.

Bicyclers truly enjoy the varied scenery on the North Bend Rail Trail, from valleys to rural communities. Head east on the trail to traverse one of the twelve tunnels and thirty-two bridges that were part of the B&O Railroad, constructed from 1853 to 1857. Three tunnels can be accessed within biking distance of the park. Bring your bike or rent one. Hikers and horseback riders are welcome, too.

Furthermore, hiking trails extend throughout North Bend State Park. View the large rock formation on the Castle Rock Trail. The Giant Pine Trail wanders through a grove of evergreens. The Nature Trail is the park's most challenging, forming a 4.5-mile circuit through the varied terrain of the park. Fishing is popular here, whether in the lake or the Hughes River.

For overnight accommodations you have two campgrounds and the North Bend Lodge. Other activities include tennis, volleyball, and miniature golf. Hit the park swimming pool or grab a meal at the lodge after your paddle. Factually speaking, there is a lot to do here at North Bend State Park, including a cool paddling adventure.

The dock at boat-rental facility at North Bend State Park

facilities. Picturesque, mostly forested hills rise from the banks, while immediately you encounter standing trees that make North Bend Lake a unique paddling experience.

It does not take too much skill to dodge the snags, but sometimes floating-fallen trees form blockades, forcing you to work around them. Scan the shore for deer, for this park is rich with the shy, tawny critters. By 0.7 mile you are working around the hilltop where stands Cokeley Campground, one of the two camping areas here at North Bend State Park. The other, River Run Campground, is downstream from the lake along a free-flowing portion of North Fork Hughes River. Cokeley Campground is on a hilltop well above the lake, unseen, although you may smell campfire smoke drifting over the water.

Rock bluffs can be spotted amid the wooded shore, while still other areas are covered in ferns and brush. By 1.3 miles you are opening onto the widest part of the lake, which is a mere 300 feet across. Here, find the main park boat launch as well as North Bend Outfitters, an on-site business renting canoes, kayaks, and other boats in season. By now you have realized that the sheer number of standing snags, fallen snags, and stumps in the lake create a significant deterrent to motorboating here at North Bend Lake, although a few anglers in johnboats may be spotted. Additionally, shallows are common. Certainly no motorboat will be going full throttle across the reservoir.

Beyond the launch and outfitter, continue along the left shore, turning into a small narrow embayment, a shallow marshy area providing additional wildlife habitat. Bring binoculars. Turning back onto the main lake, paddle along the most open portion of flatwater, nearly free of snags. Continuing the clockwise loop, you turn southwest at 2.3 miles. Snags reappear in large ranks and the park dam stands tall in the distance. Note the Fishermans Trail parallels the shore here, making for an easy exit spot.

I advise against getting too close to the dam, as fallen trees gather here in scads. After coming near enough for a look, begin your return journey, now on the north shore where hills rise sharply from the water. Paralleling the shoreline leads you past an overhanging rock outcrop at 3.6 miles then into the embayment of Lost Run at 3.8 miles. Note the island to your right, a former riverside hill now surrounded by water.

The Lost Run embayment is one of the bigger highlights of this paddle. Work your way up the pencil-thin ribbon of water swaddled in hills, finally finding a marshy wetland where the flowing part of Lost Run meets the still water of the lake. Birdsong will be ringing in the hollow.

Curve back into the main lake at 4.8 miles. From this point forward it is a matter of dancing your way among the snags, once again passing Cokeley Campground atop the hill and returning to the Third Run embayment, where the canoe/kayak launch awaits at 6.2 miles. Should you desire to paddle further, the upper part of the lake extends for over 3 narrow miles one-way, ample flatwater for extended paddling.

Skeletal tree trunks rise from North Bend Lake.

40 West Fork River Water Trail

Float your way on the West Fork River from a quiet town and old milldam past occasional rapids before briefly joining the Tygart Valley River to end on the Monongahela River in downtown Fairmont. A rail trail runs parallel to the West Fork River most of the way, making a bike shuttle practical and fun.

County: Marion
Start: Worthington City Park River Access, N39 27.051' / W80 15.937'
End: Palatine Park Canoe/Kayak Access, N36 54.875' / W82 13.276'
Length: 11.4 miles
Float time: 5.5 hours
Difficulty rating: Moderate
Rapids: Class I shoals
River/lake type: West Fork River is a medium-size river; Monongahela is large river.
Current: Slow-moderate
River gradient: 2.4 feet per mile
Water gauge: West Fork River at Enterprise, minimum runnable level 220

Season: Apr–Oct
Land status: Private
Fees and permits: None
Nearest city/town: Fairmont
Maps: West Fork Water Trail Map 1; USGS: Shinnston, Fairmont West
Boats used: Kayaks, canoes, a few johnboats, bigger boats on Monongahela River
Organization: Guardians of the West Fork; www.guardiansofthewestfork.com
Contact/outfitter: West Fork River Trail, Marion County Parks and Recreation, 1000 Cole St., Ste. B, Pleasant Valley, WV 26554; (304) 363-7037; www.mcparc.com

Put-in/Takeout Information

To the takeout: From exit 137 on I-79 in Fairmont, take WV 310 for 0.3 mile, following signs for downtown Fairmont. Turn left onto East Park Avenue and follow it for 1 mile, then stay straight, joining Merchant Street. Follow it just a short distance, going under the Million Dollar Bridge, then turn right onto Water Street and follow it a short distance to end at the boat ramp and canoe/kayak dock on the Monongahela River at Palatine Park.

To the put-in from the takeout: From Palatine Park, backtrack on Water Street, then turn right on Merchant Street and immediately cross the Monongahela River. Keep straight as Merchant Street becomes Third Street. Stay with Third Street for 0.7 mile, then turn left on US 19 south. Stay with US 19 south for 7.5 miles to Worthington, then turn left on Meadow Ridge Road. Immediately cross the West Fork, then turn right to Worthington Park. Put in just below the angled milldam. *Note:* This is also a trailhead for the West Fork River Trail, the rail trail you can use for a bike shuttle.

Paddle Summary

This paddle adventure takes you down one of the two major West Virginia streams that come together to form the famed Monongahela River—West Fork River. Starting in quiet Worthington, pick up the West Fork just below a milldam, then float your way through occasional Class I chutes between grassy gravel bars. Make a big bend through quiet country before reaching the hamlet of Monongah. The rest of the float is even more relaxed, in slower waters. Then you meet the Tygart Valley River, which together with the West Fork River forms the Monongahela River. Moreover, it is on the famed Monongahela that you triumphantly paddle into downtown Fairmont in the shadow of the renowned Million Dollar Bridge, landing at Palatine Park astride a dock exclusively for canoers and kayakers.

River/Lake Overview

The unusually and officially named West Fork River (it is referred to as the West Fork and West Fork River) starts in the hilly heart of West Virginia down Upshur County way. Gathering tributaries, the river winds north until its waters are stilled as Stonewall Jackson Lake. The big impoundment was completed in the late 1980s, controlling floods, and is the site of a West Virginia state park of the same name. Famed Civil War general Stonewall Jackson grew up hereabouts. Below the Stonewall Jackson Lake dam, the West Fork River becomes paddleable and the next 75 miles or so are part of the greater West Fork River Water Trail. The stream continues northeast, picking up tributaries and making its way to Clarksburg. Below there, the river winds past the beginning of our paddle in quiet Worthington before flowing a bit more to meet the Tygart Valley River, forming the Monongahela. The "Mon" is one of the two major tributaries forming the Ohio River at Pittsburgh. The Monongahela drains much of northern West Virginia via major tributaries of not only the West Fork River and Tygart Valley River but also the Cheat River.

The Paddling

The paddle starts at Worthington Park, a nice little 10-acre preserve on the banks of the West Fork River. The park is also a trailhead for the West Fork River Trail, the rail trail that can be used as a shuttle for this paddle. Worthington Park also has a picnic shelter, playground, and ball fields. The elevated perch of the park allows you to look down on the West Fork River and the unusual angled milldam here. The dam was part of a long-abandoned milling operation with the mill remnants on the far side of the riverbank. A gravel bar collects below the milldam and is a popular fishing spot as well as launching point for this paddle.

When starting your trip, paddle from the gravel bar over to the far side of the milldam and you can view the remnants of the operation with its stone block construction before floating under the Meadow Ridge Road bridge. A quick little riffle pushes you downstream here. During summertime when the water is low, these

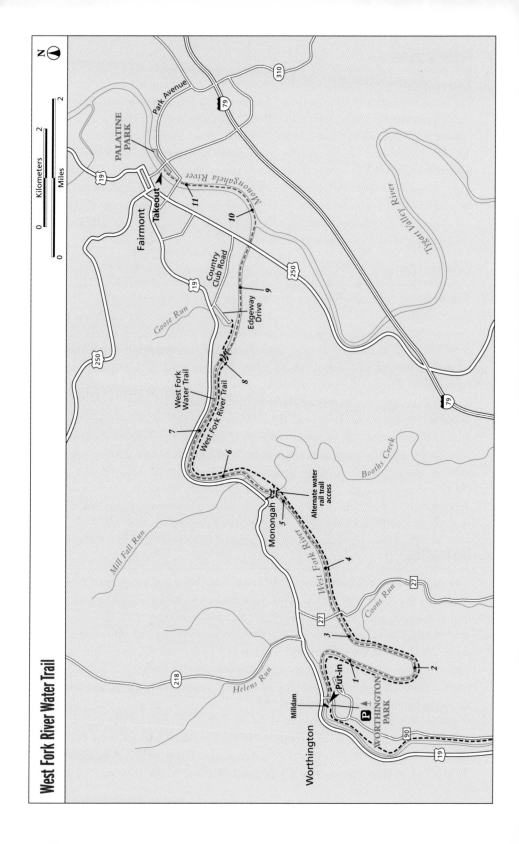

West Fork River Water Trail

Worthington

PALATINE PARK

Park Avenue

Fairmont

Takeout

Monongahela River

Country Club Road

Edgeway Drive

West Fork Water Trail

West Fork River Trail

Monongah

Alternate water rail trail access

West Fork River

Coons Run

Booths Creek

Mill Fall Run

Helens Run

Goose Run

Tygart Valley River

Milldam

Put-in

WORTHINGTON PARK

N

Kilometers
0   2

Miles
0   2

1
2
3
4
5
6
7
8
9
10
11

19
250
310
79
250
218
27
27
90
19

The wide dam just above the put-in

chutes will be narrow, bordered by sycamore and brush-covered gravel bars, while the pools of the West Fork River will be wider.

Paddle along the shores of quiet Worthington, whose houses are protected by a rock bank extending 0.6 mile. After that, Helens Run enters on river left at a riffle, then the waterway, stretching about 120 feet wide, turns southeast away from Worthington, making a big bend after passing tall stone pilings of an abandoned bridge. Steep hillsides form on river left. Pawpaw and dense woods rise on the banks. At 1.7 miles the West Fork River makes a hairpin bend back to its primary direction north, forming an appealing gravel bar on the inside bend. If it has been raining lately you will hear cascading cataracts falling from the hills into the river, including one spiller that flows just above the West Fork River Trail, the rail trail mimicking the curves of the waterway. Some of the cascades crash over 40 feet before entering the West Fork River.

At 2.9 miles Coons Run enters on river right. Look up the stream and you can see the rail-trail bridge spanning this larger waterway. Float under the County Road 27 bridge at 3.4 miles, then scoot down a little shoal. At 4.4 miles paddle by another stone edifice that once was a bridge piling. At 5.2 miles come to the hamlet of Monongah. Here, sizable Booths Creek adds its flow to the West Fork River. View the rail-trail bridge over Booths Creek. This location is also a river access for the water trail. Float under a bridge here, then pass yet more abandoned bridge pilings before Mill Fall Run enters on river left at 5.6 miles. Fixtures atop the pilings indicate power lines were once strung atop them.

At 6.5 miles the West Fork River bends east and stays in that direction, running along US 19, your driving shuttle road. Float under the West Fork River Trail bridge at 8.1 miles. If doing the bike shuttle, you will pedal over the river at this span. The lazy current moves on as you pass Goose Run on your left. The river is now 180 feet wide. Float under the US 250 bridge and find yet another set of stone bridge pilings to meet the Tygart Valley River at 9.8 miles. You are now at the official beginning of the Monongahela River. You should paddle upstream just a bit on the Tygart Valley River in order to paddle three different waterways on one paddling trip.

Now you are on the big and wide Monongahela River, northbound again. The town of Fairmont rises on high hills. Pass under a defunct railroad bridge, then turn a corner and you can see the gold-domed Marion County courthouse ahead, as well as the elaborately ornate Million Dollar Bridge, erected in 1921. Then on your right

The put-in for this paddle is a wide gravel bar.

Pass this waterfall if you shuttle using the West Fork River Trail.

at 11.4 miles, pull into Palatine Park with its boat ramp, boat dock, and paddler boat dock with a handicap-accessible boat slide.

If executing the bike shuttle back to Worthington, your biggest challenge is finding the West Fork River Trail where it begins in Fairmont. It is off Edgeway Drive, an unlikely dead-end road bordered with houses. Here are the coordinates for the rail-trail access: N39 28.164' / W80 10.543'. From Edgeway Drive, you will descend a steep gravel road to reach the actual rail trail. However, once on it you have a beautiful and pleasant ride back to Worthington, pedaling along—and over—the waterway you just paddled.

41 Cheat River

Make a fine float on a big river in a wide valley deep in the mountain splendor of the Monongahela National Forest.

County: Tucker
Start: Holly meadows access, N39 7.304' / W79 40.486'
End: Saint George access, N39 9.918' / W79 42.374'
Length: 8.3 miles
Float time: 4.0 hours
Difficulty rating: Easy
Rapids: Class I
River/lake type: Mountain rimmed valley river
Current: Slow-moderate
River gradient: 6.2 feet per mile
Water gauge: Cheat River at Parsons, 450 cfs minimum runnable level without scraping, can go down to 300 cfs but expect to scrape some,

500–1,000 cfs ideal level, stay off the river above 5,000 cfs
Season: May–Oct
Land status: Private; surrounding mountains are national forest
Fees and permits: None
Nearest city/town: Parsons
Maps: Cheat River Water Trail; USGS: Parsons, Saint George
Boats used: Kayaks, canoes, tubes, rafts
Organization: Cheat River Water Trail, 1343 N. Preston Hwy., Kingwood, WV 26537; (304) 329-3621; www.cheatriverwatertrail.org
Contact/outfitter: Blackwater Outdoor Adventures, Location Rd., Parsons, WV 26287; (304) 478-3775; www.blackwateroutdoors.com

Put-in/Takeout Information

To the takeout: From the intersection of US 219 and WV 72 / WV 48 near the county courthouse in downtown Parsons, head north on WV 72 for 5.8 miles and turn right on Location Road, County Road 5. Immediately cross the Cheat River, then turn right after 0.2 mile into Saint George Community Park and the shoreline access next to the Location Road Bridge (note that at 1.4 miles you will pass Holly Meadows Road, County Road 1—this is the route to the put-in).

To the put-in from the takeout: Backtrack to WV 72 and head south for 4.4 miles, then turn left on Holly Meadows Road / CR 1 and follow it for 0.5 mile, crossing the Cheat River to immediately turn right on Anglers Way, then quickly turn right again to reach the Holly Meadows access, a long but narrow canoe/kayak ramp.

Paddle Summary

This paddle explores the big, island-studded Cheat River as it winds through a wide valley from which rise the Allegheny Mountains within the greater Monongahela National Forest. The whole affair has a bigness to it—the river is big, the valley is big, and the mountains rising above are big. Yet the Cheat River in this section is not the

In summer, gravel bars grow over with grasses.

brawling white torrent of whitewater fame but rather the pool and Class I shoal segment that is ideal for recreational paddlers like us. Leave the Holly Meadows access, making an elongated 180-degree bend around Holly Meadows, passing the first of many islands. Meander through the wide valley, along field and hill, soaking in highland panoramas. The river often stretches very wide and shallow at cobble bars, then evolves into Class I–I+ rapids. The next segment curves around Horseshoe Bend, then navigates among some big islands, with multiple channels and routes before a final calm stretch leading to Saint George. Beware during times of low water—some channels will be impassable. Also, the route is subject to wind due to the big river and wide valley. This is a viable bicycle shuttle as the roads are relatively quiet and no big hills are negotiated.

River/Lake Overview

The Cheat River flows a mere 80 miles, but the course is memorable, wild, and in places raucous. Its headwaters flow north from spruce-covered highlands deep within the Monongahela National Forest. Here, Glady Fork, Dry Fork, and Laurel Fork flow through untamed, gorgeous montane territory, coming together—along with the

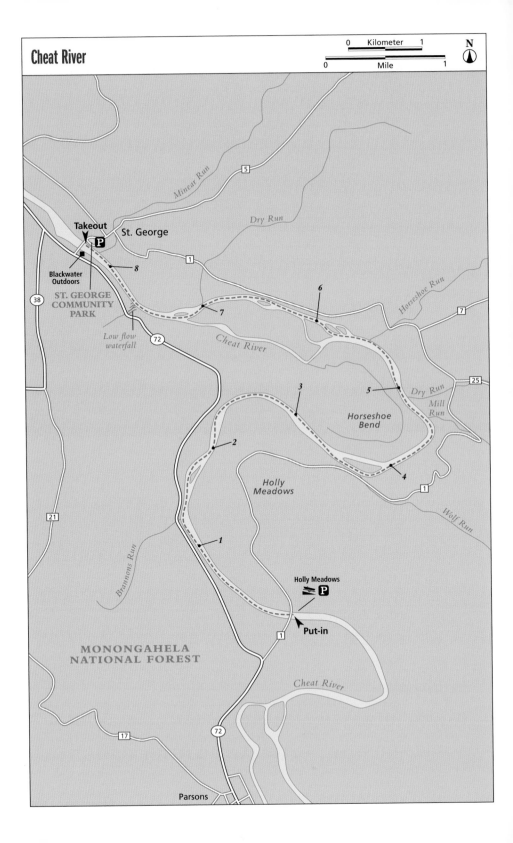

Cheat River

0 Kilometer 1

0 Mile 1

N

Minear Run

5

Dry Run

Takeout
P
St. George

Blackwater
Outdoors

8

1

6

Horseshoe Run

7

38

ST. GEORGE
COMMUNITY
PARK

7

7

Low flow
waterfall

72

Cheat River

25

3

5

Dry Run

Mill
Run

Horseshoe
Bend

2

4

1

21

Holly
Meadows

Brannons Run

Wolf Run

1

Holly Meadows
P

1

Put-in

72

MONONGAHELA
NATIONAL FOREST

Cheat River

17

72

Parsons

famed Blackwater River—to form the Black Fork. The Black Fork flows but a short distance to meet Shavers Fork—also draining some incredible parts of West Virginia, including High Falls—and together Shavers Fork and Black Fork merge at the town of Parsons, just above this paddle, to form the Cheat River, son of a mountain if there ever was one. From here, the Cheat meanders through an often wide valley fenced by mountain ridges, cutting an ever-deeper chasm. Narrow gorges form in places, then the Cheat is slowed at a hydroelectric dam, just inside the Mountain State. Released from its pen, the Cheat continues northward to enter Pennsylvania, briefly flowing free to deliver its waters to the massive Monongahela River. The whitewater section of the Cheat running from Albright to Jenkinsburg, West Virginia, is the section commonly referred to as the Cheat River Gorge. Other whitewater sections include the Cheat River Narrows (above Albright), but much of the river is unheralded as a recreational paddler stream featuring Class I–II rapids mixed in with slower segments. However, no matter where you are along the Cheat, mountain vistas will always be with you.

The Paddling

In its upper stretches the completely free-flowing Cheat is subject to seasonal variations in its flow rate. In spring a run down the Cheat can be a hard-charging, splashing affair, with multiple routes among the waterway's many islands. The water drops as summer comes along. The river calms somewhat and is often a wide, shallow, and serene experience, punctuated by lively little rapids. Island channels may become too shallow to run. By fall, paddlers will need to be on their toes as they navigate shallows among the golden-leaved trees of autumn.

Leave the put-in, entering the lower end of a shoal to float under the County Road 1 bridge. Gravel and grass bars border the 200-foot-wide river, along with a screen of trees, behind which stretch the fields of Holly Meadows. Rhododendron grows on the cooler north-facing hills. The tea-tinted water shallows, and you come to your first rapid, an even gradient Class I shoal, at 0.4 mile. At 1.2 miles come to a second, shorter shoal. Here, the river bends right and smallish Brannons Run enters on river left. Float beside your first major island at 1.6 miles. A shoal develops here, and the rapid sweeps you past the isle. Continue bending around Holly Meadows, enjoying another shoal at 2.2 miles. These rapids are composed of even-gradient cobble bars pocked with a few bigger stones amid them. Look for the deeper channels. A gravel bar good for stopping lies on river right at the base of this shoal.

At 2.6 miles look for a buckled bluff to the left of the river. The river is going east here, and you can gain views of the Alleghenies rising in the distance. Meanwhile the Cheat leads you on, under the remnants of a multi-piling swinging bridge at 3.3 miles. At 3.5 miles a wide, shallow shoal takes you past an island to your left. At 3.8 miles Wolf Run enters on river right. You are now making the 180-degree Horseshoe Bend. At 4.7 miles Mill Run enters on river right at a rapid, and at 4.9 miles the

EVER BEEN TO BLACKWATER FALLS?

Just east of this paddle on a tributary of the Cheat River is one of West Virginia's premier state parks. This highland getaway, perched at over 3,000 feet along the rim of the canyon of the Blackwater River, features a fine lodge, a wealth of cabins, and a campground, as well as trails and more.

The all-season resort features snow skiing in the winter, wildflower watching in the spring, hiking and camping in the summertime, and leaf viewing during autumn. In these northern mountain highlands of West Virginia, the Blackwater River emerges from the wetlands of the perched Canaan Valley, flows through the town of Davis, then begins its dive into the canyon of its creation.

Here, time and charging water have cut a gorge of impressive proportions, a valley where rock outcrops provide vistas into the lands over a thousand feet below, a place where immense forests blanket rugged slopes, a place where wild streams drain a wilder land.

The state of West Virginia did right by creating this state park, nearly encircled by the Monongahela National Forest. Today we can enjoy the waterfalls protected within the park as well as the other natural and man-made features that lie within its bounds.

The quarter-mile walk to Blackwater Falls is easy and popular yet still rewarding. It immediately drops into a canyon, wandering under woods then squeezing by rock outcrops befitting such a gorge. The path then opens onto a wide flagstone deck, where you can look downstream into the river gorge. From there, step-filled wooden walkways lead to multiple overlooks of 57-foot Blackwater Falls, culminating in a close-up view of the white, misty spiller. Upon reaching this closest viewpoint, the mist can drift onto you, especially at higher flows. Cap off your Cheat River paddle with a trip to Blackwater Falls.

first Dry Run comes in. Relax during a slower segment of the paddle. At 5.5 miles normally very clear Horseshoe Run adds its mountain flow to the Cheat.

Now, at 5.7 miles, it is decision time as some very big islands come up. Pick your route. I recommend far right, even though it is a smaller channel. Cruise a narrower, moving channel no matter which route, then the islands end at 7.2 miles just after the second Dry Run enters on river right. The Cheat widens as one big channel and slows. At 7.6 miles look river left for a low-flow waterfall dropping about 10 feet off a ledge. A bluff rises here. At 8.1 miles big Minear Run enters on river right, forming a gravel bar. The Saint George Community Park takeout is on river right just before the Location Road bridge, ending the paddle at 8.3 miles, across the river from an outfitter.

42 South Branch Potomac River

Make a beautiful run through "The Trough," a slender, unusual gorge, tackling Class I–II rapids for much of the paddle.

County: Hardy
Start: McNeil access, N39 8.807' / W78 55.426'
End: Harmison's access, N39 13.676' / W78 51.147'
Length: 7.1 miles
Float time: 3.8 hours
Difficulty rating: Moderate
Rapids: Class I–II
River/lake type: Gorge-lined river
Current: Moderate, slow at end
River gradient: 8.2 feet per mile
Water gauge: South Branch Potomac River near Springfield, 1.6 feet minimum runnable level, stay off river above 5.0
Season: May–Oct

Land status: Private; a very little wildlife management area
Fees and permits: None
Nearest city/town: Moorefield
Map: USGS: Old Fields, Sector
Boats used: Kayaks, canoes
Organization: Potomac Riverkeeper Network, 3070 M St. NW, Washington, DC 20007; (202) 888-2037; www.potomacriverkeepernetwork .org
Contact/outfitter: The Trough General Store, PO Box 357, Romney, WV 26757; (304) 822-7601. Offers rentals and shuttles adjacent to the takeout on this paddle during the warm season.

Put-in/Takeout Information

To the takeout: From the intersection of US 220 and Old WV 55 in downtown Moorefield, take US 220 north for 2.5 miles, then turn right on Cunningham Lane just before bridging the South Branch Potomac River and follow it for 0.7 mile to turn left on Trough Road. Follow Trough Road for 11 miles, then turn left onto the public access road just after passing Trough General Store. The ramp is down by the river past the access parking area.

To the put-in from the takeout: Backtrack on Trough Road toward Moorefield and follow it for 7.3 miles to turn right on Clover Drive. You will see a sign that states "South Branch Wildlife Management Area" and follow Clover Drive 1 mile to the McNeil access. Be careful not to get stuck in the gravel by the river.

Paddle Summary

This paddle cuts through an unusual geographic feature known as The Trough, an incredibly narrow valley bordered by parallel ridges rising over 1,000 feet from the water. The Trough is only accessible by boat or the railroad line that cuts through the gorge—no roads, no trails. The South Branch Potomac slices right through the heart of The Trough, delivering visual thrills glancing up the gorge and a healthy dose of

Paddlers relax on the South Branch Potomac.

Class I–II rapids in the first part of the paddle before settling down to more relaxed waters. Wildlife, from deer to bald eagles, call The Trough home. The 7-mile paddle takes you completely through The Trough. Trough General Store, located next to the takeout, rents kayaks and canoes and operates shuttles.

River/Lake Overview

Although it flows almost exclusively through West Virginia, the uppermost headwaters of the South Branch Potomac River flow down from Highland County, Virginia, near the town of Monterey. The waterway quickly enters the Mountain State after a few miles then keeps a surprisingly consistent north-northeasterly course as it knifes through the Allegheny Mountains. It leaves a gorge by the name of Smoke Hole, protected within the Monongahela National Forest, in its wake. Merging with the North Branch, the South Branch streams through the town of Petersburg, West Virginia, then the mountain stream by the confusing name of South Fork South Branch Potomac River gives its waters to the South Branch Potomac River near Moorefield. Here, the South Branch winds through a wide and productive agricultural valley until the river once again cuts its way through the mountains at the location of our paddle—a ribbon of water hemmed in by River Ridge and Sawmill Ridge known as The Trough. Beyond there, the South Branch passes Romney, and as if fighting its inevitable end, it begins to loop and turn in bends, getting as much river mileage in

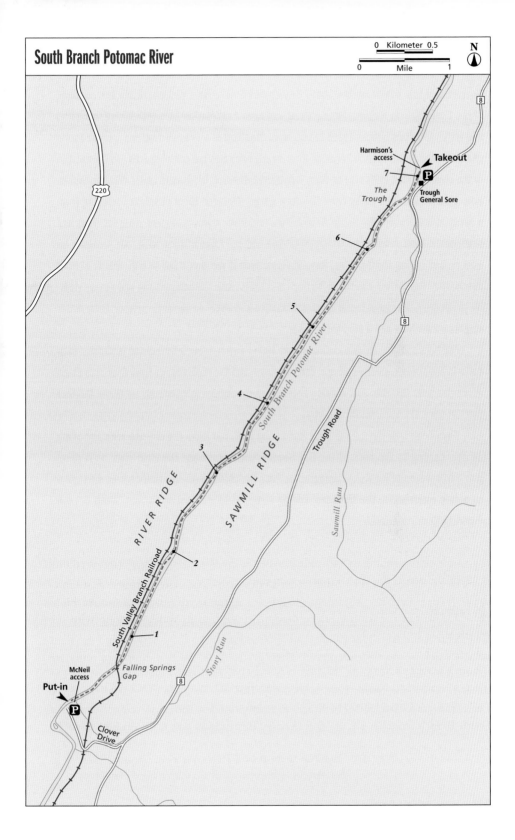

South Branch Potomac River

0   Kilometer 0.5
0   Mile   1

N

Harmison's
access

Takeout

7

The
Trough

P

Trough
General Sore

6

5

8

South Branch Potomac River

Trough Road

4

SAWMILL RIDGE

3

Sawmill Run

RIVER RIDGE

2

South Valley Branch Railroad

1

Stony Run

McNeil
access

Falling Springs
Gap

Put-in

P

8

Clover
Drive

220

HEAD TO SMOKE HOLE CANYON

Upstream of this paddle on the South Branch lies Smoke Hole Canyon, within the confines of the Monongahela National Forest. Here, you have a recreation area with hiking, camping, and water activities concentrated in one area. Standing in a dramatic setting, perched on a peninsula, the South Branch Potomac River nearly encircles the camping area. On the outside of the river, wooded cliffs rise to form a natural cathedral. Old-timers called this the Smoke Hole because the mist rising from the deep gorge reminded them of smoke emerging from a cavity in the ground. The South Branch Potomac River attracts anglers vying for trout and smallmouth bass. Around the campground you will see folks fiddling with rods, hanging up waders, and telling fishing tales. Nevertheless, even if you don't like to fish, this is a great destination. The setting can hardly be beat, and trails leave the campground and nearby vicinity. In addition, the campground itself is attractive and heavy on campsite privacy. Enjoy water spigots everywhere and a nice bathhouse.

Paddlers can also enjoy paddling Smoke Hole Canyon, though the season is shorter than down by The Trough, mostly spring / early summer, and the rapids range from Class I to Class III. Eagles Nest Outfitter just outside Petersburg specializes in river trips up there. Contact them at www.eaglesnestoutfitters.com.

Hikers can trek the 1.2-mile Big Bend Loop Trail. You leave the day-use area and climb a knob, coming to the neck of the Big Bend. From there, trace the clear river as it flows downstream around Big Bend Campground. Pass the chimney of a post office from days gone by before returning to the trailhead, adding some land-based action to your South Branch Potomac River experience.

as possible before ending its 140-mile journey at the Potomac River, staring headlong at Maryland across the West Virginia state line.

The Paddling

Be careful at the launch as paddlers have been known to drive too far and get their vehicle stuck in the riverside gravel. Then get ready as the first couple of miles are full of fun Class I–II rapids, leading you through Falling Springs Gap, a water gap through which the South Branch squeezes. But we are getting ahead of ourselves. Leave the gravel bar at McNeil access, northbound in normally clear water. The South Branch stretches about 60 feet wide. Be ready as you get a dose of Class I+

Top: The South Branch Potomac is a clear mountain river. ▶
Bottom: An upstream view at the steep sides of The Trough

straightforward read-and-run rapids in the first 0.4 mile. The shoal and ledge rapids are bordered by flood-swept stunted sycamores rising from rock bars. This is followed by another longer Class II rapid. At 0.6 mile float under the South Branch Valley Railroad bridge while simultaneously cutting through Falling Springs Gap, a water gap through which the South Branch flows. Here, River Ridge rises to your left and Sawmill Ridge rises to your right.

You have entered The Trough. And what a cleft it is, what a gorge, what a canyon! The unusual name certainly adds mystery and allure. And The Trough lives up to its billing: crystalline water with a mix of deep sections and shallower rapids bordered by boulders from which rise wooded walls of wonderment. At 1.4 miles rock bluffs rise as well, breaking the screen of trees. At 1.9 miles navigate Class I+ rapids pocked with bigger boulders amid the smaller rocks. Even though you have a railroad running parallel to the water, the atmosphere remains truly wild and scenic. The South Branch widens for a bit before narrowing again at a rapid at 2.3 miles. The river widens and shallows yet again. At 2.9 miles paddle beneath a large, almost overhanging bluff. Here, the South Branch narrows to 30 feet and gathers as a rapid. Slow down in a deep pool below this rapid. Ahead, scope out laser looks down The Trough. It seems in places the canyon was cut with precision straightness. The slow section ends at 4.4 miles with a riffle. The lower part of The Trough is definitely slower water, but portions of this slower water are often wide and shallow.

A gravel bar forms where an unnamed creek flows down from River Ridge at 5.7 miles. Your first substantial rapid in a while forms at 5.8 miles, an easy read-and-run where the river narrows. The final stretch of the South Branch flows slowly past boulder-lined banks. At 6.6 miles enjoy one last rapid courtesy of the inflow of Sawmill Run amid some islands that only become true islands at higher flows. Bluffs rise on river right beyond Stony Run. When you see these bluffs, edge over on river right as the easy-to-miss Harmison's ramp comes quick at 7.1 miles. Note the ramp is steep and narrow so try to load your boat as quickly as possible to avoid a boat/vehicle jam.

43 Cacapon River

This rapid-rich paddling trip traces the Cacapon River past rock bluffs aplenty and other attractive scenery.

County: Hampshire
Start: WV 127 Bridge ramp, N39 8.807' / W78 55.426'
End: Cacapon Crossing access, N39 27.136' / W78 25.512'
Length: 9.6 miles
Float time: 4.7 hours
Difficulty rating: Moderate
Rapids: Class I–II
River/lake type: Small ridge and valley province river
Current: Moderate
River gradient: 8.8 feet per mile
Water gauge: Cacapon River near Great Cacapon, will scrape below 2.0 feet, not recommended above 4.5 feet

Season: Late Mar through mid-July
Land status: Private
Fees and permits: None
Nearest city/town: Paw Paw
Maps: Cacapon River Water Trail; USGS: Largent
Boats used: Kayaks, canoes, tubes
Organization: Friends of the Cacapon River, Box 321, Great Cacapon, WV 25422; info@cacaponriver.org; www.cacaponriver.org
Contact/outfitter: Cacapon River Water Trail, PO Box 58, Wardensville, WV 26851; (304) 856-1188; www.cacaponguide.com

Put-in/Takeout Information

To the takeout: From the intersection of WV 9 and Moser Avenue in downtown Paw Paw, West Virginia, take WV 9 east for 3.1 miles. Then keep straight on WV 29 south and continue for 4.4 more miles to turn left on CR 29/4, Cabin Run Road, and follow it 1.2 miles to a three-way intersection. Here, turn left, still on CR 29/4, Cabin Run Road. Stay with Cabin Run Road for 1.6 more miles, veering left after a mile as a private road leads right. Finally, turn right at the signed turn to the Cacapon Crossing access on the right. Be sure to walk down to the sandbar access, located on a bend, then scout it out. The access can be difficult to recognize from the water.

   To the put-in from the takeout: Leave the Cacapon Crossing access and backtrack on CR 29/4, Cabin Run Road, and follow it for 1.6 miles. Stay straight at a three-way intersection, joining CR 45/4, P. W. Loy Road, to follow it for 2.1 miles, and turn left on CR 45/7, Gaston Road. Follow Gaston Road for 0.6 mile, then turn left on WV 127 and follow it for 0.6 mile to turn left onto the access road for the WV 127 bridge ramp after bridging the Cacapon River. A concrete ramp is located at river's edge beside the bridge.

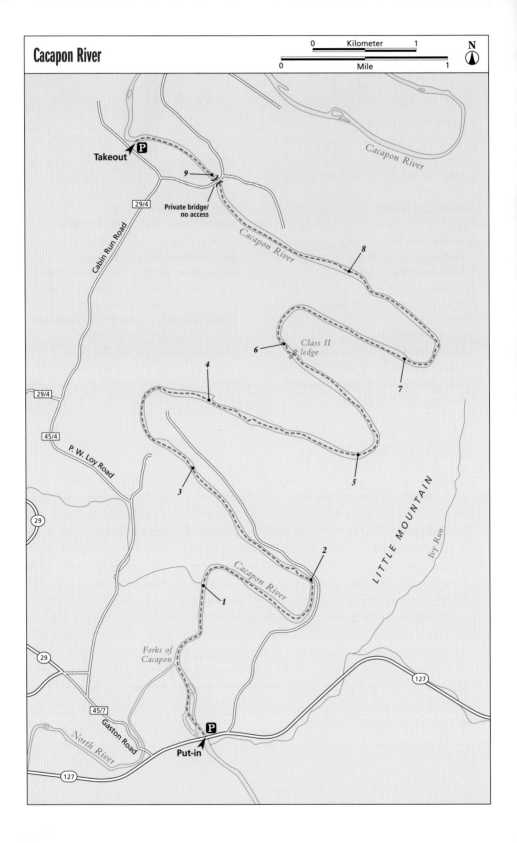

Cacapon River

0   Kilometer   1

0   Mile   1

N

Cacapon River

Takeout   P

29/4

9

Private bridge/
no access

Cacapon River

8

29/4

45/4

P. W. Loy Road

4

6   *Class II
ledge*

7

29

3

5

LITTLE MOUNTAIN

Ivy Run

2

1

Cacapon River

29

*Forks of
Cacapon*

127

45/7

Gaston Road

North River

P

Put-in

127

Slow sections of the Cacapon River alternate with lots of shoals. KERI ANNE MOLLOY

Paddle Summary

This exciting small-river paddle is rich on scenery, with tall bluffs rising from the clear, rocky waters as well as plenty of mostly Class I shoals and rapids scattered throughout the float as it makes a series of "paper-clip bend" turns. Though many fish camps and river houses are sprinkled on the banks, the river cuts through a scenic swath of West Virginia, winding its way among the ridge and valley province of the eastern panhandle. Expect to tackle plenty of rapids, both straight ledge drops and longer rapids dropping in moderate gradients. Some of the ledges on longer rapids are Class II but even at that are mostly straightforward drops. The Cacapon tends to flow too low by midsummer. I recommend running the river at 2.0 or above on the Great Cacapon gauge, hitting it in spring or early summer.

River/Lake Overview

The Cacapon River is West Virginia born and bred. Its headwaters form in the Alleghenies against the Virginia state line, flowing off Great North Mountain, Bald Knob, and other highlands. The waterway at its inception is known as the Lost River, and it heads north for 30 miles before earning its name, flowing underground near the town of McCauley, becoming "lost" for a mile before reemerging from the depths with a new name near Wardensville, now flowing as the Cacapon River, Indian for "healing waters." The river continues north, collecting more streams within its 680-mile watershed, becoming paddleable as it leaves the hamlet of Capon Lake. (The community of Capon Lake got its name from the lakelike status of the Cacapon River here, not because the Cacapon is dammed.) The 15 miles of river from there to Capon Bridge are flat and easy, interspersed with a few easy rapids. This upper river is most subject to low-water spells. For the next 12 miles, from Capon Bridge to the WV 127 bridge, the Cacapon runs wild and raucous, with attractive scenery but also rapids ranging from Class I to Class III, keeping most casual, recreational paddlers on the banks. The next section below the WV 127 bridge is where our paddle takes place and is also where the Cacapon begins its noteworthy paper-clip bends through greater Largent. Plenty of rapids occur here, but the closer to the Potomac the more long pools are found. Below the WV 9 bridge, the Cacapon bends less. Finally, the water is dammed at Great Cacapon, then is freed to make the last of the 38 miles from the WV 127 bridge and empties into the Potomac, one of that river's cleanest tributaries and purportedly the Potomac's most biologically diverse feeder river.

Rock bluffs are seen on this section of the Cacapon.

The Paddling

The paddle leaves the quality WV 127 boat ramp and immediately splits around some islands. You will find out quick if there is enough water, since at levels of 2.0 or less on the Great Cacapon gauge, you will likely scrape or even pick an altogether too low channel here. However, it is a fun ride straight out of the gate, making your way among these small isles. The best route is to the right. Shoot your way among these channels to meet the North River, quietly entering from your left at 0.5 mile. This area is known as Forks of Cacapon. The waterway stays as one channel, stretching about 60 to 70 feet wide, and normally running clear, bordered by sycamore and river birch. At 0.6 mile shoot your first Class I+ rapid as it pushes forth in a straight shot beneath a pine-and-rock bluff, the first of many such outcroppings. Continuing downriver, an unnamed stream enters on river left at 1.0 mile. Make your first bend beyond this, rolling down some shoals. Additional shoreline vegetation runs from pawpaw to pine. Rock outcrops extend to and into the water. Tackle a set of rapids ending as a river-wide ledge (best run on the right) at 1.7 miles. Beyond here, the Cacapon makes its first paper-clip bend, its curve resembling the arc of a paper clip.

WALK TO THE BIG SCHLOSS

Within the headwaters of the Cacapon, where it is known as the Lost River, stands the 2,963-foot Big Schloss (German for castle), a huge outcrop that delivers spectacular views into the Lost River watershed and beyond. You can make a 2.1-mile one-way hike to Big Schloss from Wolf Gap, where a free national forest campground is located (open year-round; bring your own water). Consider hiking to Big Schloss then camping at Wolf Gap Recreation Area, all part of the George Washington National Forest.

The hike leaves Wolf Gap near campsite #9. The wide Mill Mountain Trail wastes no time climbing the west slope of Great North Mountain, making a switchback at 0.3 mile. At 0.7 mile the path levels off atop the ridge. At 0.8 mile pass a rock outcrop with a wonderful view to Virginia's Massanutten Mountain and the Shenandoah Valley, with the heights of the Blue Ridge forming a backdrop. Traverse a narrow rock ridge with stunted tree cover in places. At 1.8 miles reach the 0.3-mile Big Schloss Spur Trail. Head right up the spur, soon opening onto a partly wooded outcrop with views in three directions. Ahead, reach a land bridge connecting outcrops. The views are even bigger at the end. You can see into West Virginia in the near and easterly to the Blue Ridge and south toward Wolf Gap. Multiple outcrops make exploration fun among the panoramas of the Big Schloss. For more information, visit www.fs.usda.gov/gwj.

River-wide shoals like this are common on the Cacapon River.

At 2 miles as you turn, run another long set of shoals, a mix of mild gradients and little ledges. The river now turns northwest, and at 2.6 miles, drop off another ledge created by another outcrop reaching down to the water. Float under a major power line at 2.9 miles. At 3.3 miles you begin another paper-clip bend as a cedar bluff rises on river left. The bend ends in a splashy rapid at 3.7 miles, with a sand beach on river right at the rapid's base. You are now looking directly east at Little Mountain. Negotiate another ledge at 3.7 miles, and keep east, passing another rapid at 4.6 miles. The river then makes another paper-clip bend at 5 miles, forced to turn by Little Mountain. Float over another ledge and you are fully heading northwest at 5.4 miles.

Come to the biggest ledge yet at 5.9 miles. This is a Class II straightforward drop amid a set of shoals preceding a bend to the right and another bluff of stone and evergreen on river left. As you are floating east at 6.5 miles, another outcrop reaches to the water and creates a ledge. This area exudes remoteness. At 7 miles Little Mountain forces a turn and the final paper-clip bend. A little rapid accompanies your northwest direction at 7.4 miles. Enter a slower section. Enjoy the relaxation near paddle's end. Float under a private bridge at 8.9 miles amid the first shoal in a while. Be on your toes at this point, as the Cacapon Crossing access is not evident. Get over river left, and at 9.6 miles reach the access, just as the Cacapon River curves right. Look left for a small sandbar and rough access, completing the paddling adventure.

44 Sleepy Creek Lake

Make a circuit cruise on this long lake bordered by steep ridges. The "no gas motors permitted" policy keeps the venue quiet and paddler friendly.

County: Berkeley
Start: Sawmill ramp, N39 31.476' / W78 8.872'
End: Sawmill ramp, N39 31.476' / W78 8.872'
Length: 5.4 miles
Float time: 3.0 hours
Difficulty rating: Moderate
Rapids: None
River/lake type: Narrow mountain lake
Current: None
River gradient: None
Water gauge: None
Season: Apr–Oct

Land status: State wildlife management area
Fees and permits: None
Nearest city/town: Martinsburg
Maps: Sleepy Creek WMA; USGS: Stotlers Crossroads
Boats used: Kayaks, canoes, johnboats
Organization: West Virginia Tourism Office, Building 3, Ste. 100, State Capitol Complex, 1900 Kanawha Blvd., East Charleston, WV 25305; (800) CALL-WVA; www.wvtourism.com
Contact/outfitter: West Virginia Department of Natural Resources, 324 Fourth Ave., South Charleston, WV 25303; (304) 558-2771; www .wvdnr.gov

Put-in/Takeout Information

To put-in/takeout: From exit 14 on I-81 near Martinsburg, take Dry Run Road west for 6.1 miles to turn left onto Swinging Bridge Road and follow it for 0.4 mile. Turn right onto Cavern Road and follow it for 0.6 mile to turn left onto Back Creek Valley Road. Follow Back Creek Valley Road for 3 miles, then turn right onto Sleepy Creek Road, CR 7/9 (you will see a sign for Sleepy Creek Wildlife Management Area) and follow the paved road, which becomes gravel after 1.4 miles. Continue on the bouncy road (low-clearance vehicles exercise caution) over Third Hill Mountain. At 6.1 miles reach a signed split in the road. To the left are the Upper Campground and Meyers Place Campground, with Piney Point Campground and Lower Dam and Pier on the right. Go right and drive for 1 mile, then turn left into the Sawmill boat ramp.

Paddle Summary

This still-water paddling adventure circles the shores of a scenic linear lake, nestled in the ridge-and-province country of the eastern panhandle of the Mountain State. Sleepy Creek Lake is the centerpiece of a natural wildlife management area by the same name. Hemmed in by Third Hill Mountain to the east and Sleepy Creek Mountain to the west, the impoundment stretches the narrow length of dammed Meadow Branch. Starting at the less-used Sawmill boat ramp, you will head south along the lake's east shore winding amid coves while soaking in the ridgeline vistas to reach and explore the marshy waters where Meadow Branch enters the lake. Standing snags are set both along the shore and in the lake center. From there, turn north, enjoying the west shore of Sleepy Creek Lake to eventually reach the widest part of the waters at the impoundment dam, then finally returning to Sawmill boat ramp. The narrow lake is a good choice both aesthetically and practically, for you need no shuttle and the scenery is rewarding. Just watch for the bumps in the road getting there.

River/Lake Overview

Meadow Branch, the stream impounded as Sleepy Creek Lake (Sleepy Creek is actually located west of Sleepy Creek Mountain Wildlife Management Area), is formed at a place interestingly known as "Locks-of-the-Mountain." This is where Sleepy Creek Mountain, which borders Sleepy Creek Lake to the west, and Third Hill Mountain, which borders the lake to the east, come together. Meadow Branch flows north from here, along with Roaring Run, a major tributary. Roaring Run comes to be at Neglar Spring before giving its waters to Meadow Branch just before Meadow Branch is impounded as Sleepy Creek Lake. The impoundment stands at 1,100 feet in elevation and covers 205 nearly linear acres. Completed in 1962, the lake, with an average depth of 9 feet and a maximum depth of 26 feet, continues to be a major fishing and paddling attraction within the 23,000-acre Sleepy Creek Wildlife Management Area.

The Paddling

Sleepy Creek Lake has several boat ramps—the primary ramp, especially for day users, is the ramp by the dam. However, Sawmill ramp is a better choice for paddlers since it is less used and more primitive, leaving it open more and allowing paddlers to take their time loading and unloading their craft. Yet another ramp is at the camping area down-lake. Still other boaters simply pull their craft up to lakeside campsites. Most boats used are either canoes/kayaks or smaller johnboats, since Sleepy Creek Lake is an electric-motors-only venue. This is especially important here, as parallel ridges hem in the impoundment, and the sounds made within—therefore the only sounds you hear echoing in the pretty Meadow Branch valley—are birds chirping instead of outboard motors roaring.

Leave the Sawmill boat ramp, nestled in a cove, and quickly emerge onto the main lake. The tarn is quite narrow and stitched in by the high ridges. Hickories and oaks dominate the shoreline, growing in thick, fragrant ranks, along with other hardwoods such as maples as well as pines. A few outcrops dot the shore. The lake dam is to the south, but it will be miles before we reach that milestone, as we are going the opposite way. The dark waters reflect the mountains above. Sleepy Creek Lake is subject to waterweeds growing in it during the warm season, therefore April through June is the

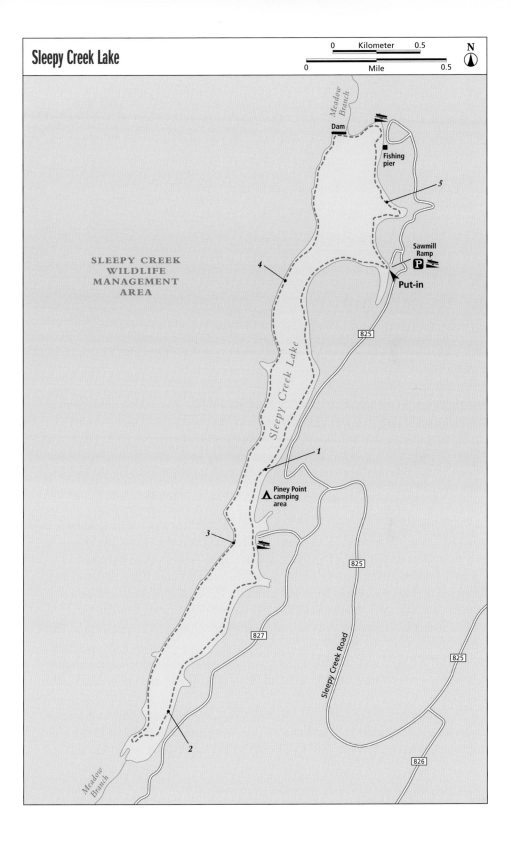

Sleepy Creek Lake

0   Kilometer   0.5

0   Mile   0.5

N

Meadow Branch

Dam

Fishing pier

5

SLEEPY CREEK
WILDLIFE
MANAGEMENT
AREA

Sawmill
Ramp

P

Put-in

4

825

Sleepy Creek Lake

1

Piney Point
camping
area

3

825

827

2

Sleepy Creek Road

825

826

Meadow Branch

Kayak fishermen on Sleepy Creek Lake

best time to visit, though later in summer and fall are fine if you don't mind pushing through the lily pads in places.

While paddling you will agree this is an underutilized resource for kayakers and canoers. The primary paddlers that do come here are kayak fishermen tossing a line along the rising shore. Continuing down, Sleepy Creek Lake stretches in the distance, with Sleepy Creek Mountain rising across the waters, forming a wooded mantle. Stopping spots along the shore are not difficult to find, especially since you will be passing camping areas. Sleepy Creek Mountain WMA has more than seventy-five campsites clustered in multiple locations. Be apprised that the immediate shoreline may be shallow in places, forcing you to paddle a little farther out in the lake.

At 1.1 miles paddle by lake access spots adjacent to Piney Point camping area. Then you actually pass Piney Point and turn into a cove, one of the few larger coves in the linear lake. At 1.3 miles paddle by the Piney Point boat ramp and then visit a second cove. The vegetation can get thick in the upper lake in the summertime. Pass a third cove at 1.9 miles. Now you are approaching the marshy head of the impoundment. This can be a rich wildlife-viewing area for both fur-bearing aquatic animals such as beavers and muskrats and avian life, from songbirds to raptors such as hawks and eagles.

Work your way to the inflow of Meadow Creek, reaching its mouth at 2.1 miles. Depending on the water level and time of year, it is possible to paddle a distance up the stream. During the warm season you can feel the cooler creek water flowing into the tepid lake. Binoculars come in handy here for inspecting this rich wetland. Stop your boat and just listen to the birds and the bees.

Beyond the mouth of Meadow Creek, you turn north, now working up the west bank of the lake. Third Hill Mountain is in view now, forming the eastern boundary of this bowl in which sits Sleepy Creek Lake. Watch out for stumps in the shallows while traveling along a nearly uniform bank of the lake, the exception being beaver lodges old and new occupying the margin between land and water. Work around a point at 3 miles. Keep on winding with the shore as the earthen dam of the impoundment draws nearer.

By 4.1 miles Sawmill boat ramp is tucked into a cove across the slender lake. You are now in the widest portion of Sleepy Creek Lake. This open area leads you to the dam at 4.6 miles. After paddling along the dam, come to the primary boat ramp for the wildlife management area at 4.8 miles. Here, bank fisherman like to congregate, especially at the fishing pier, located just beyond the dam ramp. Turn into a final cove at 5.1 miles, then work your way to the cove where the Sawmill boat ramp sits at 5.3 miles, completing this enjoyable, underutilized paddling destination in West Virginia's eastern panhandle.

The upper reaches of the lake are marshy where near the inflow of Meadow Creek.

45 Potomac River near Shepherdstown

Cruise along the big Potomac while paralleling the historic C&O Canal Trail, with opportunity for a potential bike shuttle.

County: Jefferson
Start: Taylors Landing ramp, N39 29.926' / W77 46.073'
End: Princess Street ramp in Shepherdstown, N39 26.079' / W77 48.095'
Length: 8.1 miles
Float time: 4.0 hours
Difficulty rating: Easy
Rapids: Class I
River/lake type: Big river
Current: Moderate–steady
River gradient: 1.1 feet per mile
Water gauge: Potomac River at Shepherdstown, WV, no minimum runnable level
Season: Year-round
Land status: National park on Maryland bank; mostly private on WV bank

Fees and permits: None
Nearest city/town: Shepherdstown
Maps: Potomac River Guide; USGS: Shepherdstown
Boats used: Kayaks, canoes, tubes, johnboats
Organization: Chesapeake & Ohio Canal National Historical Park, 1850 Dual Hwy., Ste. 100, Hagerstown, MD 21740; (301) 739-4200; www.nps.gov/choh
Contact/outfitter: Shepherdstown Pedal & Paddle, 115 W. German St., Shepherdstown, WV 25443; (304) 876-3000; www.thepedal paddle.com. This outfit not only rents boats and offers shuttles, they also rent bikes for pedaling the adjoining C&O Canal Trail.

Put-in/Takeout Information

To the takeout: From the intersection of WV 45 / Martinsburg Parkway and WV 480 / Duke Street in the heart of downtown Shepherdstown, take Duke Street north for 0.1 mile then turn right on High Street and follow it 0.3 mile to turn left on Princess Street. Follow Princess Street for 0.3 mile to seemingly reach a dead end, but turn right at street's end and descend to a small, often crowded parking area and the boat ramp. Be very discerning about how and where you park here. Expect the lot to be busy on nice-weather weekends. A steep concrete ramp leads to the river's edge.

To the put-in from the takeout: From the Princess Street ramp, backtrack to Duke Street and turn right, immediately bridging the Potomac River to enter Maryland, and begin following MD 34. Stay with MD 34 for 4 miles to reach Sharpsburg, and turn left on MD 65 north. Follow MD 65 north for 2.2 miles, then turn left on Mondell Road and follow it for 0.6 mile to turn right on Bowie Road. Stay with Bowie Road for 0.6 mile, then turn left into the Taylors Landing boat ramp parking area. *Note:* This parking area is also used for bicyclers on the C&O Canal Trail. The concrete ramp is at the lower end of the parking area.

Paddle Summary

If nothing else, this is a historic paddle. Not only do you end in a historic town on a historic river, you also parallel the C&O Canal National Historical Park, located on the Maryland bank. In fact, this paddle starts on the Maryland bank of the Potomac River at Taylors Landing, part of the national park. The entire Maryland bank remains a national park, where the C&O Canal and the parallel towpath once were. Now, the old towpath has been turned into a trail that you can easily use as a bicycle shuttle with just a little road riding. The paddle leaves Taylors Landing in a light shoal, then floats with the elongated curves of the Potomac as it heads south, dividing West Virginia from Maryland. The current is mild but steady with little to no rapids, making for an easy, carefree float that leads you to busy Princess Street Landing in downtown Shepherdstown, a historic as well as up-and-coming tourist destination. Add some time on either end of your paddle to explore Shepherdstown as well as Antietam

Bridges old and new are found at the Shepherdstown takeout. Keri Anne Molloy

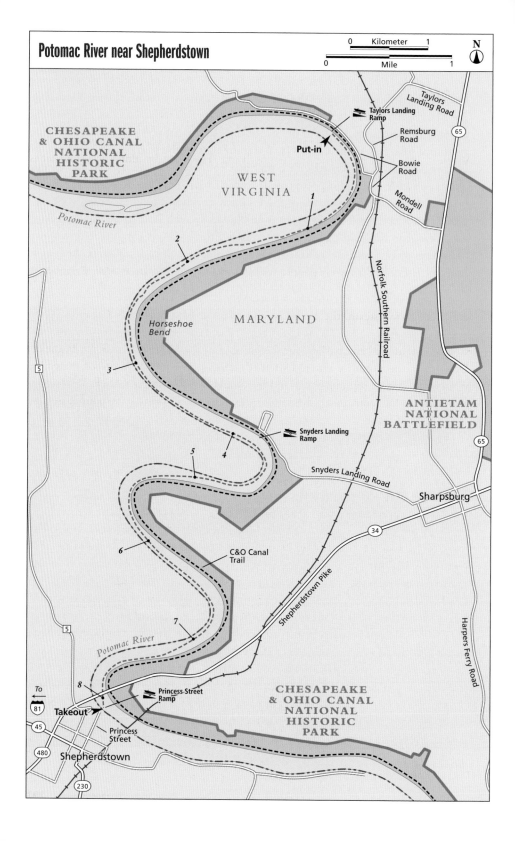

Potomac River near Shepherdstown

CHESAPEAKE
& OHIO CANAL
NATIONAL
HISTORIC
PARK

Potomac River

WEST
VIRGINIA

Taylors Landing Road

Taylors Landing Ramp

Put-in

Remsburg Road

Bowie Road

Mondell Road

65

1

2

MARYLAND

Horseshoe Bend

Norfolk Southern Railroad

3

ANTIETAM
NATIONAL
BATTLEFIELD

65

Snyders Landing Ramp

4

5

Snyders Landing Road

Sharpsburg

34

6

C&O Canal Trail

Shepherdstown Pike

7

Potomac River

Harpers Ferry Road

8

Princess Street Ramp

CHESAPEAKE
& OHIO CANAL
NATIONAL
HISTORIC
PARK

To
81

Takeout

Princess Street

45

480

Shepherdstown

230

5

5

National Battlefield, so close to the paddle that you drive by the battlefield visitor center during the shuttle.

River/Lake Overview

The Potomac River is one of America's great waterways and an integral aquatic element in the history of our country. Its headwaters are found in Virginia and West Virginia, as well as Maryland and Pennsylvania. However, its ultimate headwater is said to be near a place called the Fairfax Stone, a marker settling a boundary dispute in colonial lands that ultimately divided Maryland from what became West Virginia. Here, spring waters form the North Branch Potomac River. Yet other higher feeder branches of the river are found in the two Virginias, on its two primary tributaries, namely the South Branch Potomac River draining Virginia's Highland County as well as West Virginia mountains. The Shenandoah River, the other significant tributary, drains the high peaks of Shenandoah National Park. The river's official start is where the South Branch and North Branch merge near Green Spring, West Virginia. Gathering steam, the Potomac also takes in West Virginia's Cacapon River. The Monocacy River is Maryland's largest tributary feeding the Potomac. All Pennsylvania tributaries enter Maryland before giving their waters up to the Potomac. Downriver, the Potomac enters its famed gorge at Great Falls, a site of incredible whitewater, before settling down and becoming a wide, tidal waterway, flowing by Washington, DC, and into Chesapeake Bay. The river forms state boundaries for much of its 405-mile length, while draining 14,700 square miles of land.

The Paddling

The Potomac is flowing rapidly past Taylors Landing, this paddle's point of embarkation, situated on a curve as the Potomac is in the midst of a 200-degree bend. The C&O Canal Trail runs along the left bank of the river for the entire paddle. Through the trees you may glimpse bicyclers pedaling the path. Relics of the old and mostly dry C&O Canal are found along the trail. We drift downstream with the steady current of the Potomac, ranging upwards of 250 feet wide at this point. Gravel bars and grasses lie beneath the shoreline, which is wooded with sycamores, river birch, and ash. Maryland is to your left and West Virginia is to your right. Stunted, downstream-facing sycamores rise from gravel bars in the regularly inundated margins of the river.

By 0.7 mile you have made the first bend and are now headed southwesterly. Soak in the long downriver sweep of the waterway. The clear-green water churns and boils in spots, exhibiting the characteristics of a big river. Note the plethora of shells in the shallows. At 1.3 miles the Potomac speeds up in a narrower, shallower section. Drift over a riffle at 1.5 miles, followed by more very mild shoals at 1.9 miles and 2.1 miles.

At 2.3 miles begin a bend to the left as the waterway speeds in more shoals. This is one of the longer riffles of this paddle. Note the gravel bars on the inside bends. These will be more exposed the lower the river level. Pass Snyders Landing boat ramp at 4.2 miles, on the Maryland side of the river. The waterway is quite wide at this point, therefore you have to plan to be on one side or the other of the river if you want to take a break. Snyders Landing is also an access for the C&O Canal Trail. Begin another big, sharp bend. However, a bend can only be so sharp with a river this big. The curvature does create a nice shady gravel bar on the inside of this bend. The West Virginia banks remain surprisingly devoid of development. Of course, the Maryland side is a national park.

Make another major bend at 5.4 miles, then pass under a power line at 6 miles. The wide Potomac continues its steady push. Only two more big bends remain between you and Shepherdstown, so enjoy the ride as the scenery changes, curving right at 6.7 miles. Then that final turn at 7.7 miles reveals the Duke Street bridge linking Shepherdstown to Maryland, as well as buildings perched on the hills of Shepherdstown. You will also see the stone pilings of several other now dismantled and destroyed spans at this historically important crossing of the Potomac River, along with the current railroad bridge of Shepherdstown.

Be on guard after paddling under the Duke Street bridge and move over to river right. Come close to some old pilings before reaching the steep Princess Street ramp. The landing can be very busy in summer, so consider carrying your boat up to your vehicle. After loading your canoe or kayak, check out the historic downtown of Shepherdstown or Antietam battlefield—both are worth a visit.

About the Author

Johnny Molloy is a writer and adventurer based in nearby Johnson City, Tennessee. His outdoor passion started on a backpacking trip in Great Smoky Mountains National Park while attending the University of Tennessee. That first foray unleashed a love of the outdoors that has led Molloy to spend most of his time hiking, backpacking, canoe camping, and tent camping for the past three decades. Friends enjoyed his outdoor adventure stories; one even suggested he write a book. He pursued his friend's idea and soon parlayed his love of the outdoors into an occupation. The results of his efforts are over 65 books. His writings include hiking guidebooks, camping guidebooks, paddling guidebooks, comprehensive guidebooks about specific areas, and true outdoor adventure books throughout the eastern United States, including hiking guides to Virginia's Shenandoah National Park and West Virginia's Monongahela National Forest. He is also author of *Hiking Waterfalls in West Virginia*, another FalconGuide.

Molloy writes for various magazines and websites. He continues writing and traveling extensively throughout the United States, endeavoring in a variety of outdoor pursuits. His non-outdoor interests include American history and University of Tennessee sports. For the latest on Johnny, please visit www.johnnymolloy.com.